THE MONKEYS RULE

Buck —

May love energy
follow you always

Victoria
Barhan
1-18-2019

THE MONKEYS RULE

WHY THE LAW OF ATTRACTION
DOESN'T WORK FOR SOME . . . IT'S ALL ABOUT ENERGY

Victoria (Koegle) Barkan

ISBN: 978-1-7335243-0-8 - Paperback
eISBN: 978-1-7335243-1-5 - ePub
eISBN: 978-1-7335243-2-2 - mobi

Printed in the United States of America   0 1 1 1 1 9

∞This paper meets the requirements of ANSI/NISO Z39.48-1992 (Permanence of Paper)

This book is dedicated to Richard A. Mueller and James O. Robbins. If both of you had not been exactly who you were and behaved exactly as you did relative to me, I may have never traveled the road I did and learned what needed to be learned to write this book. I thank you both from the bottom of my heart.

This book is also dedicated to my mother, who taught me more about myself in the last year of her life than all the other years combined, and to Andy, my late soulmate, who served as my rudder and the best mentor I ever had.

TABLE OF CONTENTS

Cover Description   ix

Illustration List   xi

Preface   xiii

Acknowledgments   xix

Introduction   xxiii

PART ONE: ANGER GATHERED, ANGER STORED   1

   1) Retrospection   3

   2) A Loss of Innocence - The Continental Story   7

   3) Sexual Harassment - The Metrovision Story   23

   4) No More Naïvcté - The Cox Communications Story 39

   5) The Brand Consultancy   91

PART TWO: THE TWILIGHT ZONE   95

   6) Victimization vs. Victimhood   97

   7) Enter Native American Teachings   123

   8) Real Estate Boom or Bust   153

   9) Moving On   165

PART THREE: THE MONKEYS   183

   10) The Monkeys are Born   185

PART FOUR: THE MYSTERY SCHOOLS 203

11) So Much to Learn 205

12) Consciousness—The Shift from Linear (Words) to
Nonlinear (Energy/Feelings) 209

13) Truth—The Linear World of Words 217

14) Energy—The Quantum of Physics 233

15) Communication—There are Two Levels: Words
and Energy 245

16) So, What's It All About, Alfie? 269

Epilogue 275

References 277

Bibliography 281

Indiegogo Campaign Contributors 289

COVER DESCRIPTION

The Monkey on this cover is a painting I did back in 2012. On a trip I made to Peru in 1988, a few of us chartered a flight to take us over the Nazca Lines. During that time, I saw the many geoglyphs of Nazca theoretically created for or by ancient aliens as they can only be seen from the air. I took many pictures and used the picture of the Monkey for the basis of my painting.

The colors in the painting come from a vision I had during a cord-cutting ceremony I had done back in 2008 with my friend Blue Thunder. In that ceremony, he asked me to call up my little girl. Instantly I saw a vision of a little brunette two to three-year-old chasing a blue butterfly through a field of colorful flowers. However, everything green in a real field was yellow. This made the colors of the flowers pop, hence the background color of yellow in this painting.

This Monkey painting is called Insatiable. One modification I made to the original picture is the bulging stomach full of manna. Additionally, he is gathering more manna to eat and has gathered even more manna on which to gorge. The blue butterfly in the picture represents the butterfly I was chasing in my vision. Blue is the color of truth. So, this Monkey is chasing truth while he is consumed by never being able to satiate his appetite for more stuff. That was me in the early stages as I wrote this book.

ILLUSTRATIONS

Diagram I   Maslow's Hierarchy of Needs w/Consciousness Overlay

Diagram II   Drawing of a Diamond

Diagram III   Dualistic/Linear Thinking

Diagram IV   Positionality

Diagram V   Allowing Neutrality

Diagram VI   Communication Styles

Diagram VII   The Political Divide

Diagram VIII   Path to Enlightenment

Diagram IX   Humanity Today on the Path to Enlightenment

Diagram X   Positive vs. Negative Energy

Diagram XI   Energy Feelings/Linear Language

PHOTOGRAPHS

1)   Love and Gratitude © Office Masaru Emoto, LLC.

2)   You Disgust Me © Office Masaru Emoto, LLC.

I was angry and very tired of feeling and being victimized. Rather than buying a gun and killing people who deserved my wrath, I started writing this book. When I said, "I am writing a book," people would say, "Oh, you are a writer." "Not hardly." I never intended to write a book. I was *dragged kicking and screaming* the whole way.

I was instructed to write this book by powers beyond me...*the voice* had a lot to do with it.

Actually, writing became my form of self-preservation. One of the only things keeping me from committing suicide was this book. *One step in front of the other* I would say to myself. It gave me the purpose I needed to stay off the couch of complete and utter despair.

You know those people who are always right about things? That served me well in my profession because I was right most of the time when it came to what needed to be done from a business and consumer perspective. (Perhaps that was more talent.)

For spiritual growth, however, being right was simply a roadblock or resistance to my learning—a stop sign, so to speak. "Stop and pay attention; there is something to learn here." So, my successes in Corporate America helped cloud my spiritual growth. Actually, there was virtually no spiritual growth going on while I was in Corporate America.

Besides being a cathartic process for me, I wrote the book for all those who have been, or are being, victimized to know "You are not alone." I also wanted you to know about the Corporate World and how its structure, truths and personalities contributed to my demise and could to yours. Thirdly, I wanted you to see how I used my experiential learning, readings and helpers to get out of my black hole and how what I learned could help you.

We each have our own story and these things really happen to us. But if you come away with the idea that someone owes you something because of what happened, then you are missing the spiritual lesson that will set you free of your suffering. Victimhood only resides at the lower energetic consciousness levels. The longer one stays in that lower energy, the more prolonged the suffering. Self-examination, looking in the mirror and humility are needed for you to get past blaming others for your circumstances.

This is my story, the path that brought me here to you. Everything in here happened to me. I am an insatiable reader, and I have exposed myself to experiences and lessons no book could have ever conveyed. I am here to tell you about the insights (the word *miracle* is a more appropriate word) that were brought to me in this process.

Somewhere back in the beginning of my existence I knew I would always be alone. Actually, I believe that came from my first Christmas at one year old because the same picture keeps popping into my head. My brother was only days old. The picture shows my mother holding my brother. I am alone on a new tricycle. My dad was taking the picture. The expression on my face was one of fear. I think this was the point when the idea *I will always be alone* crept into my psyche, obviously all subconscious, I can assure you. It really did not manifest, though, until I was moved as a sophomore in high school because my dad got transferred to Cleveland, Ohio.

I had been a happy-go-lucky kid and my nickname at Kettering High School was Smiley. I left behind all of my lifelong friends and two boyfriends. (I got away with that because one was in a different school.) However, when my friends threw me a 16th birthday/going-away party, both boys were there. I freaked out but my girlfriends had it all handled. My whole English class seemed to be there. They gave me a charm bracelet with my first charm, a small silver abacus--they said it was to count all my friends. That time was one of the happiest of my life. Leaving all those friends, boyfriends and hometown devastated me. I never fit into the new high school. That devastation left me when I went to college, but only briefly.

They made me go, you know. My dad was sick with terminal cancer, so I did not want to go away to college but to stay home with him. My mom insisted I go saying, "Dad's dream has been to see his kids go to college." I'll never forget that day a couple, work friends of Dad's, drove me out the driveway to college (alone again). Dad stood in the picture window of our home dressed in his robe and pjs watching me leave. [That scene still brings tears to my eyes.] I agreed to go only when my mom promised to let me know when I needed to return before the inevitable. She didn't. I got home about an hour after he died, thinking I was home for Thanksgiving. That reinforced the subconscious alone-all-of-my-life belief. Losing my security figure turned my world upside down. Anytime a child loses a parent is devastating but, being only 19 as a freshman in college during the *make-love-not-war* era with the training *good-girls-don't-and-bad-girls-do* was much worse than devastating. It was catastrophic...for me.

My relationship to carefree dating and having fun with boys I dated walked out of my life the day my dad passed. Unknowingly, I was now trying to replace the security I had lost with the guys I dated. Forget that, they were sowing their wild oats; they weren't there to meet my security needs. I felt this as a betrayal. (None of this was conscious on my part.) I was really confused, like I was walking on quicksand and there was no solid land to steady myself.

I dated a lot but had only one or two steadies and the one I was *in love* with lived in Chicago. I remember my cousin telling me once that he didn't think I was capable of a long-term relationship. What? I was aghast. I said, "I can't help it if the one I love lives in another state." Later all of this would make sense when my counselor suggested, "You only bring unavailable men into your life." Unavailable—to prove my underlying belief that I am unlovable and meant to be alone.

In the early '80s, and early in my career, I realized I was no longer perceived by some as the happy-go-lucky person deserving the nickname Smiley. When I realized something was *off*, I was on the beach at Ponte Vedra, Florida, on a boondoggle with The Movie Channel (TMC), and two of my female TMC reps. At that time, I was President of the Atlanta Chapter of Women in Cable and these two were on my board. We were laughing and cutting up under the perfect full moon watching the gentle waves come in and lap the beach when I noticed they kept saying how much fun I was, over and over and over. Finally, I asked, "Am I that much of a bitch at other times?"

They were both silent.

Then one said. "Well, you are intense."

Yes, that was true. On the job, all I could see was getting the tasks done. Apparently having fun doing the work was not a skill I had.

That was an awakening to the fact that what one thinks is happening in the world may not be what is perceived by others.

In my effort to do a good job, I spoke my mind and took positions when I felt I was right. My successes had given me a lot of ammunition to support that thinking. I would say I was somewhat of a pit bull. When I thought I was correct, I was not inclined to compromise. I saw the middle ground as watering down the success. In my mind, that was a typical Northern behavior. However, when I found myself in the South, Southern genteel I was not. I spoke the truth as I saw it, not realizing people do not like the truth. I did not know how to sugarcoat it. I was unaware speaking the truth was getting me into hot water. I had no real idea how much people hate the truth, especially if it has anything to do with them and their behavior.

My drive to succeed was the underpinning of the need for security because if I were going to be alone all my life, I knew I would need to make a good living to take care of myself. If I could not do something to take care of myself, I would have to hire it done and that would take money, often a lot of money. So, anything that happened to me to affect my ability to make a living was a threat of significant magnitude. Being a woman in the 70's and 80's in Corporate America should not have been an issue…but it was, big time.

I was not alone in the discrimination. All minorities were experiencing it to a greater or lesser degree, depending on who their individual manager was or the direction of the corporation. The difference for me—I confronted the issue rather than quietly leaving. Each situation made me more and more determined to bring the behavior into the light so it could be eradicated.

What follows is what happened to me and how I coped or didn't cope.

ACKNOWLEDGMENTS

There are many people who had lots of influence on me as I was learning what I was to write about. I want to thank those who were extremely influential in my growth and who supported me all of the way.

First, I thank Sylvia Johnson Gemmill, my psychologist, and Ruth Zanes, my one and only coach, who was coaching before it became the thing for even the most uneducated to do and who introduced me to Landmark Education. Without these two working together to diffuse my rage while keeping me on a straight path, I may have bought that gun and used that list.

The three years doing Landmark Education work enabled me to crack my hard shell. Thank you to all of those in Landmark dedicated to the process and the Leaders who had to put up with my cracking shell. Without those years of work in Landmark and the coaching I received, I would never have been able to work with Gary.

I thank Gary Adler Fourstar. Without you, I never would have learned many of the distinctions needed to crack the pain around my father, suffering I did not even know I had. Thank you for all of the Native American Teachings. Your explanations of Native tribal life opened up an understanding of the word love that I never knew existed until my time with you. I will always love you for putting up with me! I thank Debbie Bullock Fourstar for giving me permission. It made all the difference!

Without the help of Cheryl Burney, I would never have been able to get through the years with Gary Fourstar. I described working with the two of them as Gary blowing up the dam and Cheryl helping me to put it back together. Being as raw as I was at those times, she helped save my life. May you rest in peace Cheryl.

I thank Bernice and Yoni Werzberger for introducing me to the wonderful world of Psych-K. Thank you for your support and encouragement in allowing me to immerse myself in the Psych-K process. Bernice, thank you for allowing me to continue to work with you even though I did not have the money for the sessions; very appreciated!

I must mention Bryan Mercer and Clinton Wade Thornton, who refocused my earning thinking from the world of jobs to the world of projects. That shift in thinking really allowed me to dissipate the mindset that having a job was the only way to earn a living. Coming from a family who only understood jobs, there was no support for the shift. Only entrepreneurs seem to understand this concept and my family has none of those. The world of projects that Bryan and Clint introduced me to lends itself to the creative.

I thank my many friends who were there to help me with their support in talking things out, giving me gas money, food or just a shoulder to cry on. Thank you Montana Popienko, Lin Lemmer, Cathy Conn, Deborah Hirsch, Cheryl Burney, Nancy Sellers and especially Cindy McEntire. Cindy was the one who was not only there but never failed to lift me up no matter what was going on. You are all special to me!

I thank Dr. Dwana M. Bush, M.D. for all of her help during my trying time and her hand-written prescriptions of support.

J. Curt Hockemeier deserves a special mention because he was the miracle sent to me when I was at my lowest. His phone call and consulting job offer came at a time that literally saved my life two days after I asked God for a miracle.

Thank you to my Indigogo campaign sponsors for your trust and support of my project. Your support helped me get finances out of my head while I wrote. They are all listed on a separate page in this book. Thank you.

I thank all of the wonderful people in the Atlanta Writers Club and, in particular, my Northpoint critique group, especially Harold "Buzz" Bernard, John Sheffield, Dr. Terri Segal, Jim Seltzer and Susan McBreairty. Your input was invaluable. I had no idea about the complexities of the act of writing a book until I received your help.

Thank you to all of those who go unnamed here because of the numbers that touched my life in ways that helped me learn the lessons I needed to learn.

And then there are the people in my Hawkins study group, who have been my rock for the last seven years. Like any group, the people in it come and go and each one was helpful in his or her own way. Thank you to: James Dudley for helping me find the references in the many books by Dr. David Hawkins; Chris Cobb, Caroline Van Sickle, Karen Paul Holmes, Blair Enfield for helping me with the muscle testing of my comments and diagrams throughout the book; Judy Corkle for reading the entire book while it was in a confused state; Melodie Ransom, Pari & RJ Jyotishi, Laura Gomez, John Gano for overall support.

And, of course, I must thank my editor, Geleta Fenton. Without her help, this book would probably be unreadable and very confusing. It was at times a difficult process but we got it done. I can't begin to thank her enough!

It is with much gratitude I salute you!

INTRODUCTION

As You Read This Book, Remember This:

EVERYTHING IS ENERGY...
EVERYTHING

Everything is energy and everything has an energetic outcome. So, pay attention to the energy coming from any interaction. This book is about positive and negative energy, using as an example my experiences in Corporate America and the resulting path I took. As you read this book, go through life, are contemplating action or witnessing the outcome of somebody else's actions or interchanges, ask yourself:

> Does the energy coming from this interaction result in negative emotion, nonloving energy, such as separation, anxiety, fear, anger, secrecy, exclusion, special consideration for some, judgment, fighting or violence; OR does the energy from this interaction result in positive emotion, loving energy, such as acceptance, inclusion, unity, equal treatment, nonjudgment, joy or love?

Your answer will tell you who the false prophets are. Pay attention to the energy...it does not lie.

FIRST PART – ANGER GATHERED, ANGER STORED

Written in 1999, Part One tells of my poisoning by negative energy in the form of discrimination. Each succeeding case slowly destroyed my trust. Each situation was different and, in the end, the harder I worked and the more successful I was, the more I seemed to be pushed down. Until, in the end, I no longer trusted men, women or worse—myself. My confidence was totally shattered.

When I was told early in my career that I would threaten people, especially men, I had no idea what was meant. Yes, I wasn't out to be liked; I was out to get the job done. When I did, it threatened a lot of people—not just men.

Hillary Clinton said it best in a recent interview: "The more successful a man is the more likeable he is. With a woman, it is just the opposite."

And, of course, there is karma, the residual effects from past lives that come into play in this life. All of us are sons and daughters of God on an evolutionary path of consciousness, trying to get closer to our Source. Earth is a school we attend to help us accomplish this over many lifetimes or sometimes few.

SECOND PART – THE TWILIGHT ZONE

What happened to me in Corporate America was the precursor to my spiritual path. I was heavily inspired by experiential learning, which helped this human being awaken to the truths of the Universe.

I felt like I was in a Twilight Zone because there were so many things happening that I could not explain. For example, one night I asked God where to start reading in my new Bible. The very next day Jehovah's Witnesses knocked on my door with a little book entitled *Know Your Bible*. [I wasn't used to the concept of synchronicity or the law of attraction, that there are no coincidences and that everything happens for a reason.]

My first read after the Bible, *The Celestine Prophecy*, explained the spiritual process at a level I could understand—I was being guided. I call it the voice. Don't get me wrong, I was not hearing voices; I was being infused with directions…do this, go there, study with this person, don't study with these people, etc. *The Celestine Prophecy* helped me to trust the process.

You will be surprised, as I was, at where I was being guided to go to learn. When I was guided to the Native American teachings instead of the so-called *right* church, I was perplexed, until I started learning their *ways*. Besides working with a psychologist and life coach, the Jehovah Witnesses and Native Americans, my Twilight Zone included courses, such as Landmark and Psych-K.

During my Corporate years, I had become a multimillionaire. That allowed me to travel to exotic places, like many areas in Africa, including the Sahara Desert and New Guinea, and invest in real estate. Both experiences not only taught me about me and life, but how life and money are fleeting. The Twilight Zone was a place I learned to trust the Creator, to *keep my hands inside the boat*. I did not understand the reason why something was happening but all I had to do was wait and float down the river a little ways and there would be the answer.

THIRD PART – THE MONKEYS

Why Monkeys to describe our fears and state of resistance? We all have Monkeys. You may not be able to see your Monkeys but other people can spot yours. In fact, many of us spend lots of our time pointing out other people's Monkeys in a subconscious effort to avoid acknowledging and dealing with our own Monkeys. You may call them your demons, buttons, insecurities, fears. They are the negative nonlove energy, subconscious, jumping in to affect your life. I had a very scientific mind so the realm of the mystical and the Monkeys was very woo-woo to me at first.

When I left Corporate America in 1997, I started awakening to the existence of the Monkeys. You will read how their antics slowed me down and kept me from discovering my path to happiness--kept the Law of Attraction from bringing me what I consciously wanted. You will see the Monkeys pop their heads up occasionally and you will see that I do not recognize them.

Brackets. I used brackets [ ] to give statements about the preceding paragraph(s) to inform you about what I did not understand at the time, like you are in a movie and the voiceover is explaining your motivation but you, as the character, don't know it yet.

FOURTH PART – THE MYSTERY SCHOOLS

During my journey, I became aware of four distinct, but intermingling, concepts — Consciousness, Truth, Energy and Communication. All these topics intermingle, so pulling them apart for clarity was/is very difficult.

In this introduction, I am going to explain only one thing: the use of applied kinesiology and VTK because I used Applied Kinesiology to muscle test statements throughout this book—VTK means Verified as True by Kinesiology.

My first exposure to Kinesiology was in the early 80's with a chiropractor who had studied in China. It freaked me out then simply because I was uneducated. Good thing my best friend was a chiropractor who explained that we are learning new things daily. I trusted him and its use *felt* right.

As in all science… "we don't know what we don't know." If something has not been proven by science means it does not exist, then God does not exist in whatever form or name you choose to use. It simply means that there is no understanding or method of proof *at this time*.

My experience is all I have to go by and my experience has covered over 35 years. More recently, through the practice of Psych-K and the study of Dr. Hawkins' work, my experience with VTK and muscle testing (kinesiology) has expanded.

I am well aware of the limitations of the art of getting correct muscle readings, e.g., people trying to prove a point rather than seek truth will get false readings, people who are nonintegrious (calibrate below 200) will get false readings and cannot use the method. The body does not lie; however, the practitioner's interpretation is subject to review and challenge. Intent is very important and one must seek the truth above all else.

The muscle testing I completed for this book follows these protocols:

1. done by a group of people who study Dr. David Hawkins' work;

2. done using the two-person arm method;
3. results were verified by separate individuals; and
4. done in 2015-2017.

Applied Kinesiology is a tool and should be used as such. If the answer does not feel right, then rewording of the statement being tested may be in order.

Every person has a choice between love (positive) energy or nonlove (negative) energy. Energy does not acknowledge justification. It is either one or the other.

If you find parts of the book troublesome or hard to understand, do not worry. Some will call parts hogwash, woo-woo or even blasphemy. It is simply a reflection of where you are consciously in your ability to understand.

One man who wanted to read this book stopped after he crossed into the Twilight Zone. He could not understand or relate to the happenings and started rejecting my experiences. This was completely understandable given where he was consciously.

Remember as you read, your reactions to where you are in the book can be a guide to you as to the level of learning that lies ahead for you.

THE MONKEYS RULE

Part One

Anger Gathered, Anger Stored

Chapter 1

Retrospection

Karmic Payback

I know I was a male chauvinist pig in a past life. Now was karmic payback time—being brought back as a woman in male dominated Corporate America. What was worse, there were very few women at the higher levels, where I found myself. Wow, what a punishment. I played the game by the men's rules. I functioned like the men and succeeded. Unfortunately for me, I was in a woman's body. A man succeeding in Corporate America can be a threat to many, but imagine the threat a successful woman posed, especially in the '70s.

A comment from the best mentor I had early in my career was, "You will always threaten people, especially men."

I thought, *what is he talking about? How am I threatening people? Better put, how can I stop it?*

[I did not know about the Monkeys then...mine or theirs.]

Doing a great job was all I thought was required to get ahead. I clearly remember my parents' counsel: "Work hard and do a good job and you will get ahead and the company will take care of you." That was the perspective of two people who had worked during the Depression for AT&T, one of the few companies that did not lay off people. Instead, they cut hours, thus allowing everyone to work, a much more humane answer to the challenges of that period.

> *Those were the thoughts going through my mind that fine October day in 2007, as I sat in the pew of the All Saint's Episcopal Church on one of the infamous Peachtree streets in Atlanta,*

3

Georgia, listening to Duffy Leone eulogize James O. Robbins (JOR), the Past-President of Cox Communications.

Jim was President when I was there as Director of Marketing Operations of the Western Division and, at a different time, Director of Marketing for one of their cable systems in Oklahoma City, Oklahoma. Knowing I considered Jim a friend, another friend, Angelina Li, former VP of Research at Cox, had informed me that Jim had passed and when the services were, in case I wanted to pay my respects.

Duffy was talking about how great working for Jim had been, "It was like going to JOR University." (Duffy in the earlier days, when I was in Oklahoma City (OKC), had been a peer of mine as the Director of Marketing in the Cedar Rapids, Iowa, cable system, which was much smaller than OKC.) JOR University seemed to have a major positive affect on his career.

As Duffy said that, my Monkeys came out to painfully remind me I did not have an opportunity to go to JOR University, and the indignation began to rise. Feeling the anger was not difficult because I had a whole well full, an accumulation of years in Corporate America being subjected to various discriminatory behaviors. All inhibited my ability to make a good living and secure a good retirement for myself. You betcha.' I was angry!

BEFORE THE CORPORATE WORLD

In 1965, during my freshman year and at age 19, my father's death impacted me greatly. Losing my dad at that time, which translated to losing my security, had me all confused about the opposite sex. I had fun dating until the death of my father. It was the middle of the love revolution, make love not war, and I was brought up with the teaching—good girls don't and bad girls do. But when my security needs were no longer being met by my father, I sought to get them in the boys I dated. They were not ready for that. They were still sowing their wild oats. I took that lack of interest in me as a person, as betrayal. The confusion was paramount.

In 1969, I graduated from Bowling Green State University with a degree in Art Education and a focus on Advertising Design. My experience student teaching showed me that I had no desire to teach kids who were that close to my age. I was not mature enough to handle their problems--I had many of my own.

So, I went into advertising not knowing I was *jumping from the frying pan into the fire.* Now I was dealing with men and not boys. The good news—I knew none of these men, like the boys in college, had any interest in me as a person. The only thing they wanted was to get me into bed. Back then I had the same measurements as Marilyn Monroe so there was very little interest in even knowing my name, or that is how it felt to me.

After several years in that rat race, I fell hard for a client. He was interested in me as a person, or that is how it felt, and he was married. I was so frightened about my feelings and the fact he was married. To get away from him, I jumped into a marriage with John Barkan, Jr., who appeared to be the first person who was interested in me as a person and genuinely cared. Because I got married for all the wrong reasons, the marriage was destined to end.

I remember one day after seven years saying to myself, *there has to be more to life than this.* So, I walked out, saying to John, "I'll be back when I get back." I walked out that day having no idea what I was going to do. I ended up going back to my alma mater resurrecting contacts at Bowling Green and in Toledo where I had been in the advertising field.

I ended up contacting an old friend, Jim Krone, who I had a crush on while in school. He was the sportscaster at the TV station where we worked together and also the commentator at the Rossford school football games, where I had student taught. The relationship became just friends when he showed more interested in my roommate. By this time he was a bigwig in the athletic department at Bowling Green. Jim gave me a great deal of time to ask lots of questions: "What do you want to do? Where do you want to go? I was just seeing what would come up.

That trip proved very fruitful -- a week or two later he called and told me that a mutual friend, Tom Willett, had a position open with Continental Cablevision in Findlay, Ohio. Tom later called me and we set up interviews, which seemed like a long agonizing process, probably because this was not just a new job for me, but a career decision and the possible end of my marriage. When Tom finally offered me the job, the decision was huge. John was in therapy, so this was just a separation as I went off to Findlay, Ohio.

CHAPTER 2

A LOSS OF INNOCENCE
THE CONTINENTAL STORY

JOINING THE BIG LEAGUES

In 1977, I procured my first position in a true Corporate environment with Continental Cablevision. If you have had any exposure to the series *Mad Men,* then you will have an understanding of why I wanted to get into what I thought was a more stable working environment than the fickle advertising field.

I became the Advertising Manager for all of Continental's cable systems across the country and number two of two in a Corporate marketing department. Located in a regional office attached to a cable system that Continental franchised, we were smack dab in the middle of rural farmland; the rest of the Corporate offices were in Boston. At that time, most of Continental's cable systems were in small rural towns across the midwest and as far away as California. The large city franchising frenzy was a couple of years away.

Before she left, Pam Euler, whose position I was taking, gave me a pep talk as I was training with her. I would remember her advice for the rest of my career. She said over lunch one day, "The guys are great guys and they don't mean anything by it but they will not invite you to meetings or social events you need to be at. You need to go anyway. It will be awkward at first but they will not say anything or challenge you. Just go. After a while, the guys will expect you to be there but they still will not invite you."

Well, she was right. The first time I walked into a social event uninvited, a sudden silence fell over the room as everyone turned to look at me. Being on stage was not fun for me. I pretended nothing was wrong or awkward and entered the reception. If I had not broken the silence, I do not know how long it would have gone on.

As time wore on, as Pam said, the awkwardness disappeared. Going, even though I wasn't invited, turned out to be some of the best advice I received early in my career. I will always be indebted to Pam for that advice.

I had no idea that was only the beginning of what I would have to do to get my job done. Wasn't I lucky to be replacing a woman unafraid to talk about the reality of what I was getting into? That was about the only time I had someone who understood the situations, and instead of pretending things did not exist, advised me.

Pam and I had been in the same graduating class at Bowling Green State University. I learned later she had told Tom Willett, my new boss, that I was considered the top design student in our class, a nice compliment coming from a peer, and one that, I am sure, helped me get the job.

Tom was the VP of Marketing for all of Continental's cable systems. Tom also graduated from Bowling Green and we had worked together at WBGSU-TV with Tom, our on-air talent for the nightly news show. I had been a graphic artist who did about any task needed behind the camera, a fun job for college.

Tom was a good-looking man of slight build and an immaculate dresser with his three-piece suits and, of course, his unmistakable pipe. He was very organized and precise in his work. He turned out to be a great boss from the perspective of pushing people to their capacity and fostering their growth.

He was also the consummate politician. I remember the comment of a female council person at a Cinevue launch in Tiffin, Ohio, when he forced me to make a speech in front of all of the city dignitaries. She was so impressed that they had a woman as a spokesperson. Back in '78 that was a rare thing. If only she knew the practice I had to go through in prep for the speech. I was terrified and Tom and Chuck Younger, Vice-President, Ohio Cable Systems, stood by me through all of the agonizing redos.

Tom gave me a wonderful compliment once saying, with a bit of awe in his voice, "I have never seen anyone grow as fast as you have." That was nice considering the enormous hours I was expending to learn the business and hours doing the job at the same time.

I had been on the job for Continental many months and was traveling to several of the cable systems to manage Pay TV launches. Our company created its own pay TV service called Cinevue rather than pay Home Box Office (HBO) license fees. This was early in the growth of pay TV and HBO was not even delivered by satellite yet, so to run and deliver our own pay TV service the same way they did -- manually -- was easy.

ENTITLEMENTS

In 1977, I was making only $11,000 a year, not even enough income to qualify for an American Express card. I had a personal Visa with a limit of $800. Given all the travel I was doing, I asked for a company credit card, because I was running up Travel & Entertainment (T&E) expenses. The answer to my request was a firm, "No. You don't travel enough." I felt like someone's daughter being told I was not ready for the responsibility. Please! No good reason was given except that I did not need it.

Because I was in a Corporate department located out in the field hundreds of miles from the Corporate office, I had to submit my T&Es to Boston for reimbursement. That meant a two-to-four-week turnaround. My checks never came in time for me to pay the credit card bills. I was not in a financial position to be floating the company loans and now I was paying interest on those loans, in order for me to do my job.

[Yea, I know this is hard for you young ones to believe but, trust me, this happened.]

By this time, I had several advertising campaigns under my belt. Tom hired a New York marketing firm to evaluate our advertising for suggestions on improvement. We were crossing over the bridge into Manhattan and I was looking all around at my new surroundings when Tom said, "Oh, you have never been here be-fore?" Apparently, he had been trying to discuss business when he realized I wasn't paying attention to him. Yep, it was my first trip to the Big Apple.

Later that day in discussions with the consulting agency, they picked all of the campaigns I had done and said, "This is the type of advertising you need to continue doing." All of my campaigns were benefit-oriented. I got a raised eyebrow from Tom because I had been refusing to make the subtle move from the advertising aspect to the marketing aspect of cable TV. My fear was, as I moved more into marketing, I would be moving further away from my art. With the vote of confidence I received from this agency, my path towards marketing solidified.

Things were heating up in the industry. HBO finally went to sat-ellite delivery and suddenly everyone was exclaiming, "Wow, let's put some programming up on the bird," as satellites were affection-ately called back then. With HBO on satellite, which made delivery easy, we discovered people would pay for both Cinevue and HBO. Our launch schedule doubled overnight. This phenomenon blew our minds—the idea of convenient scheduling for the consumer was not a concept back then. Remember, we were coming out of the 3-5 channels off-air era. So, paying for two different channels with basically the same programming, only at different times, was an unfamiliar consumer convenience.

Once HBO went to satellite distribution, the boom was on. Every programming idea known to man went on to the satellite for distribution. For the first time, cable TV had something to offer the larger cities. That started what we in the industry called the franchising frenzy. Almost overnight (that's how it seemed) every big city in the country was putting out Request for Proposals (RFPs) for cable franchises. Corporate manpower needs skyrocketed so anyone who had any experience was in great demand. We went from franchising two cities a year to over 60. That's how quickly things happened. As a result, I was running all of the marketing and launches and Tom was all over the country franchising for the company.

TITLES

Tom came to me one day when he was in town. "We really need help. Can you hire people under you faster than I can find a peer?"

Well, we all know the answer to that. Of course, I could hire help faster, and I did. I had hired one full-time employee and a part-time employee, weeks before he hired my so-called peer.

By now things were running smoothly and then my peer came on board, a nice man with a wife and two kids. I am sorry I cannot remember his name, maybe some psychological reason for that—ya think? Oh, now I remember. Bob.

He was given the title Marketing Manager, which implied he was my boss because my title was still Advertising Manager. That is what some of the people in the field thought. Maintaining my decorum was s-o-o-o difficult when one of the general managers asked how I liked my new boss. What frosted me the most—his first week he was given a company credit card and he wasn't even traveling!

I decided that was enough bunk, so the next time Tom came to send me to one of the systems, I told him I couldn't go. He was not happy and treated me like I was refusing to do my job. Then I explained, "I am at my limit on my one personal credit card and the company has several of my T&Es that haven't been paid, so I have no money." He *was* angry but...I had a credit card within a week, faster than my T&E reimbursements. Fancy that.

Playing such games to get the tools I needed to do my job brought up a great deal of resentment in me. To my knowledge, none of the men had to play these games. They were afforded the respect and the tools their positions required. Of course, those are assumptions on my part and, remember, this is the late '70s.

Bob came on board and I turned over the letter shop functions to him, which required him to coordinate many launches at a time and schedule our direct mail drops. These duties consisted of taking the printed direct mail pieces, inserting the correct pieces into the correct envelopes, and preparing for insertion into the mail.

Each launch had three specific mailings timed according to our Free Previews of HBO and Cinevue. There were a lot of elements that required tracking. We hired an outside company to do the letter shop functions.

Several months went by and things started happening. There was concern coming out of our letter shop—"Bob isn't keeping his hands on the pulse of the launches." They were apprehensive that mistakes were going to happen because Bob was putting insertion instructions in memos and then the letter shop would not hear from him. There was no checking to see if anything had changed or everything was on schedule, no follow-through.

I started getting calls from suppliers fearful they would lose the account if Bob blamed them for his not checking for mistakes or changes. Staying out of it, I referred them to Tom.

Bob didn't have any feeling for what I called *current events*. One day all hell broke loose around the office. A political situation had come up and we had to stop a Pay TV launch in midstream. The city fathers of this small rural town in Ohio were shocked at the R-rated product available on the Free Previews of our Pay–TV launches, which were uncut and unedited, so they wanted to stop our launch. In the late seventies, unedited R-rated material had never been shown on Free TV before. [Frankly, it was a kinder and gentler time.] Sex on TV was a real *shock*, especially in rural America.

Our launch marketing material consisted of a series of three direct-mail pieces scheduled to drop at specific intervals during the launch. We would usually have all of the three mailings processed by the letter shop sitting waiting until the drop date to insert into the mail. Apparently, Bob did not understand when one is told to stop a launch that one needs to tell the letter shop not to drop the next mailing. So, the next scheduled mailing dropped according to schedule. We were crucified by the city and the press. The city fathers saw that as a deliberate action on our part. What a political disaster. Not on purpose, just Bob's oversight.

Tom came to me madder than a disturbed hornet and asked,

"What the hell happened?" My response, "I don't know, Tom. Why don't you talk to Bob?"

He walked out snarling like a dog about ready to tear into red meat. I do not know if he was madder at Bob or me for reminding him I was not responsible for that function anymore. Frankly, I think it was the latter. That discussion with Bob resulted in Tom conducting an investigation, which resulted in meetings with suppliers and letter shop management. The letter shop's concern that something like this would happen had come true. This was certainly a current event that had needed major attention. Bob's future employment became questionable.

EQUAL PAY

While all of this was going on, review time came around. I received a great review. By this time, I had a staff of three. I got a $1,000 raise, a little over 9%, bringing me to $12,000 a year. (Still not enough to get a personal American Express Card.)

One day I came back from lunch and, on my desk, turned upside down, was a copy of Bob's review. I had enough time to read it and make a copy before the secretary discovered her mistake (I think it was a mistake). He had received a bad review and a $2,000.00 increase, almost 12%. He was being moved from $17,000 to $19,000 a year. I was being moved from $11,000 to $12,000 a year *and* I was told he was my peer. Hmmmm! I had suspected this all along, because I was only making $11,000 and could barely make it financially. A man, wife and two kids had to be making more. Corporations must think their employees are stupid when it comes to salary information. Like, we can't figure these things out?

Well, here I was faced with the very thing I was reading about in the papers, magazines and seeing on TV: wage discrimination. Women were reported to be making a little over $.50 for every dollar a man was getting in the same position, or for the same work.[1] Well, that was about where I was, somewhat over $.50 on the dollar.

I didn't want to jump to conclusions on this. I went to a dear friend of mine who was the head advertising guy at Caterpillar Corporation and asked, "What should I do?" He helped me with a salary survey. We took my responsibilities, the scope of my job, the fact we were a national organization and industry factors to get a feel for where my salary should be. The results--I should be in the $25,000 range. However, my industry paid lower than others so a more realistic number was $19,000. Interesting, that is what Bob was making after his raise and bad review.

After my salary survey and the launch fiasco, Tom came to me. "We are going to let Bob go and we want you to take over his responsibilities. For that we are going to give you a 25% increase, which will bring you up to $15,000 a year."

I was delighted at the confidence he was showing in me but my off-the-cuff reply was, "Well, you know, 25% of nothing is nothing. I am extremely pleased you recognize my ability and for that I want *his* title and *his* money."

You would have thought I had asked for ownership in the company.

"I can't give you that kind of raise," he blurted.

"It's not a raise; it is a promotion. I am being asked to do my job *and* his. I am not asking for his salary *and* my salary. I just want his salary and his title."

They were giving me the responsibility; why not acknowledge it with the money and the title? A promotion was worth the increase. Not for Tom; he was positioning it as a raise, as if my responsibilities would remain the same and not increase.

Later, Tom must have had an idea he was on thin ice. He came back to me and justified Bob's higher salary by stating that he was in a management training program.

THE EEOC

That threw me for a loop, so I went to the Equal Employment Opportunity Commission (EEOC) to see if this was a legitimate justification. Going to the EEOC, even to gather information, was tantamount to treason. [I suspect it still is.]

The EEOC told me the management training reason was legitimate, under certain circumstances.

"What are the circumstances?"

"Is there a *written* company management training program?"

"No."

The company didn't even have a human resources department back then.

"Have you been offered to participate in a management training program?"

"No."

"You have an open and shut wage discrimination case." (Remember, I had a copy of Bob's review.)

They were very realistic about the situation and advised me to try to work it out with the company. "The realities of a lawsuit are: (1) it will probably take years to settle; and (2) while the case is going on, you will probably find it difficult to find work."

The words *blackballed* came to mind as he spoke. I was starting my Corporate career and separated from my husband, so I opted to negotiate. If I had had a stable marriage and reliable income, I might have considered a different course.

I talked to Tom several times, trying to reach some common ground, but he wouldn't budge. From my perspective, there was some underlying need to win driving him and there seemed to be no concern for what was right in the situation. In asking for Bob's title and salary, I was doing nothing that he or most other management people would have done. I didn't understand why he would not recognize the inequity and negotiate, but then I did not know his pressures. Maybe if he had told me, we could have worked things out. I mean, a stepped-up increase plan and a title change would have been acceptable.

I told him I would be looking for a new position because I could no longer work for him and give him the 110% I had been giving him and the company and feel good about it. I think Tom felt I was taking advantage of him because the company needed me so much at that time. To show how badly he needed me, he wanted me to sign an agreement to stay until the end of the year or until he could find someone to replace me. "Oh, sure, I'll do that!" I did not sign the agreement.

OPPORTUNITY STRIKES

The company was growing by leaps and bounds and the different company divisions were talking about hiring their own marketing managers. After a meeting of the Ohio management team, the Senior VP of the region, Chuck Younger, jokingly commented that all the Ohio managers wanted him to hire me for the Ohio marketing job. Given that I was now looking for a new position, I asked, "What are you paying?"

He did a back step as he blurted out, "I can't come after you; Tom would kill me."

"What if I come to you?"

"Let's have lunch."

Chuck was a great guy and a good person, very Ivy league type, a bit less formal than Tom. He was a family man with a wonderful wife. [I still use her spaghetti recipe.] I think he felt sorry for me because he viewed the job as keeping me from my husband, John, who lived in Cleveland, Ohio.

When I had taken the position three hours away from John, I knew we were both headed for a divorce after seven years and our separation agreement was that we both could date. John was a union representative at the fire department where he worked, working on a degree in labor relations. Continental was having rumbles of unionization. John's and my marital arrangement became a company issue when Chuck tried to hire him to help keep the unions out of the Ohio region. Chuck thought it was a good fit and, of course, he probably thought he would be helping me out by bringing us back together.

I'll never forget the Christmas party where I started listening to the conversation Chuck and John were having. I thought, *Oh, shit, he is interviewing John.* Not too long after that he came into my office and told me he was going to hire John and if this were a problem, I needed to speak up. OMG...a problem! Chuck had no idea I was seeing someone and this would spell disaster. I didn't know what to do. I didn't want to get in the way of this opportunity for John, but it would complicate my moving on with my life after John.

So, I went into Tom's office and asked, "Can I have tomorrow off?"

"Why do you need tomorrow off?"

"Because Chuck is going to hire John and I need to get a divorce."

Well, you can imagine the closed doors that caused. It could have been a real disaster of soap-opera proportions. As it turned out, what happened was bad enough. Chuck ended up not hiring John. Thank God for me.

***

So, Chuck and I went to lunch. We talked about the position in Ohio and the responsibilities. There always seemed to be an amount of tension between being centralized versus decentralized in corporations during their various growth stages and Continental was no different. There was an undercurrent of seceding from the union coming from Chuck. The company was in the process of moving the Corporate marketing department to Boston and I was evaluating how much higher the costs of everything would be for the different cable systems.

Finally, Chuck put it out there, "I am offering you the position starting at $18,000 and I will give you 30 days to make the transition but, after that, you work for me. No going back and forth helping Tom." This is where decentralization is a disadvantage for some young companies because they do not talk to each other or have anyone making sure these mistakes do not happen.

This position was paying a whopping $3,000 more than the *raise* I was being offered for the national position. And this was for a regional position, handling about 1/3 less than what I was handling. Up until then, all the marketing was centralized. With Ohio being the biggest region, it was a big chunk out of the printing quantities.

I accepted. Chuck gave me 30 days to give my notice and go to work for him, knowing what a bind it would put Tom and the company in. I cautioned him. "You know Tom will have to stop this. I just don't know how." Little did I know I would be my own undoing. You see, I loved this company and I didn't want them to get into trouble, so when I gave Tom my resignation, I told him why I was leaving.

[I was *s-o-o-o* naïve but I thought I had it all figured out. I believed people would think like I did--a mistake most of us make until we get a few years under our belts.]

I knew Tom would tell the President why I was resigning. I thought when Tom told the President what I was about to tell him that the President would ask, "What did you do to drive her to do this?" The President was a man named H. Irving "Irv" Grousbeck and his office was at Corporate in Boston.

[I thought he would be a fair judge. Again, *s-o-o-o* naïve. But then, I had a mother who taught me life was fair, and I had believed her. There was no reason to believe the President would act in any different way. At that time, I did not know about the powerful energy behind fear and how that affected an individual's Monkeys.]

On Friday night before a function Tom and I had to attend, I finally informed Tom, "I am resigning because I can no longer work for you in good faith. What you have done is considered wage discrimination by the EEOC and is illegal. I am not going to sue. However, I want you to know what needs to be done to protect the company in the future." I proceeded to tell him all the things that needed to change.

All he said was, "I wish you hadn't told me this. I am an officer of this Corporation."

My mentor at the time told me, "In the end, it always boils down to personalities when these things play out," and he was right.

[Each individual's Monkeys come out to play the game. Soon you will see everyone has Monkeys and they subconsciously affect how we all behave. But I did not know about the Monkeys then.]

The Monday after I gave Tom my resignation, Chuck, who had hired me the week before, came into my office. "The Ohio position no longer exists." I couldn't believe my ears. I protested, "I told you Tom would have to stop this and you needed to be prepared." He acted as if he did not know what I was talking about. Needless to say, I lost all respect for those men on that day.

[But who was the dummy here? The experience was my first taste of what happens to people when fear takes over—communication ceases to exist. This, by the way, is why women do not bring these things up. You are immediately relegated to a position of the enemy.]

My mistake was giving too much credit to the President.

Instead the President reacted from fear. He told Chuck not to hire me because he did not want anyone in management who *thought like that*. So, Chuck pulled the job.

[There was no understanding on my part that each of us have our own individual views of what happens to us. In other words, we each have our own Monkeys. I was convinced the President would ask questions about what brought me to my behaviors. I was wrong. He simply reacted in fear.] He also did not deserve my respect.

Fortunately, on my behalf, all the managers in Ohio, when they found out what had happened, called Mr. Grousbeck in my defense. So, the President did something he'd never done before--he reconsidered. He told Chuck that he could hire me, but he also said, "…but you know how I feel about it." Well, Chuck was coming from fear, too, and he would not do anything without the complete blessing of the President, so I still lost my job.

WOULDA COULDA

This, in the realm of the EEOC, was considered retaliation. With the copy of my peer's review, I was told I had an open and shut wage discrimination case and with retaliation, where the big money is when it comes to a lawsuit. [Man, if I knew then what I know now, I could have sued and won big.]

In a small industry, news travels and Pam called Chuck telling him she heard I was going to sue. He laughed. "No, but if she did, she would win."

I had no intention of a lawsuit. I was thinking of my career and knew if that road were chosen, I would never work again.

How do I know what happened behind the scenes when Mr. Grousbeck changed his mind? The beautiful part of things boiling down to personalities is how it allows people to see the injustice and actions which go against their moral senses. Lyle Kneeskern, VP of Engineering for Ohio, another executive in a position to know, took me to lunch one day and explained the behind-the-scenes activity. "If anyone else was the VP of Ohio right now, you would be working for us. Of course, if you tell anyone that I told you this, I will deny everything."

[Well, enough time has gone by for the truth to come out without people suffering. Most of the players (except me) are deceased or retired millionaires now and the company has been swallowed up by one of the larger media conglomerates.]

DMMA AWARD

There was a *coup de grace* for me while everything was happening. We got notification we had won an award from a competition I had entered, put on by the Direct Mail Marketing Association (DMMA, now known as the DMA). Still young in the industry, I did not even know what the DMMA was. When I told my rep in New York from HBO about the award, he started laughing. By his reaction, I thought *this must be some fly-by-night competition*.

"Are you kidding? HBO would give their eye teeth to get an award from the DMMA." Then he explained—the DMMA was an international competition and we had been competing with the best in advertising and direct mail. "I just think it is funny that someone from Findlay, Ohio, won." (The arrogance of some in New York always amazes me.)

I believe we won because I had used a clear plastic bag as the envelope, which allowed people to see the announcement of our free preview and guide without opening the bag to get the message. In direct mail, getting the consumer to open the envelope is the first big hurdle. I have not seen a similar use since, probably because of the more restrictive mailing requirements. That, coupled with a telethon during the Free Preview, garnered us an 8.4% return when a 2% return on direct mail was considered good.

Timing was perfect for me. However, I believe, to put me in my place one more time, Tom put another hot poker in my side as he announced, "Since her resignation is in, I will send Carol [my assistant] to pick up the award."

I went into his office, "What are you trying to do, push me into court? I am picking up that award whether you pay for it or not." All this and he had wanted me to sign a contract to keep working for them until they did not need me. What a crock. I think my value at the time really irked Tom.

[Remember, it always boils down to personalities and their Monkeys. Monkeys were running rampant in this interchange.]

The Awards Convention in New Orleans was exciting because I was at the winning table with Wilkinson Sword LTD of London, England, and the U.S. Johnson & Johnson Co. Having these companies as my peers was thrilling. President Ford was the featured speaker. I shared a room with Carol and she picked up the restaurant tabs. So, the company did pay. "What a way to go out."

That thought brought me back to the church, hearing Duffy go on about the wonderful aspects of Jim, our Past-President. I did not disagree with anything he was saying. I reflected on how I viewed Jim as somewhat of a personal friend probably because we had worked together at Continental Cablevision. Since my employment at Cox, he seemed to take a personal interest in me and my career. When in Cox's Corporate office interviewing for the position as Marketing Director in Oklahoma City, I think people were a little surprised when Jim requested to see me. I mean, when does a Corporate President talk to an interviewee looking at a position in the field? That was an unusual path for interviews. Because of this, I always felt a special professional relationship with Jim.

Listening to Duffy speak, I remembered how shocked he was when he and I were both marketing managers (he was responsible for a much smaller system) and we were talking about salary increases. I shared that I had received a 4% increase. (We never talked numbers—that was verboten.) He couldn't believe it. You should have seen the look on his face. In his shocked state, he blurted out, "I have never gotten lower than a 6% increase."

I chuckled thinking, I lack a certain part of his anatomy and it's worth a minimum of 2% a year. No wonder the U.S. Bureau of Labor Statistics claims women were still earning only 74% of what men made doing the same job. Clearly my Continental experience supported this.

As I sat there listening to Duffy talk, my mind slipped back to the time I almost ran into Jim as I came out of a budget meeting. I remember him making a comment about "not missing my headlights." I remarked to another executive who was walking with me, "I don't seem to be able to get away from that behavior even after I had a breast reduction."

CHAPTER 3

SEXUAL HARASSMENT
THE METROVISION STORY

NORTH MEETS SOUTH

After leaving Continental in 1980 (without suing) and working for five months in Denver for another Multiple System Operator (MSO), I received a call from Metrovision, in Atlanta, GA, about the position for which I was waiting. This time my title was Director of Marketing, making more money: $23,000, much closer to, but not the $25,000 my Continental salary survey had indicated it should have been two years prior. Not the best money but, at least this time, I had the title.

I guess going to work for a southern company was no accident. These boys, southern gentlemen for the most part, were the management team that was so successful at Cox they split off and started their own company. I first talked to them before I went to Denver. They were busy winning franchises then, but, with no customers, they didn't quite need me and my talents. Several months later, they purchased a group of cable systems—the largest purchase the industry had seen. Now they needed me. So off I went to Atlanta.

My boss, Ernie Olson, was a terrific guy, a wonderful person, good ole northern boy from Connecticut. Not a southern bone in his body.

[The Monkeys are different in the North than they are in the South. This was my first real exposure to cultural differences in the Monkeys.]

23

He was President of the Cable Television Administrative Society (CTAM). That was an added perk for me, elevating my exposure in the industry rather quickly, and bringing really fun times.

After several months of ownership of the newly purchased cable systems, Henry Harris, Metrovision's President, decided to bring all management to Atlanta for everyone to meet each other, the goal—to form bonds and working relationships, as well as get business done. We had the management from the newly purchased cable systems, the management from the new build (newly franchised) cable systems, and the Corporate employees.

As Director of Marketing, I had a place on the program to present the marketing plans for the year. Directors Don Smith and Ron Sumrow, my peers, were in charge of putting the meeting together. At the Corporate office, Susan Wallace was the fourth director, Director of PR.

Don wasted no time letting me and Susan know we were on different levels even though we had the same director titles. When he was around, he clearly put himself on a higher level from us ladies.

A memo came out that everyone was supposed to clean up after themselves in the break room because they felt no need to hire a cleaning person. That was fine with everyone until *everyone* didn't actually include *everyone*. I remember how appalled Don was when I confronted him on *his* memo.

"Well, you don't expect Henry to clean his own dishes, do you?"

The problem? Once someone is special enough to be exempted from the everyone list, then the rest of the executives start to show why they are important enough to be exempt. Interestingly, the line always seems to stop between male and female. A question of leadership arises—where the leader goes so goes the flock. If you are not exempt, where you are in the pecking order becomes clear.

I took a stand. "I will not clean until *everyone* really means *everyone*. I won't use the facilities and will have my own coffee cup so I won't have to clean except my own cup." No one cleaned except the women, who felt obliged to do so.

[Their Monkeys told them where they were in the pecking order. Clearly, somewhere along the line, they started believing their Monkeys. Just like the men's Monkeys made clear that they were superior to the women, the women's Monkeys made clear that they were subservient to the men.]

Well, you can see why this northern lady with the acute sense of fair play was not a favorite among the southern genteel. So, was this sexual harassment? Sexual discrimination? Or was this a politically stupid little girl bucking the status quo?

The management conference was upon us fast and I was too busy getting my plans and presentation ready to notice I had not been given any details of the meetings or social functions. When the conference arrived, I discovered all kinds of events, none to which I was invited, in fact, none of the women were invited. I wasn't even given an agenda, and I was *on* the agenda. I felt odd, déjà vu, knowing I was to speak but not told when or where.

Well, remember that great advice I got from Pam while I was at Continental about going to meetings I needed to be at where I wouldn't be invited? That advice worked for me at Continental so I figured it would work for me here. So off to the meetings and social events I went, tired of the games I had to play but knowing I had to play them. Susan had her own way of getting there—as the PR person, she had to coordinate the pictures of the function.

The first thing that happened occurred at a luncheon. Don Smith, one of the gentlemen who put the meeting together and also my peer, came over and sat next to me. He put his arm around me and said, "So good of you to join us for lunch, but you aren't staying for the meeting, are you?"

I was so shocked he had the gall (I'd like to use a different word here that rhymes with gall) to say that. In the time (a split second) I turned to answer him, he had his back to me and was talking to someone else. Wow, that never happened at Continental. Pam had said they wouldn't challenge me and they didn't in the North.

[This was my first introduction to the Southern Monkeys.]

Even though I had not planned to attend that afternoon's meetings because I had other work to do, I went and was there in all my glory. I had come to expect this behavior from the men. (By the way, this was not deliberate with most, they just weren't paying any attention, unlike my put-his-arm-around-me southern gentleman.)

WOMEN MEET WOMEN

However, I was greatly surprised by the way I was being treated by the other women in the organization. *They were ignoring me.* The next day, when one of the other women passed by my office, I called to her, "Why aren't you at the meetings?"

"Oh, I have so much work to do. I don't have time."

I gave her the time-out sign. "Time out! I wasn't invited either."

Then her *real* feelings came out. I found interesting that the women apparently snubbed me because they thought I had been invited. Well, for the rest of the week, I let her and all the other women know they should be at the functions. The system managers were people they worked with every day and they also needed to establish relationships, not only the men. By the end of the week, all the women were attending the functions, thanks to me. Chuckle!

[And I wondered why I threatened people! What I had not faced at that point was that *I was a change agent.* Apparently, part of my karmic payback was to seek to turn around behaviors I probably initiated somewhere in my past lives.]

I was not going to let things drop there. When the conference was over, I had a meeting with Ernie. "Did you want me at the conference?" He looked at me as if I were crazy. "Of course! You were making a presentation. You are the Director of Marketing. Why are you asking?"

"Because I was not invited to anything and not given an agenda." I proceeded to inform him of what had happened and what I had gone through. He was appalled (remember, he was from the North). He called Don and Ron into our meeting. The reason they gave—"We were trying to keep costs down." They had a budget. (So, they had excluded the women deliberately.)

I said, "Interesting that you drew the line at male/female and not at manager/director or some other more reasonable delineation." Hell, we were such a small company. Why not let the rest of the employees meet everyone at a social function? Whatever happened to morale and camaraderie?

[Notice that this decision boiled down to two personalities. Southern male personalities, like I said, their Monkeys are different.]

That was the first time I had been exposed to blatant discrimination. Don was a true southern gentleman. If I dropped a hankie, he would have had it returned to me before it hit the ground. He was a real pleasure to be around as long as you did not step out of his bounds for you. He made very clear that, although I was a Director like him, he was on a different level.

And he was. He got to participate in the hunting and fishing trips and the like; I did not. Ernie often joked he would buy me a pair of stuffed ducks to put in my office so I could fit in.

There was good reason I did not get to go on those hunting and fishing trips—it was dangerous for men and women to bond because the men had an unspoken rule that the women were open game for sexual exploits. That age-old game played among men and women had not been expelled from the board room. Not all of the men played around, but most (at the higher levels) did. Some of them treated the women in the Accounting Department as their own personal harem. Ernie did not—what a joy to see someone happily married, who enjoyed a healthy respect for himself and his wife. [The Monkeys were clear.]

PASSES HAPPEN

My lot was to have passes made at me by the President, Henry Harris. Henry was a good ole southern boy and very well-respected in the industry. He was a nice-looking man and married.

The first time he made a pass, we were stuck in the office because of a snow storm in the early '80s. I discounted that time because of the alcohol, porn flicks and lack of food. For Christmas, I had given Ernie a bottle of Crown Royal, which he kept in his office. When the word got out that he had that bottle, its contents did not last long.

Because I was in charge of keeping track of the different programming going up on the satellites, I had a couple of complete porn flicks from one of those new services. There were new channels of programming going up on the satellites daily and most sent samples of their programming. I was the keeper of the movies.

Once into the liquor, the boys raided my office for those movies. For them it was one big party. Booze, pornography and no food was an accident waiting to happen. I finally took my chances with the storm. I felt it was safer.

Waco, Texas. The second time Henry made a pass was when we were doing a launch of new cable services in Waco, Texas. Because I ran from the first encounter and did not face it, I now found myself dealing with it again. I did not make it clear that I had no interest because he was married. I was looking for a partner who could commit to me not one who played around. This behavior infuriated me.

At that time, TV stations would not take our advertising because they saw us as competition. So, as Director of Marketing, I had to create an event the news had to cover. I went to Henry— could he get Ted Turner to appear at our launch? Henry was good friends with Ted but, for whatever reason, he refused to ask his friend for the favor. I was on my own to make this happen.

We were in contract negotiations with Turner for carriage of their new services and Susan Korn, our rep from Turner, was heavy in the negotiations. I called her and asked if we could get Ted to do a press conference for the launch in Waco. After much negotiation and back and forth, the deal was done. Ted was coming to Texas. I had my media event. Back in the early '80s, Ted coming to Waco was a big deal for middle Texas.

Back then, as Henry knew, Ted was not reliable as a spokesperson because he spoke his mind, regardless of who might be listening, and he was known to drink, which added to the complexity. Susan knew all of this, so I had to work with her to do exactly as she said when Ted was involved. We were launching a tier of new services, several of which were Ted's, like CNN and WTBS. "Write down what you want him to say," she instructed. "This will keep him focused."

Ernie asked, "Who's picking Ted up at the airport?"

"Bob and I." Bob was the Waco Marketing Manager. "We need time to brief Ted on what we want him to say. If you and Henry pick Ted up, you will be talking about where the quail hunting is good in Texas."

Bob and I picked Ted and Susan up at the airport and took him directly from the plane to the press conference. We used this time to coach Ted on what we wanted him to say. We gave him the paper with the information on it. I remember my reaction when he studied the paper then said, "Suckervision, new channels with all the same stuff on it." I was horrified. I found myself saying, "Of course, Ted, we do not want to say that to the press."

I prayed all the way to the press conference. God, please have him in good form tonight not rare form. I will never forget that night as I led Ted into the studio where we had the press conference set up. The guys at the system did a great job setting up a backdrop of TV sets displaying all the channels we were launching. We had press there from all over Texas, every TV, radio station, and newspaper from all around the area. I felt like I was introducing the President of the United States—a career high for me.

Ted was perfect in front of the cameras. He couldn't have done a better job if I had scripted everything myself. Henry came up to me later and asked, "How did you get him to do that?"

"That is why you pay me the big bucks and, frankly, I got tired of wearing that blond wig."

(This was way before Jane entered the picture. Ted was ru-mored to like blonds and his going after blonds was certainly my visual experience of him. It was my way of making a joke.)

That night, after dinner, Henry made his move. Already close to midnight when our dinner with Ted broke up, we were all on our way to our hotel rooms when Henry asked me to go out for a drink. Let me put this request in context. We were in Waco, Texas, in the mid '80s. We were in a dry county. There was no place to get a drink unless one had a club card, which none of us Atlantans had.

I told Henry to find out where we could go and to call me in my room. This will give me an opportunity to have a conversation with him where I can disarm the situation without destroying his ego and stop the behavior. He called my room a few minutes later. "There is no place to go. I'm having some beer brought to my room. Come over."

"Call me when the beer gets there."

Meanwhile, I was trying to figure out what to do and how to do it. At the same time, I was flattered—as he was an attractive man. I also was devastated. *No matter how I handle this, my career has no place to grow with this company. If I allow the situation to progress, I will be dead, and if I do not allow the situation to progress, I will be dead. One way I will lose my respect and the other way I will become a real threat.*

For if I showed a higher level of ethical standard, I would always have something on him. Who with that kind of threat hanging over his head would allow me into his inner circle? My God, I was already at a disadvantage because I could not go on the hunting trips. Now my career at this company was in peril. Anyway, that is how I felt.

[Maybe someone with different Monkeys could have handled this without much thought but I was coming from a belief that the world was fair and had no training on how to handle these situations in a Corporate environment.]

The question of what to do was not an issue for me. He was married. My dilemma was how to do it and keep my career path open. I wanted to disarm the situation. I did not want to be a threat. I wanted to talk to Henry about what had happened and disarm any potential negativity, but I did not know how and, frankly, it scared me.

He called, "I can't get any beer."

"No problem. We can have a drink some other time."

I was saved but the damage had been done.

There were not many women in the industry in higher management to turn to for mentoring, especially on these kinds of issues. I was lucky to have Gail Sermersheim, head of the Southeast region of HBO. (I do not think she had her VP title at that time.) After I got back to Atlanta, I called her to have lunch to ask her how I should handle the situation going forward and hopefully keep my career at Metrovision.

After I told her what happened with Henry, she related, "Some have, some haven't and you better not."

Well, no lie, I already knew that. I wanted to know how to save my career with this company. I was left to figure that out myself. The answer—I couldn't save it. Leaving was only a matter of time. I wanted to sit down with Henry to tell him how flattered I was with his attention, but I would not involve myself with another married man. I had learned that lesson the hard way. (I called my affair with a married man the best mistake I ever made, because we were deeply in love—a true tragedy. It was nonetheless a mistake according to society and I was determined not to repeat it.) Anyway, I was looking for the right opportunity to talk to him. But the time never was right, so things were left incomplete. Clearly, he could never feel safe with me again because I had something on him. That, unfortunately, was my downfall. I would never be able to be in his inner circle and that left me vulnerable to anyone who was in the inner circle.

Our southern gentleman, Don, of the meeting planning sort, did get into the inner circle and when he did, he manipulated me right out of the company. I never understood why they asked me to resign, except that this guy was saying things that clearly undermined my credibility with the boys. He not only held the confrontation about the company meeting against me, but there were complaints about him and other issues in the field that were coming to me. And, stupid me, in an innocent effort to help the field people, I brought these issues to Ernie.

[I was taught to take care of my little brother, which apparently, I transferred to everyone else in need. So, when this happened, my Monkeys became active and my Joan of Arc tendency came out. I look back now and think what a naïve fool I was, but then I was coming from the world-is-fair teaching, so I had no idea about the dangerous territory I was in.]

I told him what was being said. Instead of going to the field himself, like I thought he would, he sent Don, our Southern friend, to find out what the issues were. Don returned stating there were no problems. When I called the boys in the field to find out what happened, the boys said, "He didn't ask, so no one said anything. Everything was very cordial and nice but no real issues were discussed."

Of course, the field was not going to stick their necks out and bring up the problems unless the man in charge made the place safe to do that. Don availed himself, but because no issues were brought up and discussed by the field, he returned with a clean bill of health, stating there were no problems—such typical behavior in Corporate America.

Now, I was the troublemaker. I felt I had led the Charge of the Light Brigade only to turn and find the boys in the field hiding behind the rocks while I rode alone on my white horse before the enemy. I never forgave those boys who complained to me; notice I use the word boys here. I still consider them cowards, but then who was the real fool?

[The situation showed how very naïve I was. I thought I was helping. In reality, though, in a Corporate environment, I was very stupid. I thought those guys in the field wanted help. Well, they did but they did not have the courage to speak for themselves and the way I went about helping sealed my fate with my fine Southern gentleman.]

If I did not have an enemy by calling attention to the discriminatory practices of this man during the meeting debacle, I certainly did now. This peer of mine wanted me out, and no matter what happened, I was going to be out. A few years passed but the fact I was never in a position to counter whatever he said about me behind closed doors took its toll. In time, I was asked to resign. I was never given a reason.

ENTER THE LAWYERS

I needed some official advice on my situation, so I called a friend whose husband was an attorney. She sent me to an attorney who handled these types of things. I started to tell him the story when he interrupted me. "This isn't happening to you because you are a woman, is it?"

He caught me off guard. I balked and didn't know what to say, so I started laughing, my usual response when I am nervous.

His retort was, "My dear, I see this all of the time."

He went on to advise me that I needed to get a separation agreement, or the minute I walked out the door of the company, the severance they promised me could totally disappear and I would have no legal recourse.

Well, Henry was also a Southern gentleman, and when I asked him for a separation agreement, he got furious. Guess he took it as an affront to his word. I told him I trusted him, but the rest of the executives, one of which was Don, my other Southern gentleman, I didn't trust (none of them knew Henry made passes). And God forbid, if Henry got run over by a truck, they may not honor his severance agreement. I thought I almost had him as he thought for a moment, but then he still wouldn't do it. A few tears did get me a couple of more months' severance, which I offered to use only if I needed it. Tears were not my usual style, but by now I had learned that the direct Northern way was not effective with Southerners.

I went back to the attorney and told him what had transpired and that I was unable to get the separation agreement. He said, "Under the circumstances, you will need to do one other thing. Is there anyone in the organization who you trust?"

"Yes, my boss, Ernie."

"Tell him that if they don't follow through with their severance agreement, you will sue them for sexual harassment and sex discrimination and you will let everyone in the industry know."

I was horrified. "I can't win that."

This man taught me one of the biggest lessons in my life that day when he said, "My dear, we are not in this to win; we are here to play the game. I simply want you to let them know you have an ace up your sleeve and you're not afraid to use it."

[That was my first introduction to the fact that life is a game. I wish I had paid more attention then, to that lesson. I would have been able to take things less seriously.]

Well, I thought long and hard about the advice I had been given and didn't get much sleep as I remembered what a can of worms I had opened at Continental. People do not realize the emotional stress and strain situations like this create. I recalled the drain during the confrontation with Continental, so I finally decided not to say anything and hope for the best.

Probably a quirk of fate but Ernie decided to take me out to lunch the next day. You see, he tried to stop things from happening, but Don had done his damage and Ernie woke up too late to the circumstances around him. A quadruple bypass slowed him down enough to finally see what was happening. Until then, he seemed oblivious to Don's slow usurping of his responsibilities. Unfortunately, by then he was powerless to alter the events already set in motion.

At lunch he asked, "How are you doing?"

"Fine, but I didn't get much sleep because of a phone call I got yesterday."

"What phone call?"

"I thought long and hard and decided not to discuss it with anyone."

Well, that was like putting a red flag in front of a bull. I no longer remember exactly how the conversation went, but I recall thinking *it couldn't have gone better if I had scripted it myself.* He pulled the information out of me one piece at a time.

I do remember his shock when I said, "I'll always wonder if this happened to me because Henry felt guilty about the passes he made at me and so would not let me into his inner circle."

He became very focused, his eyes got as big as saucers and emphatically he asked, "What passes?"

"Oh, you remember, I told you a long time ago." In reality, I had not told him.

He stated in a very stern voice with distinct emphasis on each word, "Refresh...my...memory!"

You see, several of the senior executives had affairs and one of the officers had one with his secretary. His wife was a smart cookie and had her own old southern money. She hired detectives and even bugged the company phones. When she collected all the proof she needed, she called to tell her husband she was coming in to confront him with the evidence. He had just enough time to get the secretary out of the building. When his wife arrived, she went into his office, shut the door and proceeded to break every object available that could be destroyed. All people could hear was crashing glass. It must have been an interesting experience. Since Ernie and I were out of town, we missed the fireworks. Anyway, there was a great deal of sensitivity around such issues because some of the guys had been caught.

I told him the whole story and when finished, I said, "Ernie, don't let them *fuck* with me because I *will* fuck back." I actually used those words for emphasis.

I got everything they promised. You see, the ace I had was not the threat of a lawsuit but the possibility the wife would find out. Even an allegation in that environment would have been a disaster for Henry. I find shameful that I was forced to operate that way. All I wanted was to be part of the team but I had forgotten––I was not a man. I was a man in a woman's body. (Remember, my karmic punishment.)

Sexual harassment? Sexual discrimination? Or was this bucking the status quo? [My assessment in hindsight -- a combination of all three. I clearly did not know how to make my points without making enemies and, given the times, I am not sure that was possible to do without totally caving to the status quo anyway.]

THE GOOD TIMES

Lest I sound like all the times at Metrovision were negative, I must tell you about some of the good times.

My position was one of the best I had up to then. Because of my position, I was privy to many opportunities in the industry that most would not enjoy. One of my duties was keeping track of the programming that went up on the satellites and on which bird they were being delivered. Back then we were smack dab in the franchising frenzy so offering the latest programming to the cities requesting RFPs was paramount. This responsibility was time-consuming but had its perks.

I remember one day I received an invitation to the Playboy Mansion during one of our Cable Conventions. It seemed real hush hush. Names had to be provided and cleared. We were picked up by Playboy limousines and names were checked. When we got to the Mansion, we had the run of the place. I must say our expectations were somewhat out of place. There were no stars. There were no famous people and Mr. Hefner was nowhere to be seen. Just us cable people. We had no idea why we were invited. We suspected that Playboy was going to announce some kind of new channel.

We explored the game room, with connecting all-mirrored bedrooms off the side. One could only imagine what had taken place there. We explored the famous grotto off the swimming pool--all temperature controlled to eliminate the need for clothes or suits. Orchids seeming to grow out of the stone cave-like walls with comfortable lounging areas alongside the stream just big enough for two…or three.

All of this was really exciting for me…to see how the other side lives. However, the visit was still disappointing with only us cable folks. Then Ted Turner showed up with his latest blond date, who happened to be a past playmate. Then and only then did Mr. Hefner show his face while dressed in one of his famous silk smoking jackets and pajamas.

Listening to Ted and Hugh was fun as they tried to one up

themselves by discussing who had the bigger mansions. Mr. Hefner did announce the coming of the Playboy Channel later at the convention.

I was invited to a second party at the Mansion. This time I took my good-looking cousin, who happened to live in San Clemente at the time. I warned him that there was no need to bring his camera because there would be no *pretty* people there. No stars. No famous people…just us cable people. Well, Hugh was filming the party for the Playboy Channel that had been launched for several months. What did I know? Hugh came out with five gorgeous playmates on his sides, all scantily dressed. There were stars there and famous people. "No famous people, huh?" was the only comment from my cousin.

There were many other opportunities like this because of my position, which I suppose added to my anger when I lost the position through no fault of my own--except, of course, not knowing how to positively manage the Corporate politics.

ACKNOWLEDGEMENT STOLEN

I left Continental when I won the award from the Direct Marketing Association. Now I was going to be awarded one from the Cable Television Administration and Marketing Society before I departed Metrovision.

[I must tell you about this as what happened fits with one of my most prominent Monkeys…lack of acknowledgement.]

The award ceremony in San Francisco was a somewhat formal event. A few of my friends and I sat in the audience waiting for our category to be called. I felt we had a good chance of winning something because I was a pretty good judge of marketing programs and only entered when I felt I had a good campaign with extraordinary results.

We sat enjoying our camaraderie when our category came up. Wow, there it was—Metrovision, winner of the top prize. But there was a problem: someone else's name was listed as the Director of Marketing on the slide, not mine. And as I hesitated to get up for it, not knowing if the company name was wrong or the Director of Marketing name was wrong, some man was running up on stage to get my award. They had listed the incorrect name for Director of Marketing. The award was ours. My few seconds in the limelight were taken by someone else and a man to boot!

The officials from CTAM wasted no time getting to me to apologize for the mistake. They retrieved the award from the gentleman and gave it to me during a small ceremony at the cocktail reception that night. Needless to say, not many were paying attention, so CTAM decided they would do a big article in the next newsletter about me and the award. That was all well and good but when the word got out that I was *resigning* from Metrovision, they decided not to do the article. The story of my life—the recognition always eluded me. All of this added to my anger.

[I had no idea my individual Monkeys kept the pattern in place for me. And, as I said before, I did not even know about the Monkeys then.]

That burst of remembered anger brought me back to the church and the continuing eulogy for Jim. Duffy was finished and now the priest was talking. As I sat listening, I could not believe my ears. The priest was telling the story of how Jim called him a few days before he died and asked if God was mad at him. Had he, Jim, done something to displease God?

At that moment, I wanted to jump up and yell out, "I know why he is mad at you."

[That was definitely a moment when my Monkeys were in total control.]

I do not know if God was mad at Jim but I know I was. He recognized the job I was doing for Cox but did not protect me from those who were threatened by my performance. He let them, in his words, slot me.

CHAPTER 4

NO MORE NAÏVETÉ
THE COX COMMUNICATIONS STORY

DECENTRALIZATION

Cox Cable, as it was called in those days, [now Cox Communications] was a Multiple System Operator (MSO) having many cable TV systems across the country. As a cable system, we procured the rights to carry and redistribute all satellite-delivered channels, like HBO, CNN, Discovery, Nickelodeon, etc., as well as all off-air networks, like the local ABC, NBC, CBS affiliates, and any other networks in the viewing areas. Cox was poised for great future growth.

James O. Robbins, President of Cox, was tall, lanky and seemingly down to earth, easy to approach. People joked that the hat he usually wore made him appear to be an everyday Joe, not the CEO of a large Corporation--he looked ready for a fishing weekend and only needed a few flies hooked on the brim. Jim had a military background and a family with two daughters, so you might think he would have a tendency to support women in business, or maybe not. Jim received some of his direct line experience at Continental Cablevision, where I had functioned as Director of Marketing, though my title was the lesser Advertising Manager.

Jim gave a speech at an intimate breakfast meeting of Women in Cable (WIC) in the mid-1980s, while I still was working for Metrovision and President of the Atlanta Chapter of WIC. At that meeting he said, "If you (women) want to get ahead and break the glass ceiling, you need to get field experience."

Jim was speaking from the position of the president of a

decentralized corporation. At Cox, the field had all the direct line responsibility—the money makers. The people in the Corporate office were *in theory* only advisors, so getting field experience was highly regarded.

Having a previous professional relationship with Jim, who was I to argue with his advice, even though the majority of his own staff did not have experience in the field and, of course, his whole staff at this time was male. This counsel was clearly for the females as an explanation of why we were not getting to higher levels in our organizations. Taking Jim's advice literally, I later took a position at Cox Cable in Oklahoma City as Director of Marketing.

This would turn out to be a wonderful reprieve from the different discriminatory behaviors I had faced in my previous two positions and the best and most fun position I would hold in the industry from the standpoint of getting direct results for my actions.

Remember that dear mentor of mine who once told me, "It always boils down to personalities in the end." I would add that it boils down to an individual's Monkeys. And lucky for me my new boss, I would find, either had a great deal of respect for me or didn't have the usual discriminatory Monkey behaviors, or a combination of both.

OKLAHOMA CITY

So off I went, kicking and screaming because who wanted to go to the Dust Bowl of the Midwest? Not I! Unfortunately, or fortunately, depending on your perspective, I had found the position I was looking for in what turned out to be this wonderful wind-blown city. My new boss, J. Curt Hockemeier, VP and General Manager, had the cable system ready to be marketed.

Curt was a couple of years younger than me. Though short, he carried the persona of a very self-assured man. I found him to be a very proactive supervisor. There were no games--he was upfront, personable, very businesslike and would constantly challenge you to do your best--always asking questions. He treated

his staff like the advisors they were to be for him. He would ask
for their opinions, contemplate what they had to say and then
make his decisions. Curt acted and dressed the part of the VP and
General Manager of a large cable system and you could tell he had
professional exposure. To learn he came from farm life in Mis-
souri kind of threw me; it did not seem to fit. He ended up being
the best supervisor I had in my career, a clear leader and not a do-
it-my-way boss.

He once told me I was the only person who interviewed for the
position who did not have their tongue hanging out. He was
right--I did not want to go to Oklahoma City, so I questioned them
from every perspective looking for the reason not to go. I couldn't
find any good reason. The job was perfect for me at the time.

What a great opportunity to put my money where my mouth is. I had
been at the Corporate level my whole cable career, always in a
position of telling the field what I thought they needed to do, but
I had no direct line responsibility. In this new position, I was an
officer of the Corporation as Director of Marketing and I would
be getting, as Jim would say, *real field experience* with that coveted
direct line responsibility. I finally had this great opportunity to
put my thoughts and beliefs into action—sink or swim time. In a
Corporate position in a decentralized corporation one can only influence the people in the field. There is no risk in advising someone as I had done from the Corporate level at Metrovision and
Continental Cablevision. This time the responsibility was mine
and mine alone. My neck was on the line. That was scary and exciting at the same time.

This relatively new cable system was in trouble and clearly a
turnaround situation. I had to laugh when I was out on one of my
interview trips. I had called the cable system's travel agent to
change my flight schedule only to have their agent tell me, "You
don't want that job. That place has revolving doors. No one stays
there." What a great endorsement.

I knew that and I knew why.

This was my dream job, not only because it was a challenge I was up for, but, for the first time in my career, I was being paid what the job was worth. Working for Cox, I believed the only reason I wouldn't reach a top position would be my performance. (Remember my belief system: Life was fair and hard work was rewarded.)

I had a great boss in Curt, who got out of my way and let me do my job. He had done all he could on cost control. Revenue was now the issue. This was during the mid-'80s and the region, with its oil-based economy, had been severely hit with a downturn. Conditions were so bad, people walked away from their homes. At one time, we estimated that 20% of the homes were boarded up and empty. In my mind, despite the abandoned homes, the time was perfect for cable TV. People needed something for entertainment, and cable was cheap, relative to everything else. (Basic cable was $12.95/month. Add all of the pay channels and it totaled about $50.)

The first thing I had to do when I settled into the new job was hire a new General Sales Manager. I brought in Jim Lisko from Metrovision where he had been the most promising Sales Manager in the field. He was excellent at sales management and knew how to motivate a sales team.

I did not know he was going to be the catalyst for my first disagreement with the Senior VP of Marketing, Daman Gupta, born and raised in India, who was a very intelligent man, but he had an incredible need to be viewed as the expert. (This came out years later when the Corporation put us through Birkman Method Testing.)

[Unbeknownst to me at the time, he carried all kinds of cultural Monkeys on his back. India is a caste society and the highest regarded woman was still lower than the lowest man. His ingrained beliefs kept women in a place to be controlled and under his thumb. But this was camouflaged by the fact he hired lots of women. His Monkeys around needing total control started to surface early with me and what I felt needed to be done to complete the job I was hired to do.]

He started by insisting on interviewing my candidate for General Sales Manager. What Senior VP of Marketing of a big Corporation inserts himself into the interviewing process of a General Sales Manager out in the field? Well, for whatever reason, he did, and gave a thumbs-down on Jim. I found myself in a position of going against Daman right out of the box, not a place I wanted to be. I will never forget Curt's reaction when I went to tell him I was hiring Jim.

He said, "You know *we* are making a career decision here."

I was extremely impressed that he included himself in that statement, a quality of a real leader.

"Yes, sir, I know, and I also realize you don't know me any better than you know Jim, but you hired me to do a job. I am the only one who is aware of his ability and it's my neck on the line."

So, he turned around to the phone and called Daman to tell him Jim was being hired. That was the beginning of my being on *the other side of Daman*. Not a good place to be, especially as a woman.

My job, as I understood it, was to turn this fledging cable system around. To achieve that, I needed to do some unorthodox things. I knew it would take some time and patience, something of which Corporations have very little. As usual, in a Corporate environment, things are slow to change.

The first thing I did was stop all marketing. That was a popular move--Not! Not only unpopular, but people thought I was nuts. I am sure some were questioning their decision to hire me. I had to do it, though, because the market was really confused.

Another franchised cable system was in the area but in another part of the city—Multimedia. Because of that, any time either of us went into the media with an offer of reduced installation costs, in effect, both of us were in that same offer because most consumers did not know which cable system serviced their area. When we got calls off Multimedia's advertising, we would honor their promotions as they would ours. By doing this, we were virtually in promotion mode all the time and giving away installation of the product on an ongoing basis. Both cable systems were having revenue issues and were in dire need of new customers.

I shut down all media marketing and kept direct sales and telemarketing going. I did not want any advertising in the media, no promotions of any kind. I was resting the market while negotiating an advertising co-op with Multimedia. We could do this because both companies were in different franchise areas and not in competition.

I put all the immediate pressure on my new General Sales Manager, Jim. He was great and really understood the plan. I told him, "Get me a net gain every month, even if it is just one customer. We need to send a signal to the Corporate office that something different is happening out here."

Jim and I both knew, in the short term, we would not make any of our numbers, which usually got people fired, so we had to show them something different was going on to give them pause. It's fun to look back on our monthly customer net gains because they were sparse, like one or six or twelve (and that was a good month), but there were no net losses, so we were growing, a major difference from before.

Of course, two or six customers per month was not going to *cut it* over the long term, so market preparation was in the making. I had to appease my company, but what I had not expected was the problems I started to have with a certain supplier, Home Box Office (HBO.)

Enter the Big Boys–HBO. When I joined Cox Cable, I was told it was a decentralized organization, meaning all of the decisions regarding the bottom line rested with the field. When I got to my new position, however, and started unraveling the issues, I discovered a lot was coming down from the Corporate office as off-the-record Corporate agreements and, interestingly, those terms were being delivered by one of our Pay TV suppliers, HBO.

My HBO rep informed me, "You are an *HBO Cinemax market* and have to sell HBO and Cinemax before you sell other services, per our agreement with your Corporate office."

My rep was a nice guy. I was not sure if he was right out of school because his boyish features and clean-cut appearance surely gave me that impression. I liked him and had no real fear of HBO's position. However, because I came from a free-market mentality, their posture did not sit well with me. I believed the consumer should be able to choose and let the viability of the product determine their choice.

HBO was clearly the leader at that time but Showtime was a close second choice. Showtime's philosophy was to buy only movies for which they could get exclusive rights. Thus, if the consumer got HBO without Showtime, they would get only half the movies made in Hollywood. Back then, the product on both services were just movies and a few sports shows. Showtime was fighting for survival and second position in the market. HBO was attempting to secure Cinemax's survival as the number two pay-tv service. To accomplish this, there was a battle to push Showtime out of the second position.

Along I came, not having any interest in the fight between HBO and Showtime (which did turn into a lawsuit and later was settled in Showtime's favor). All I was concerned about was the consumer and how I could sell the most product to the most people. I started to equalize the playing field for all the products we had available—HBO, Showtime, Cinemax and The Movie Channel—by creating price-point packages rather than product-based packages. HBO started pushing against what I was doing. They were trying to dictate to me what and how I should market.

So, you can imagine the pressure I got when I stopped signing up for the HBO marketing campaigns. When I had signed up for their campaigns and they were putting money toward our marketing, I would, in theory, have to follow their *rules*—no selling the other services, like Showtime, when in an HBO Cinemax promotion.

I was always amazed how many executives actually accepted that bunk. Coming from Metrovision, we always did multipay promotions (selling all pay services at the same time). The strategy, followed for years was: we are doing a multipay promotion and, if HBO wants to be represented, then they have to kick in advertising support the same as the other pay channels or they would be out of the advertising.

With me at a local level and not at the Corporate level, HBO may have felt they had more clout. Well, they did with my Corporate office but we were decentralized, so I had the authority as long as Curt, my General Manager, backed me. What they did not seem to get—this was my neck on the line, not theirs. My job was to help get this system turned around and, if I failed, I would pay the price like everyone who preceded me.

I had no idea Daman had negotiated the contract with HBO and promised Oklahoma City to be an HBO/Cinemax market. My focus was turning the market around and so was Curt's.

[Unbeknownst to me, I was, for a second time, positioning myself opposite Daman, thus setting myself up for later problems. Remember, he had a need to be viewed as the expert and came from India where the highest woman was still lower than the lowest man.]

As part of my strategy, we did not sign up for the HBO campaigns knowing that Multimedia would sign up. Because they did sign up, HBO had to put all kinds of media in the market to support them. Knowing this, I would do my own direct mail and run it off Multimedia's HBO-supported advertising. Remember, the consumer, for the most part, did not know which cable system they were in.

Curt came into my office one day. "I just got a call from Atlanta (headquarters) and they want to know why you are not in the HBO campaign." This questioning became common place and my pat answer was, "I am in the HBO campaign. I just did not sign up for it."

Fortunately, Curt understood what I was doing—shifting the negotiating leverage. It got to be a joke with us and HBO was getting more and more frustrated. They were used to getting their way.

My poor rep, who was between me, my staff and his humorless results-oriented bosses in Dallas, cordially put up with our abuse. Jim suggested one day to take him to the Pink Pony for one of their *great hamburgers*. Jim and Scott, his Direct Sales Manager, pulled that stunt on me one day. Agreeing to go for the great hamburger, I went with them to the Pink Pony, knowing something was up. As I walked in, I was greeted by a naked woman on a flying trapeze, coming right at me in all her glory. Yes, Oklahoma City had no restrictions on what a stripper was to wear or not wear at that time.

Our poor rep took it all in stride…especially the table dance. I guess, subconsciously, we were letting him know what we thought about the policy he was trying to get us to honor. I don't think he minded.

He still had to do his job. When pushed, I would say to him, "They hired me to do the marketing in this system, so I will be doing it my way. When they hire you, you can do it your way." I did not mind losing my job if my way did not work. However, I did mind losing my job because I was forced to listen to someone who didn't have the responsibility.

HBO became so desperate they sent in my friend, Gail Sermersheim, the head of the HBO office in Atlanta. Gail and I had been friends during my days at Metrovision and Women In Cable (WIC). She was very instrumental in encouraging me to use my skills to organize the Atlanta Chapter of WIC, which was having a difficult start. I became the only two-term President of that organization at a time when stability was needed. As a result, it became the cable force in Atlanta.

When they sent her in to deal with me, rather than a round of golf like the men, we did a spa day. She presented her position, or I should say HBO's position, and I stated mine. Mine was that I was not going to support HBO's attempt to put Showtime out of business. She informed me she was simply doing her job.

Under the spa face mask, I remarked, "It is time that you understand I also am simply doing my job and that job is to help turn the OKC cable system around." From that point forward, she treated me like I did not *like* her or HBO and that I openly favored Showtime, which I didn't.

[Shows you what happens when one side takes a position and the other simply wants to remain objective. Sort of like drawing the line in the sand and saying, like President Bush did after 9-11, "You are either with me or against me." With that stance, there is no room for being objective.]

By this time, I had stayed out of three campaigns, and my rep said to me one day, "HBO will do anything to get you back."

That is where I wanted to be! By now I had cemented the advertising co-op deal with Multimedia and had let them in on what I was doing with HBO. We had agreed to go into the market together with TV and radio only four times a year.

I also had time to evaluate the research about the system Cox had. Daman, coming from Coca Cola, brought research to Cox and later was credited with bringing research to the cable industry. I had plenty of data to reference. There was an incorrect price perception in the market. Because of earlier top-down selling, the consumers thought cable was $50+ a month.

In September of 1986, basic cable (all available channels except the Pay channels) was $12.95 a month. Even though our medium was television, we had never used it for advertising. That was due to the fact that: (1) TV stations would not take our ads in the early days because they considered us competition; and (2) we, as an industry, simply would not spend the money.

I finally had HBO where I needed them. We wanted them to help us advertise the cable product to turn around the misperceptions the customer had about our prices. We negotiated the production of television spots to clear up the price perception and all at HBO's expense, a real coup. I knew if we could turn around the misunderstood pricing, we could start moving the market.

So that winter, we, Multimedia and Cox, went into the media for the first-time advertising on network television in a coordinated effort. It worked. I remember Jim sharing with me that one of his salesmen had a potential customer who had turned him away the night before but called the salesman back because he had seen one of the commercials and wanted to sign up. He had been unaware that cable was so inexpensive.

From then on, we were in charge of the marketing and not HBO, not to mention well on our way to shifting the consumer value perception of our product.

> *I drifted back to the church as the eulogies were continuing, thinking to myself, Wow! Up until now I have not focused on the fact that I set myself up as an adversary to Daman so early on in the process. Being blind to political implications and to other people's Monkeys, my only focus was to help turn the OKC cable business around, what I thought I was hired to do. I was not paying attention to whose toes I might step on in the process. And that toe-stepping was only the beginning.*

Once we got the market calmed down and Multimedia and Cox were coordinating our advertising efforts, I started looking for what else was inhibiting Cox's growth. One day when monitoring the customer service reps to see what I could find, I noticed that they were quoting pricing that even I did not understand, so I started digging and asking questions. I had no idea what a can of worms was about to be opened.

Working with our computer manager, I studied the pricing codes. Whoa! What a mess--old rates, grandfathered rates, new rates and everything-in-between rates. Nothing made much sense. I might as well have said, "Want a piece of candy, little girl? I have any kind of candy you could want." And that is how the customer service reps acted with the customers. "Let me see what kind of price I can get for you."

I believe this particular mess was caused by: (1) miscommunication; (2) change in management; (3) change in customer service personnel over time; and (4) most importantly, no one officially in charge of paying attention to the changing rates and how that affected the computer codes. There were no policies in place governing code changes; they all continued to exist in the computer. Many were not supposed to be used anymore but, because the rate codes remained, and there were customers still in those codes, they stayed active, which meant our reps could still access and put new customers into them. The computer could not keep new people from going into a rate as long as the code was active. The only way to keep the customer out was to make sure management and reps understood that no new customers should be put into those rate codes. Well, over time, with turnover, that communication had been lost.

Additionally, when they launched Cinemax and created an HBO/Cinemax package $3.00 cheaper than any other service combination packages, it was implemented incorrectly. They ended up creating two packages with the same product. If the customer asked for Cinemax first, they would get a package $3.00 cheaper than if they asked for HBO first. Same services, but different prices. What a mess!

Jim Lisko and I flew to Atlanta to make a presentation to the marketing and operations staffs about the situation. In that presentation, I tried to add comic relief by creating a cartoon of the shyster on the corner with a long mustache and a big black coat hiding stolen or fake watches, who, when he opened his coat to show his wares had all kinds of different rates instead of watches.

When I presented the situation with the HBO/Cinemax package, Daman was adamant that I was incorrect. He postured, "You are wrong. The pricing was created so the HBO/Cinemax package was $3.00 cheaper than HBO and any of the other pay services, like Showtime."

With a smile on my face, I countered, "That may have been the intention; however, that is not how it was implemented."

[Here I was again bringing to light a situation that Daman thought had been done differently. I was not being political. Had I known this was such an issue with Daman, I would have gone to him first with this information so he would not have been caught off guard. Fortunately, or unfortunately, my focus was the predicament and not politics. He certainly was not at fault because things had not been implemented as he thought. These kinds of miscommunications happen all of the time.]

I had a second agenda at this meeting. Remember, Daman was against hiring Jim, my General Sales Manager, when I first joined the company. I wanted to use this meeting to expose Jim and his ability to Daman so we could start to dissipate his negative view of Jim. I had Jim do a presentation on his analysis of the market from the direct sales perspective. He really did a great deal of work on this situation, so you can understand my dismay when Daman got up and walked out just as Jim started to present. I was not a happy camper and was upset with what I perceived as Daman's rudeness. But then he was the Sr. VP of Marketing, so what could I do?

Fortunately, Daman returned to the conference room as Jim was recapping. This caught Daman's attention and he had Jim repeat the whole presentation for his benefit. Thank God! The exposure did the job intended. About a year later, Daman came up to Jim and me at a company meeting and told us he had been wrong about Jim and he was the best General Sales Manager Cox had. That ended up being one of two times I received positive feedback from Daman. I was thrilled for Jim and myself.

Once back in the cable system, I proceeded to start the pricing cleanup. In 1987, only a couple personal computers existed, in the Accounting Department, so all the analyses had to be done by hand. I had to figure out how many customers were in each different rate code and how many different rate codes were attached to each customer, who fell into what group, etc. It was complicated. Once I had a good understanding of where everyone was with their prices, I had to figure out where they would be going when I created the new packages.

To minimize confusion and sticker shock, I created what I called *value-added packages* and analyzed what would happen to the customers' rates as I moved them into these new combinations.

Many different products would be added to the bundles to give the perception of value but did not add a lot of cost. I would include a guide, a remote, additional outlets or all of them. From my perspective, consumers absolutely hate a-la-carte pricing. They want to get the lowest price for the most stuff. Only accountants or bean counters like a-la-carte pricing. (The airlines nickel and dime the customer to death today—I mean paying extra for more leg room—please. Sorry, I digress.)

The analysis was extremely complicated. However, I seemed to have a real knack for it and I absolutely loved it!

After creating the new packages, I looked at where customers would move once the change was made. Movement was all over the map--some people were going down in price, some were staying the same, some were going up and about seven hundred were going up a lot.

Our billing computer company, Cable Data, had created a program that allowed a complete download of the customer rate data from the billing computer into a personal computer. This download ability enabled us to have the data in a format that would give us a great deal of flexibility in terms of marketing to the different affected groups. So, we hired a computer programmer and had a program written that would allow us to send specific marketing messages to each set of subscribers.

For the 700 people who were going up as much as $7.00, we called them personally in hopes of controlling the downgrades. To our amazement, the vast majority of those customers were so surprised we personally called them ahead of the rate realignment, they kept their service levels and accepted the rate increase. That result was totally unexpected, so the tactic became part of the marketing plan for all other rate realignments I was involved in later in my career.

This rate realignment was a marked success, so I wrote a case study about it. In 1988, it won a Cable Television Administration and Marketing (CTAM) Case Study Award. That was the first time a download of billing information from the billing mainframe computer to a personal computer to segment the marketing messages was used. The case study was the highest rated that year. I was not supposed to know, except one of our executives was on the judging committee and he let me in on the secret.

In 1989, I wrote another case study called System Turnaround, which won a second CTAM award. I wrote this to promote the job done by all those involved in our turnaround. The buck stops at the top and most of the success kudos needed to go to J. Curt Hockemeier, who hired and supported me and those under me in doing our jobs.

Jim and I, in the first year, used to joke about whether we would last a year in our positions since the turnover was so great before we arrived. We had a job to do that was going to take longer than most corporations had patience, certainly longer than a year. While Curt, Jim and I were spearheads of the effort, if it had not been for the complete cooperation of all the department heads and their staffs, the job would not have been completed.

I am not a maintenance manager who is satisfied dealing with the status quo. I am a troubleshooter and I love troubleshooting. After almost four years of things turning around and business significantly improving, the everyday running of the cable system took on a more mundane tempo and I started to become somewhat bored. So, I put my hand up for one of the three Director of Field Marketing positions located in Atlanta at the Corporate office. I would be able to help many systems at a time and happily get back to Atlanta. *I would, however, also be working in Daman's department.*

OFF TO ATLANTA

I had a conversation one day with Curt before raising my hand for the Director of Field Marketing position in Atlanta. We were discussing my next career move possibilities and he had reservations about what I was contemplating.

He proceeded to tell me, "You know Daman is a male chauvinist. Are you sure you want to work for him?" I stood up for

Daman and said, "Are you kidding? He hires women, in fact, his staff is mostly women."

Curt smiled, "I said he was a chauvinist, not stupid. He knows he can hire women for less and they will work harder."

Curt's comment was shocking. I couldn't believe I was hearing this admission from Curt but I knew he was right. Daman's behavior seemed to bear out the Indian caste system that women were inferior to men.

I should have seen the *writing on the wall*. Gretchen Shine, the Director of Field Marketing for my system had told me that Daman was trying to hold her back. She had to do all kinds of things, like getting support from the men in Operations, to get out from under his control. For her, moving into Operations was the only way out and, to my understanding, it was without Daman's support.

I was blind to the knowledge I had and to the warnings I was getting. They did not matter to me because I was so motivated to get back to Atlanta. This move was the only way I saw to do that and still be employed. I kind of had the *can't-happen-to-me mindset*, a fatal flaw in thinking for anyone. Besides I would be working directly for Morgan Taylor, Director of Marketing, not Daman.

Morgan was a beautiful lady, a feisty petite redhead, always well put together, with a flair for simplicity--choosing a lone pin to offset her ensemble rather than a lot of jewelry. Clearly, she looked the part of a Vice-President and I recall the battle she had over the years to get the VP title [another warning I ignored.]

Cindy, who had the Director of Marketing position previous to Morgan, gave up the fight and left the company (which is what many good women do rather than fight). She actually had a potential lawsuit against the company. When she was Director of Marketing and Daman was promoted to Senior VP of Marketing, he had four directors under him. He promoted the two male directors to VP but not the two female directors, arguing that the two men needed the title to do their jobs. I guess the women were better at their jobs because he didn't think they needed the title to do their jobs! She chose to leave Cox rather than sue.

[All of this was more information I chose to ignore in my overwhelming desire to get back to Atlanta.]

At any rate, working for Morgan, I thought I would be insulated because she was active in Women in Cable and pushing women's issues.

[Not knowing it then, that actually was a detriment rather than an advantage.]

***

By the time I was promoted to the Corporate office as Field Marketing Director over the Western Division, Oklahoma City had dramatically turned around. We had increased penetration by 20%. We had cleaned up all of the pricing and packaging and other marketing and advertising issues, won awards for two case studies about the process from CTAM, our Cable Marketing Society, and all because Curt allowed me to do my job.

Now, in my new position, I was in my element. I was to oversee the marketing and troubleshooting in the Western Division, which had six cable systems: Lubbock, TX, Oklahoma City and a slew of systems in California—San Diego, Bakersfield, Humboldt, and Santa Barbara—Yea!

My successes in the field came, for the most part, from not listening to Corporate marketing and doing what my field experience showed me I had to do. (I was considered a maverick in my days at OKC.)

In the position of Field Marketing Director, I had a direct line of responsibility to Marketing and a dotted line of responsibility to my Divisional Operations VP, Bob O'Leary, which meant my direct line could fire me but my dotted line could only advise. Bob was exactly what his name implied—a gregarious Irishman who loved to laugh, party and play golf but never in excess because he was also a very health-conscious man. We would always meet in the wee hours of the morning while on the West coast, him running and me walking.

I still functioned as somewhat of a maverick and Bob seemed to like that. Under him, my direction was to improve the viability of the system's marketing operations. The marketing people at Corporate, most of whom had no field experience, had a somewhat different vision of what made up my job. The difference did not come to light until a couple years later, but I will point it out now because it was at the bottom of my success.

I asked Morgan one day, "What is your view of the scope of my job?"

"You are to get the systems to participate in the Corporate marketing campaigns, review telemarketing and direct sales operations, and make sure they are taking advantage of any supplier monies directed at Pay TV marketing. What do you think your job is?"

"Anything that affects a system's ability to sell a new, or keep an existing, customer is my responsibility."

"That is pretty broad."

"If I don't restructure the pricing and packaging, review restrictive collection policies, evaluate how the technology is affecting consumers' use of their new electronics, etc., all of the greatest marketing in the world would go to waste."

[My understanding of the consumer was the basis of my successes and, I might add, I believe the reason she was threatened by me. But that will play out later.]

Lubbock, Texas. Once in the new position, I was approached at a company meeting by one of the General Managers in my division. He wanted me to come to Lubbock. "Do for Lubbock what you did for Oklahoma City."

I made a trip to all of my new clients to introduce myself and get to know everyone and I immediately put a specific focus on Lubbock. Thanks to Daman's research and after Lubbock's management evaluated their bottom line and research trends, they saw that if they did nothing and the arrows kept going the way they were, they would be out of business in a few years. They wanted me to figure out what was happening so they could reverse the downward spiral.

Their research indicated the perception of cable-TV's value

was diminishing and at a rapid rate; because of that, they were losing customers. To make up for the customer loss and make their numbers, system management was raising the rates and charging for things they formerly did not charge, *nickel and dime-ing* the customer, I called it. These actions worsened the perception of the product's value. Interestingly, at the same time, the research showed new entertainment equipment was going into Lubbock homes at a faster rate than anywhere else in the country.

While in Oklahoma City, I had not focused on Lubbock, where the company had put in what was considered by the engineers a new state-of-the-art engineering of the cable system. They ran the plant *hot*, which meant the signal was going out scrambled on all lines. When customers wanted cable, they would come into the cable system office, pick up a converter box and hook it to the existing cable wire coming into the home, which unscrambled the signals. Simple, no need to send a technician out, plant costs went way down. It was great from the engineer's perspective. The guys in the plant department spent a lot of time washing their trucks; Lubbock had the best plant numbers in the company, the lowest costs and the cleanest trucks. It was an engineer's dream. The divisional engineer and Daman were in total support of this running-the-plant-hot move [an omen of things to come for me].

On one of my first trips to discover what was happening in Lubbock, I found myself in a meeting of all of the direct salesmen. I learned early on, when troubleshooting a problem, first talk to the customer service reps and direct sales people. They always know what the problems are. Management usually does not listen to them, or even ask.

So, I asked the salesmen, "Why can't you sell cable anymore?"

They all piped up almost in unison, "Because you are giving it away."

"Giving it away? Giving it away—what do you mean?"

They proceeded to tell me about many channels *in the clear* (meaning it did not need a cable box to receive it). Someone only had to hook up the wire to their TV and they had what they *thought* was cable TV. This was the time when the new TVs had the ability to receive many, many more channels without the cable box than the old 12 channel TVs.

We had a TV in the conference room, so I had them disconnect the cable box and hook the TV directly to the line. Whoa! CNN was clear and so were Nickelodeon, all the networks, and several others. So, if you had one of the newer TVs, which got the higher channels, you were getting the cream of cable without the converter box. When I called in the System Manager and showed him what I had found, there were the usual explanations: "We decided to put the networks *in the clear* because we got so many complaints from the customers and the City." That was at least five channels––ABC, CBS, NBC, FOX and PBS. I do not remember the exact number.

I asked, "OK, what about the cable networks?" He had no answer, so we went to find out what the issue was. Apparently, there were several scramblers down (not working) and they were waiting for new ones to come in. Who knows how long that had been going on, but there did not seem to be any sense of emergency to get them back up and running.

Remember, I told you that new technology in the form of new TVs with picture-in-picture and other features were going into the homes in Lubbock faster than anywhere else in the country? Well, our new state-of-the-art cable plant disabled all of those new features on those very expensive TVs. No one seemed to pay any attention to that fact. We were a monopoly back then and the attitude was *the customer will have to get used to it*. No customer-driven focus there; it wasn't necessary. That technology glitch greatly affected the consumer's perception of our product. The customer thought our *state-of-the-art* engineered cable system was archaic, *out of the stone age*. Don't you love perception? It blinds many corporations.

So here we were—new consumer electronics going into the Lubbock home faster than anywhere in the country, loss of customers, raising rates and fees, value perception of our product dropping rapidly and system projections dismal.

The solution was multi-faceted. First, we had to change the plant configuration. Secondly, we had to do some significant value pricing and another rate realignment. Remember, they had just changed to a hot run plant a few years' prior. Well, here I was coming in, telling them they needed to change it back. Fortunately for me, the system management, because they were facing the decline of their livelihood, were ready to look at any solution. Together we convinced our Divisional Operations VP, Bob O'Leary, that we needed to change the plant arrangement and do some value packaging and repricing like we had done in Oklahoma City. During budget reviews, the President and Chief Financial Officer signed off on our plan. Before they did, they asked me what would be the first signs that this change had worked.

I exclaimed, "The customer satisfaction survey results will jump."

About this time one of the engineers who had worked on getting the plant hot in the first place and Daman got wind of the changes about to take place. They were both against what we were doing because they were the ones supporting the hot plant, but the proverbial snowball was already speeding down the hill. It was a done deal.

[What I didn't know was that I was continuing to make enemies. I thought I was doing my job and didn't realize carrying out my responsibilities had so many political pitfalls. Again, I certainly was not paying any attention to whose toes I might be stepping on. They sent me in to fix a situation and that is what I was doing.]

The plant changes and repackaging were a definite success. We followed the same marketing plan that was so successful in Oklahoma City and it went extremely well. Several months later, a customer service survey was conducted and presented at our budget review. The results were off the chart, in statistical terms. In survey-land, a five-point move was considered statistically significant. We had moved toward the positive from 12.5 to as much as 25 points. The customers were extremely happy with our changes.

A couple of years later when the government decided to reregulate the cable industry, they gave that option to the local franchise-granting authority. In Lubbock, the city administration chose not to regulate our cable system because we had done everything the government was requiring a year earlier. The municipal authority of Lubbock thought we were good community citizens because we did what was right before the government required us to do it and, as a result, did not require any changes.

This was clearly a huge success from both the perspective of the customer and the public relations franchise authority.

Bakersfield, CA. Almost at the same time as Lubbock, I was working on pricing issues in Bakersfield. Things were different there. They were the only system we owned that had what the industry called at the time *effective competition*. The system had an over-builder (another cable company building a duplicate cable plant), a satellite-delivered offering and a microwave-transmitted offering. The customer had essentially four different options in some sections of our delivery area. This was a very early taste of things to come for the industry in terms of competition.

Because our industry had been a monopoly from its birth, the executives functioned without any concept of how one must operate differently in a competitive environment.

In one budget review, the CFO of Cox Communications was looking at our budget for Bakersfield, which factored in the effects of the competitive environment. With a dumbfounded look, he asked, "Do you suppose this is what our system budgets will look like when we have competition everywhere?"

I had to laugh and thought, Yes, my friend, this is the future.

Bob O'Leary, who was a financial man, acted as if he wanted to build a wall around our system and tell everyone to leave us alone--the classic ostrich-head-in-the-sand approach. I laughed at that, too. "Being an ostrich will not work because the vultures will sit on the wall and wait until you are not looking."

So, we embarked on a pricing and restructuring of our offerings to make us more competitive. The Disney Channel at the time was a Pay TV Channel; customers had to pay extra to get it. Because we had the computer program in place to analyze the bottom line when we made changes, we evaluated the possibility of incorporating it into the basic lineup so it would become a value-added service. Disney had been talking about this direction for its service for a while now and wanted to convert its channel to one available to everyone and was very interested in helping us accomplish that in Bakersfield.

With the system management running the numbers, we finally came up with a plan to put Disney on basic and do similar value pricing as we did in OKC and Lubbock.

After implementing our value-packaged competitive pricing realignment, Disney did an Area of Dominant Influence (ADI) study that indicated our cable system was the only competitor that had increased its penetration during the rate realignment period. Placing Disney on basic gave the customer the impression they were getting a pay TV channel for free, which definitely improved our customer perception scores. (Putting Disney on basic became the norm for the industry in the following years.)

By now we had won another award for the case study about the Lubbock turnaround. I was very happy and in my element-- these were some of the most productive and rewarding years I had in the industry. I was good at what I did and I seemed to be recognized for it outside the company.

[What I was not aware of was the growing fear or disdain of my abilities that Morgan and Daman seemed to be harboring. Frankly, I am not absolutely sure what it was. I know the more successful I was and the more the President recognized me for it, the more distant those two became. I was about to find out how threatened they felt.]

Pricing and Packaging. Because of my experience in Oklahoma City and now in Lubbock and Bakersfield, I focused on value-based pricing throughout my division rather than on this or that campaign. It was a big deal back then, in the very early '90s, because we were coming into the personal computer age, so the systems had very few computers and even fewer people who knew how to use them. So, pushing in this area was sometimes like pushing a granite boulder up Mt. Everest.

Sales were suffering because of the confused pricing, so this was my focus. Because of that direction, my division was the only division to have computer programs in place that allowed a quick evaluation of the pricing and packaging showing bottom line impact when the industry was reregulated by the government. The systems were able to evaluate their situation very quickly and make changes, which reduced the negative impact of the requirements the government had instituted.

Morgan wanted me to get the program out to the other two divisions pronto. Unfortunately, each program was written specifically for that system and most of the work took up to a year to accomplish. Remember, personal computers were very new and most of us did not understand how they worked. I think Morgan thought all I had to do was put a floppy (gives you an idea how far back this is going) in the computer to copy the program, take it to another system and it would work—hardly.

[I think Morgan thought I was trying to undermine her in some way by not getting the program out to the other systems. At this point I was not solidly accepted into her camp. I wasn't sure why. Several outside the company told me she was very threatened by me. That seemed to flow with the treatment I received from her. But those were her Monkeys. I could not change that and, if I could, I certainly did not know how.]

You see, at this stage of female acceptance (or nonacceptance) into the Corporate structure, the good-ole-boy network was alive and well, but there was no good-ole-girl network. In fact, we were our own worst enemy. We were taught by our mothers the other woman was the competition. Much as we wanted to rid ourselves of that training, it was alive and well, though often at a subconscious level. I'm not saying that is why she and I didn't click. Ours was more an issue of thinking differently. I remember an HR counselor trying to teach us about how we thought through a problem in two different ways. The counselor explained: Morgan would take research and develop a marketing plan from it, whereas I would go into a situation in the field and immediately *know* what needed to be done and look for research to support it. This talent was very threatening to those who didn't have it and did not understand it. As the counselor put it, "You see things other people can't see."

[It served me well understanding consumer behavior. Unfortunately, it was a double-edge sword when it came to politics in the Corporation and people being threatened by it.]

Obviously, my successes caught the attention of Jim, the President, because he was singing my praises, which made me happy, but it ended up being another double-edge sword--in Corporate America, when a higher up, especially the president, reaches down through several layers and recognizes someone, the ones in the middle start to become nervous. I wanted to be accepted and be on the team but it never happened, except on a very superficial level. I got no support from Morgan; if she wasn't threatened by me, she sure behaved as if she was.

By this time Morgan and Daman finally understood the issue was very important, so a new position was created called Director of Pricing and Packaging. This person would work nationally in all three divisions. Even though Jim had asked me to put my hand up for the position, when I did, I was denied the opportunity. Can you believe it? I created that position and had already proven my ability in the area with Oklahoma City, Lubbock, Bakersfield and two case study awards on the matter. No one else in the company, or the industry for that matter, was working on value pricing with emphasis on creating computer programs that allowed evaluation of the bottom line impact. Morgan never acknowledged my work in this area. I started to build a great deal of resentment as this flew in the face of my family teachings--do a good job and you will be rewarded. Bunk!

One day when both the VP of Research and one of the Engineering VPs were coming from a senior management meeting with the President and his staff, the two came to my office. Both expressed how the President was praising the work I was doing in the field and how he wanted everyone to be doing what I was doing. I took *everyone* to mean the three Directors of Field Marketing, one for each division.

The Engineering VP stated, "Morgan will be giving you lots of kudos."

"Maybe when Hell freezes over," I blurted.

I was horrified to hear she had been at the meeting. I was happy and horrified at the same time because the President was reaching through two levels to acknowledge my work. Of course, I never heard one word of praise or acknowledgement from either Daman or Morgan. All I got from them was a *no* to the opportunity to do for the entire company the job I had created in my division.

[Morgan's Monkeys were definitely interacting with my Monkeys. The less she recognized me for my ability and what I was doing, the more my respect for her plummeted. Most of this was subconscious to me at the time, other than the fact I liked her less and less. I know now it wasn't her I disliked, but how she treated me. What I did not face was that she was bringing out one of my worst needs—acknowledgement. I only wanted to be accepted for me and what I could do. Recognition was apparently important to me then. What I didn't know was my Monkeys were keeping the acknowledgment at bay. Can you imagine being denied the very opportunity you created? Needless to say, all of this added to my gathering anger, which surely didn't help my situation.]

By now there was a distinct problem in the organization and consultants were brought in to help find a solution. The problem, from my point of view, was a communication issue between Marketing and Operations, primarily precipitated by Daman, who had (1) a real need to be viewed as the expert and (2) what communication experts call a *violent* communication style—he would dominate a conversation, monologue, interrupt, and talk over to continue to force-feed his position rather than try to understand the other side and work out a compromise. This behavior would wear down the Operations' VPs until they would go silent. Daman viewed their silence as agreement. Because they did not feel heard, they were NOT in agreement, and they were so angry at the treatment, they would actively work against Daman. As part of the attempted fix to the constant agitation between Marketing and Operations, the President and his staff moved the Field Marketing Directors from under Marketing and put them directly under the Operations' VPs.

Because the President and staff did not know how, or, more likely, would not deal with the personnel issue, they tried to fix things by changing the structure of the organization. All it did was put the people who were in the Field Marketing positions at risk. You can't solve a personnel problem by changing the structure of the organization.

We now had a dotted-line to our old bosses in Marketing, Daman and Morgan, and a solid-line to the Operations' VPs, which included Bob O'Leary, who made very clear that I was to follow his directions. Given both Daman and Morgan were expecting the three Directors of Field Marketing to follow their directions, we were put in a nebulous situation at best, which certainly did nothing to help me cement good relationships with Morgan or Daman.

Southwestern Bell Partnership. Around this time, we partnered with Southwestern Bell on the first cable TV/phone combination. Another first, it would be built in the United Kingdom. Our competition would be British Telecom, which only had phone at the time. From a competitive view, this was a golden opportunity for the partnership. Both companies wanted to learn each other's business, because they knew the future would produce an environment that would include phone, cable and all forms of communication [like we have today.]

The two companies agreed upon an executive exchange. As part of this exchange program, the head executive in England for Southwestern Bell, Mike Turner, came to the home office in

Atlanta to interview our executives for positions available in his operation in England. Everyone knew anyone who got one of these jobs would become invaluable to either company. So, I put my hand up, volunteering for a position requiring 2-3 years' commitment. (I was concerned about leaving my mother, who was getting up in years, and I was also concerned about putting my dog in quarantine for six months, a requirement of England at the time.)

My interview included our VP of Human Resources, Barbara Hyde, as well as Mike. As the interview proceeded, he obviously recognized an expertise in me he wanted. As we discussed my concerns about the dog and my Mom, he came up with a solution– –he created a new position right there in front of me and the HR VP: I would come over and consult for a year.

He asked Barbara, "Is this okay?" She responded, "We'll do whatever necessary to make the partnership work."

Bob was not keen on the idea. He asked, "What am I going to do without you for a year? That really leaves me in a bind."

After Bob's input with the staff, they agreed to allow me to consult by sending me over for 2-3 weeks every couple of months. I was absolutely ecstatic. That took care of all my issues and I would be troubleshooting and using my proven skills for the good of the new partnership. I was on cloud nine to say the least.

Unfortunately, when the word got around about my new responsibilities, other people's issues (Monkeys) started to come out. The day before I was supposed to go to England for the first time, I was called to Barry Elson's office, the SVP in charge of partnership arrangements. When I got to his office, Morgan was sitting with Barry, talking. I knew something was up. I was right. She was in the process of convincing Barry that if anyone was going to consult, she and the rest of the department should be doing it.

To talk with me, Barry stepped out of the office and said, "Postpone your trip for now. We are rethinking our situation and will let you know what we decide." I can't begin to tell you how deflated I was. I knew Morgan was about to get in the way, again.

Later, Bob O'Leary came to tell me the Marketing Department would serve as consultants and Morgan would head up the effort. Well, that did it. She would sit on me like she always did. She seemed always two years behind me in understanding the needs of the consumer. Once at a company meeting when Morgan was giving a speech on the direction we were going to go in the next year, one of my peers said, "You were saying that two years ago. Ah, our silent leader."

Yes, the key word there was *silent*.

Bob came back to me. "Barry has tried to convince Mr. Turner to use the whole department to consult, but he only wants you."

"Bob, I do not want to be part of this. Morgan will shove me to the side and I will not be able to help in the way Mr. Turner thinks I can."

Morgan never learned how to use my talents--she suppressed them. Now that I did not report to her, she acted more like a competitor than a team player.

Bob went on, "There will be no consulting without you. Turner made that very clear." I was given the old *ra-ra-do-it-for-the-Gip-per-team* talk. I reluctantly agreed to be part of the so-called team, however, my resentment continued to build.

[Oblivious to me—this would be one of my biggest mistakes in standing up for myself.]

There was no *team* when it came to me. For the second time, I lost a position created for me and the talent I had exhibited. I was beyond resentment, tired of working hard, succeeding, and watching someone else get or take the rewards and credit. To say I was becoming unmotivated and angry was an astronomical understatement. I was, however, not really aware of the damage taking place within me.

Times Mirror Acquisition. While all of the Southwestern Bell business was going on, each division was part of a different due diligence team investigating different acquisition possibilities. Our division staff was looking at Times Mirror. (I became a Platinum

Member on Delta because I was flying from Atlanta to Times Mirror and my systems on the West coast, then back to Atlanta, then on to England and back—lots of miles in the air.) After much time evaluating the Times Mirror deal, it closed in February 1995. Bob O'Leary was put in charge of the Times Mirror acquisition transition.

One day he had a meeting with his staff—the division engineer, division finance person, and me—to announce, "I want you all to be on my transition team." What a great opportunity for us.

I was surprised and proud when Lacey, the division finance person, put a qualifier on our participation. "We'd love to, but we don't want to become *gofers*."

"What do you mean by that?" Bob asked.

"We want real responsibility and authority to carry out that responsibility."

Bob was somewhat of a loner and definitely a doer. He did not seem to understand how to delegate. He definitely needed our help, however, and reiterated, "You'll have all of the authority you need."

I was extremely excited that Lacey got that out into the open, but a lot of good it would do me. Shortly, I would see where I stood with the gofer analogy.

Bob sent me to California to meet all the people at Times Mirror in the Marketing Department. I was to soothe any anxiety. Under the circumstances, that was almost an impossible task, so I set out to become friends.

Meanwhile, back at the ranch, Bob was in the process of relegating me to gofer status without even knowing what he was doing. Bless his heart, he did not comprehend the distinction between directing and delegating. I was in a somewhat different situation than Lacey or our engineer, as Bob did not know what to do in the marketing arena. As a result, I was able to go off on my own, do my thing and apply what I knew needed to be done without his direction, and he let me.

This situation, though, was different because it involved

personnel. If he truly had delegated to me, he would have come to me to discuss how *we* were going to incorporate the Marketing Department (Morgan and Daman) into the decision-making process of evaluating the merger of the TM marketing personnel or he would ask me for a plan on how I was going to do that. This would have been a great opportunity for me to be able to build bridges or mend fences with the two people I needed in my camp and who were clearly not there.

Instead, he went directly to them while I was in California and enlisted their aid in helping him with the merger. Notice I said, him not me *or* us. Once he did, they started doing their own planning without consulting me. He tried to make clear I was to be involved. Being involved to them meant I was allowed to tag along. They made sure I had been stripped of any real responsibility, at least that is how I felt. Unfortunately, I was now a lame duck, as they say.

One person in the department couldn't resist rubbing it in when he said to me, as we were leaving for a meeting in California, "So what are you going to be doing on this trip?"

When I told Bob about this comment, he did not *get* that he had shifted my short-lived authority to Morgan and Daman rather than creating a team and allowing me to take the lead. So much for the opportunity to work as an equal with the two people I desperately wanted in my camp, or to be solidly in their camp. I had been relegated to gofer status and Bob was clearly oblivious to this fact.

[I must say here now that my Monkeys kept me from knowing how to turn this situation around. By now I was too poisoned by anger, unable to see out from under the Monkeys' invisible cloak and see where I was party to what was happening. In my mind, all was *their* fault.]

Going Public. As part of the Times Mirror deal, privately held Cox spun off its cable holdings and created a new public company incorporating Times Mirror's cable holdings. Going public shouldn't change the operation of a Corporation but it does. There were many changes both obvious and subtle. The most obvious was how the pace of work increased. We were moving fast before but now it was as if we were projected into warp speed. Of that part, everyone was keenly aware. The subtler side effect of the increased speed was only observed by a few, the minorities.

The company always had a good focus on equal opportunity. It had concentrated on breaking down all of the old belief systems around discriminatory behaviors. In the discrimination seminars, we learned two things: (1) When things happen fast, people tend to group where they are comfortable and can work quickly. (2) To maintain equal opportunity, one must maintain focus on it. Attention is needed to continue to break down barriers. With the added speed, no priority is on equal opportunity. "Get good people as fast as possible."

[With speed, the Monkeys rule to a much greater degree. There is an understood commonality when the Monkeys are similar. White males bond with white males. Blacks go with blacks and women go with women...well, sometimes. It is a natural process.]

Those of us who had been with the company for years had believed the rhetoric that there would be many opportunities for those of us working hard to make all of this growth happen because it had occurred in the past.

For a while the opportunities were coming to fruition. However, only white males, a lot coming from the outside, were getting all the plum positions and promotions. Newsletters became comical to us because of all the white male faces. This was not happening because of a sudden drop in the value of minorities or because of an old bigotry resurgence, but speed. Yes, in many cases, bringing people in from the outside was a strategic necessity; however, rewarding those who made all this happen seemed to be just talk. They were people with phone experience or something else the company needed and the rest of us, really many of us, didn't have. Frankly, with my experience with the Southwestern Bell partnership, I did not feel the phone people brought much new to the table, except a more profound monopoly mindset than we had. But telecommunication experience was not the dominate need in all positions.

Once we went public, the natural course of action took over. Morgan was one of the first to experience what I would call *the shaft*. The pressure was high to grow and, with growth, more people were needed. They split her job into two parts, Strategic Marketing and Marketing Implementation, and gave her the implementation side. I always thought that Daman was supplying the strategic element and not Morgan anyway.

In my opinion, Morgan wasn't very strategic from a marketing perspective but compared to the buddy of Daman's, she was *strategy on steroids*. She could run circles around the guy with both feet and hands tied behind her back. He was the epitome of the classic yes-man. (The company came to realize this, too.) Because of dividing in half what she perceived as her job and giving the plumb portion to this Coke guy, she resigned her position and left the company after being with them for many years. (For the first time, I developed a healthy respect for her. *Good for her for not letting them do that to you.*)

Daman seemed proud he was having his friend from Coke follow in his footsteps. [Daman's *"I know what is best for you"* Monkey was running his decisions around the suppression of females. His cultural Indian Monkeys were active but different. He had a history of supporting males for advancement and suppressing females, to keep them under his thumb.]

I put my hand up for the VP of Marketing Implementation that Morgan had vacated. I didn't get that one because the "company needed to bring someone in from Times Mirror to help the merging of the acquisition." What never seemed to occur to those making the decisions—promote from within to the higher positions then bring those from the acquired company into the positions being opened up by those being promoted.

When I put my hand up, I figured the position was not mine to get—actually I was building a case and learning fast that these decisions aren't based on performance.

[Somewhere in the depths of my mind, I was starting to believe I was not good enough for that position forgetting I had done the same job at Continental and Metrovision]. Of course, all of this was completely oblivious to me because I was focused on what *they were doing to me.*

An industrial psychologist once told me everyone at the higher levels is assumed to be capable of performing the job. Whether you get it or not depends on whether "they" like you. I will go one step further and say it is whether they feel *comfortable* with you.

[When it comes to feeling comfortable, the Monkeys are pressed into play and in this case the cultural Monkeys from India worked to keep the women from any advancement or even position change.

Pay attention to what I am putting out here in terms of my personal energy. My assumption was that I would not get the position. I knew nothing then of the Universal Law of Attraction— everything coming into your life is coming there by your own energy and focus.]

There were lots of positions opening up so I talked to Daman about where I could go. There was a position for Data Services Marketing, which I saw as interesting. My old boss from Oklahoma City, Curt, was telling me I was perfect for that position. No one had ever done it because the service was new, plus data and the internet were just coming into play. It fit my innate ability to understand consumer behavior in an unknown environment. I was a little surprised at what I was told—No.

I was shocked! By this time, I had been blocked from so many jobs that, with my history from the other companies, I was carrying a small tape recorder with me into these meetings. (Yes, folks, I recorded the conversations. I thought, *who knows if or when I will need it?*)

For this data position, Daman proceeded to tell me, "You can't be considered because you don't have an MBA." Of course, there was no written description of the job or the fact an MBA was required. "Daman," I countered, "Most of the people in positions at that level or even higher do not have MBAs."

Daman replied, "Name one." With his response, I couldn't believe he was opening himself and the company up to this kind of exposure.

[Goes to show you that when the Monkeys are in control, how illogical they can have us acting.]

I countered again, "Okay, let's start with my new boss, Dave Limebrook, the VP of Marketing Implementation. He has no MBA."

Daman justified himself all over the place by saying, "We had to bring in someone from Times Mirror to help the merger, so we overlooked it."

[See how arrogant the Monkeys can be in their effort to be right.]

I couldn't believe my ears, "Name another one," he said.

"Okay," and I named one of the engineers.

He justified that pick because he was in Engineering and not Marketing.

"Look, we can go through the list of people around here who don't have MBAs and you can systematically justify each one of them, but the fact remains, this and none of the other positions at this level require an MBA. This position needs someone who understands consumer behavior and what makes consumers act and that is my expertise."

Well, guess what they hired? Yep, a white male without an MBA. My frustration, disgust and resentment were at a zenith. This was a company that prided itself on equal opportunity, but then they were not paying attention to what Daman was doing. I had this one on tape. I had no intention of using it but it surely gave me more confidence.

My Dream Came True...Well Maybe Not Totally. The position I had created, Director of Pricing and Packaging, came open again. This time Daman reached out to one of his white male buddies and asked him to apply, even though this guy had no experience. Despite Daman's knowledge of all the celebrated work I had done on rate realignments in Oklahoma City, Lubbock, the

Western division, the U.K and the two case studies I had won from CTAM on the issue, and the fact the President asked me to apply again, he still passed on me. My suppliers, executives from Showtime and Starz, who also were working on pricing and packaging by then, kept telling me the new person didn't understand the issues. They couldn't understand why I was not put in the position. All of this added to my gathering anger--so much for doing a "good job and being acknowledged and rewarded." Daman had no intention of giving me any opportunity.

The only position he would support me for was Marketing Director in Cedar Rapids, Iowa, which was akin to being given a tour in Siberia. Oklahoma City, where I started with Cox, was a much bigger responsibility than little old Cedar Rapids and I would be off the radar of not just the President but EVERYONE. Now if he would have talked to me about being General Manager of Cedar Rapids, that would have been a good career transition, not to mention I would be out from under his yoke. But, he appeared to have no intention of helping me in a *good* career move– one *good for me* anyway.

Later, I had conversations with the President and made my issues as plain as I could without using the "D" (Discrimination) word.

Jim stated, "You are *being slotted.*"

I replied, "You know, in different circles we use different words to describe that."

Unfortunately, most men do not get any form of subtlety and either he was missing the point or he deliberately was not getting involved. I think it was the latter because that is why the company had so many consultants in trying to fix the dysfunction. For whatever reason, Jim would not do what needed to be done when it came to Daman.

Under his Indian programming, Daman did what he thought was best. What got me was the company looked the other way when he did things that were, well, questionable. I suppose they had their horse blinders on and refused to acknowledge what he was doing, or they didn't know—maybe a little of both.

I wasn't the only woman to get this treatment. One woman, because Daman would not promote or change her title, got a job with CTAM, the Industry Marketing Society. When he found out, he threw such a fit with the Society's President coming after *his* people, CTAM pulled the position. Our employee couldn't leave our company and couldn't get promoted.

Another woman, I'll call her Barbara, came to me and asked if she should tell Daman she was interviewing with a supplier of ours (also because she was not given other opportunities). I told her "No, he will stop it and hold it against you."

So, Barbara interviewed, got the position with the other company, and then gave Daman her resignation. He was furious. He called the President of that company, one of his buddies, and raised hell. Angie, the person who had hired Barbara, was called in on the carpet. She shared with me later she thought she was going to lose her job. The President of Angie's company was too smart to put himself in that kind of position so Angie kept her job and Barbara got the new position.

When I was turned down for a position change the fourth time, I started looking at how many women had been given *other* opportunities by this man, not necessarily promotions, but other assignment opportunities. We all know, if you do not have opportunities to add to your experience and skill base, your days are numbered.

The Marketing Department was about three women to every man. In the seven years I had been there, two women had been given title changes to VP with no change in their responsibilities, after major, long-term battles to get the title. Out of the rest of us, 70% of the men were given other opportunities (including different assignments and promotions). None of the other women were given any opportunities or position changes.

[Notice I am looking for reasons to blame him rather than looking for other ways out.]

I didn't do anything with this information until another structural attempt to correct a personnel problem surfaced. Six of us were being restructured out of the company including me, being the only woman and the only one 50 years old.

Interestingly, all of the men were rehired or found other positions. One was let go with me, I assume to embolden their case with the EEOC, but was hired back later. Earlier, when I had thought of suing, I saw the writing on the wall and decided not to lose my job, and probably my career, in vain. But this time, I was very angry, frustrated and had **nothing to lose**.

[That is when people get dangerous, when they have nothing to lose. Remember, my mom had taught me life was fair, and Disney had me believing that knight in shining armor would come rescue me and save the day.]

So, when Jim saw what was happening and did nothing, I was beyond anger. Especially when he was the one outwardly touting what a great job I had been doing. I had lost faith in him and his leadership ability. Of course, the real issue was he, as President, was the problem because he was allowing the situation to happen, *being slotted*, in his words. He had the power and the authority to make something different happen, but he didn't.

The consultants were moving slowly as everything was very political. I was in an executive development program and the consultants were concerned I would lose my job before the coming changes took place and, unfortunately, they were right.

About this time an anonymous letter found its way to top management complaining about the current lack of advancement for women and minorities. I think I was credited for writing this letter but all of my letters were signed. I did walk in on the people in the process of writing it though. Because what *they* were writing about was true and surely affected me, I stayed and witnessed the editing. (I suppose, in a court of law I would be found an accessory to the fact.)

Unfortunately, the typical Corporate behavior when something like this happens is usually to ask *who wrote it* not *why it was written*. That was the case here, so it clearly was not safe to bring up these issues with management in an upfront open manner. If someone did, s/he systematically would be removed.

[The *you-are-either-with-me-or-against-me* mindset never allows safe dialogue about the issues. More on this later.]

I had seen this happen in OKC. There was a union scare and our head of Human Resources came out to thwart the unionization attempt. Once the threat was put to rest, they systematically came up with reasons to get rid of those perceived as the leaders. To my knowledge, no attempts were made to try to understand the grievances and fix them.

Remember, there were not many women at the top levels in these times. In fact, there was only one on the senior staff at Cox, the Vice President of Human Resources, Barbara Hide. A rumor circulated that when the President promoted her to his staff, he was credited for saying, "Well, now that I have a *skirt* on my staff, maybe they will leave me alone," they being the parent company, which was putting pressure on him to hire and promote women and minorities. I don't know if this was true, but my experiences with him did indicate it was very possible, if not probable.

[I know most of you today may find this crazy talk, and I'm sure it does sound foreign if you have never encountered these behaviors. But they are real and still exist. Remember, it always boils down to personalities and each individual's own Monkeys.]

Because I still was in my Joan of Arc state-of-mind, I tried everything I knew to stop what was happening *to me.* I didn't want to leave this company--I loved it. My sense of fair play and the history I had didn't allow me to walk away with a check and a smile. I tried every way I knew how within the company. I talked to the same union-killing head of Human Resources, Barbara Hide. When I went in to talk with her, she was too busy to communicate with me. I told her I had deadlines imposed upon me I had to adhere to and time was of the essence—didn't matter. She did not even have someone else talk to me, so apparently my issue was not important.

I suppose you are wondering, after all of this road-blocking treatment, why...why the hell I stayed! Clearly most men would not have put up with what I did. Well, I guess that is at least partly the reason…I am not a man. I am a woman and we are wired differently. This was not a company of business acquaintances for me. *It was my family*—dysfunctional, but mine, nonetheless. So, I was fighting to keep my family and friends, and you know what they say about a momma bear.

[Of course, I did not know at the time that I had misplaced emotions. That understanding came later.]

I am not saying all women behave this way, but I did. The company and my career were all I had. I was programmed with a sense of fair play, and when that didn't happen and the knight in shining armor did not show up to help, I was slowly being destroyed. What was happening was the slow poisoning of a human being. I was being beaten down and dismantled bit by bit. [Note the victim attitude.]

My mentor friend told me once early in my career, "You will never make it to the top." Those were fighting words back then and, in my naïveté, I said, raising my voice, "Why not?"

"Because you won't go for the jugular," he replied.

I remember being taken aback by the truth of his words. "If that's what it takes, then I don't want to get there." Getting to the top was never my goal. Being recognized for doing a good job at something I loved was.

EEOC Time Again. Before I filed a claim with the EEOC, I went to the head of the EEO Department at our parent company, Cox Enterprises. The woman in charge of looking at these issues, after reading the three-page letter explaining what had happened to me, acknowledged, "You know, I see a lot of frivolous EEO complaints come through this office, but this is the real thing. I'm supposed to talk you out of this, but I'm not going to."

Nice words of validation, but no help. I thought they were there to investigate and clear up these situations. Did she do anything to help me? No. She easily could have talked me out of filing by just bringing the issue to light. I was still on my own.

She did tell me, the other women at the parent company did not respect Barbara, our VP of Human Resources, because she was always saying there were no qualified females around. [Unfortunately, the rest of us women were subject to her Monkeys.]

When she and I used to talk, she expressed that she never felt accepted by the guys on the President's staff or the President.

[That was because somewhere back in the recesses of her brain, one of her Monkeys was telling her she was not worthy of being accepted and at some level she believed it. Subconsciously, if she was not worthy and she was the only one at the higher levels, then no other female deserved to be there. Isn't it insidious how the Monkeys work? Of course, the men did not treat her like she was an equal. They certainly did not think her area of expertise was of much value in the company, at least not as much as theirs.]

Sadly, for the first women who broke the glass ceiling, most did it by mimicking the men more than being a woman with a different perspective. As a consequence, being supportive of other women or minorities was a subconscious no-no if one was to survive in those early days. Those frontrunners usually did whatever they could do *to be like the men.*

Getting no help from Cox's EEO Department, I went to the Head of Human Resources there. That avenue wasn't open either. She said, "You better know what you want. I've seen what the guys do in these situations—they draw a line in the sand and prepare to shoot." *A very military reaction.*

No one cared what was happening to me, except me. Any one of these people could have stopped this from going further but they didn't. I didn't want to file anything and I did not want to hurt the company but no one would talk to me, no one would help.

So, I filed a claim with the EEOC and proceeded to talk to all of the women in management and tell them what I was doing. I was prepping them to be ready to act when the knowledge was out. As you know, I had been through this a couple of times before and knew how the guys would react.

[Because that is what people do when they come from fear—react.]

I knew President Robbins well and knew he would drag some of the women, one in particular because he respected her, into his office to talk, and he did. She was prepared and she let him have it. She called me later to tell me what had happened.

He asked her, "Is this thing with Barkan real or is Barkan going off the deep end?"

Her response caught him off guard. He must have been expecting her to say "It's just Barkan." He must have had his head in the sand when it came to our interactions about my situation. She said instead something to the effect of, "It's not her. Do you really think I like being called *chick* and told I can't travel because I have kids?"

"Yes," she said, "he was floored."

Then there was the young attorney who called me, absolutely blown away at the reaction her boss had when she told him she had been talking to me. She called me up, shocked and upset, and told me what happened. Rather than listening to what she had to say, he immediately criticized, "You shouldn't be talking to her. You are an attorney for this organization."

[Totally fear-driven, but then he was a lawyer, too.]

I laughed. "You never would have believed me if I had told you what was going to happen. You had to experience it yourself."

Because she was so upset with the situation, the next day she came in and talked to her VP again. She expressed the sentiment that if we cannot talk to each other about these things, then what could we do to avert these situations? So, he took her to talk to Jim and they talked about the issue. I do not know what happened at that discussion but it obviously didn't change my state of affairs.

If only I had been given the courtesy due an 11-year employee rather than being treated like a traitor and systematically killed. The dye was cast--I had become a change agent: (1) Things were already starting to change for those left behind; and (2) at least this issue had been brought out of the closet. But I was becoming very tired of being burned at the stake for what seemed like the benefit of others.

Before I pulled the trigger at the company and knowingly became a threat, I talked to about every woman in management at the Corporate level and even some in the field. Almost all knew of, and benefited from, the awareness that my actions had brought to light. None of them tried to stop me or offered to help. Most were very willing to sacrifice me (make me the victim) and at least one of them encouraged me to do so. Most of them went on to become VPs, SVPs and the one who suggested I sacrifice myself became EVP. I am not saying they wouldn't have gotten there without what I did, but I do know what I did increased the speed and opened the door previous nonawareness had closed.

What did I do? I filed a claim. I became a threat. Why did I do it? No one would talk to me or help me with what was happening so I wasn't going to go in vain. I unwillingly allowed myself to become the sacrificial lamb.

[All of this is typical. Fear brings the Monkeys out and people assume they know the intent of the perceived offending person rather than actually communicating and finding out what the person is thinking or if the grievance has merit.

When the lawyers enter the mix, the fear really kicks in. One must remember, the attorney's job is to paint the worst-case scenario. Unfortunately, they all live in the worst-case rather than living with the possibility things could be worked out. I had a real grievance and that is what drove the fear...the fear that I would take advantage of that situation.]

Hell, I just want the **slotting** to be stopped and to be given the opportunities I had earned.

Enter the Lawyers Again. The female (me) got pushed out along with five men but the men all got hired back! Yes, *now I am a threat. No one would help me before and now no one will talk to me.* Those who were still my friends would talk to me only from home or away from the office, thinking (or knowing) they were being watched.

All I ever wanted was to continue to work for the company. That was no longer an option or, if it were, I did not know how to get it done. When no one would help me, I was running out of time. When I filed the claim, there was no going back. I had to hire an attorney, or so I thought.

The attorney I hired knew the law but he was not a negotiator. Half the time I felt he was in bed with Cox's attorney, who I never met. He was friends with this person, so when I asked for something from the company and their attorney said, "No," my attorney rolled--an interesting negotiation tactic. Unfortunately, companies in these situations seem to treat the people on the other side as if the only reason they are doing what they are doing is money—big mistake. There are people out there who do things for reasons other than money, like me.

I was tired, extremely tired of having my livelihood affected by something other than my job performance. This last situation was hard to take when I had Jim touting my job accomplishments and yet he did nothing to keep the person who was slotting me from exercising that discriminatory behavior. Well, like I said, I was not going to be sacrificed in vain.

I was asking for what I believed was being stolen from me. Five more years and I would have received health benefits and most of my options would be vested. At 50 years old, I would have to start over again with pension and benefit accrual. So, yes, now I was asking for what I believed "nonslotting" behavior would have given me. One of the points of contention were my stock options.

I was becoming emotionally drained almost as much dealing with this attorney, who did not seem to be interested in helping my case, as I was dealing with the company. So, I agreed to sign the papers.

Then something happened...on June 9, 1997, a press release came out--"Microsoft Invests $1 Billion in Comcast." That changed everything. Our stock shot up along with Comcast's and every other cable company's. Why was this significant? Because our options had a *Special Accelerated Vesting Rule*: if the stock reached 140% of an individual's exercise price, and the price remained at or above that amount for ten consecutive trading days, we would automatically be 100% vested in that stock option grant. Wow! In a matter of minutes of that announcement, the stock shot up way over 140% on all of my options' exercise price. I was about to get what I thought I wanted and the company could not argue about it.

The countdown was on. Ten days to wait. Now, I became as elusive as my attorney had been for two months. My goal—hide and watch the price of the stock; do not answer my phone for anyone. As usual, my attorney did not contact me until day seven of the vesting period. I did not answer and I did not call him back until 3:00 pm on day ten. He wanted to set up a date for me to sign the separation agreement.

With a big smile on my face, I coyly announced, "Well-l-l-l...we now have a situation."

"What do you mean?"

I told him what was happening and, barring a significant drop in the market in the next few minutes, all my options would vest.

He was silent. "Is this happening for everyone?"

"Yep."

"Well, looks like I need to make a phone call."

That was on Friday. The next contact with him was the following Wednesday. He called. "You are right, the options are vesting but Cox is not going to vest your options. There is a clause in your employee manual on page nine that they are exercising."

I didn't know what he was talking about so I had to look up page nine. I read it all and found nothing that pertained to me. I called him back. "What are they talking about? There is nothing in there that pertains to me."

As if I hadn't already been abused enough, his next words hit me like a ten-ton truck barreling a hundred miles an hour down a freeway on ice. "They are saying you were *let go for cause.*"

As if it wasn't enough that they were supporting someone slotting me, not investigating the allegations, and interfering with my career, now they were *blatantly lying* about the cause of my being let go. Come on, you mean this whole restructure affecting six people was just to get rid of little ole me? Couldn't be. The restructure was in the works way before I filed a claim or made any waves.

I went off. The attorney told me, "Calm down. I've already let them have it stating they were way out of line." He asked, "Who are we dealing with over there?" as if the situation was getting out of hand.

"I don't know for sure, but most likely the union-killing VP of Human Resources, the only female on the senior staff, Barbara Hide."

"What's with her?"

"From my perspective, *the boys* probably felt she should have known about me and what I was going to do. Because she didn't, she needed to redeem herself. I suspect she was trying to nail me to the wall as best she can to look better in their eyes." (She was the woman who was telling personnel at the parent company there were no qualified females.) Isn't it wonderful to have that kind of support from the only woman at a higher level?

[We all have Monkeys and she was dealing with hers, the ones telling her she was not qualified or valuable, which she projected onto the rest of us.]

I shot off a letter to my attorney to forward to the company and their lawyers requiring an apology and retraction of the allegation. Of course, they wouldn't do either because they would be admitting they did something wrong. They did do something wrong! I realized this woman had probably tagged me as the one (it wasn't one, it was two, and not me) writing the anonymous letter, hence the let-go-for-cause *leap*. I had watched her function in Oklahoma City when she came in to help break the union attempt from the plant personnel. From my perspective, she fashioned herself to be quite the Sherlock Holmes.

[Like I said, she and the company always asked "who" instead of "why" and went after the "who" with a vengeance. I remembered my mentor's words, "It always boils down to personalities in the end and if they can't attack the job you are doing then they will attack you personally."]

Anyway, their attorney went on to say, regardless of the facts, they were not going to vest my options and he wanted to set up a time to sign the papers. Are you kidding me??? I was so blown away at the arrogance and treatment I was getting and so emotionally drained, I wanted some time.

"I have to take the weekend to think about it."

A Long Weekend. I took the weekend to think about what was happening, lazily enjoying the lake on my girlfriend's boat. I prayed and prayed and prayed and prayed. The answer was coming to me slowly and the more I thought, the better I felt. This was huge because the company was giving a year's severance to us, which was a lot of money. After agonizing over this for the weekend, I made my decision.

On Monday, I called my attorney. "I have decided *not to sign the papers.*"

He was speechless. He literally could not talk. After what seemed like hours, but were probably seconds, he finally said in a weak scratchy tone, "Do you realize what kind of money you are giving up?"

"Yes, sir, and don't think I don't need it, but they are asking me to sign a piece of paper stating I cannot say anything *disparaging, denigrating or untrue about the company or its employees.* Telling the truth about what was happening could be viewed by some as just that...disparaging and denigrating. They are treating me like the enemy rather than an 11-year employee who has an issue, and they are not even going to look into or investigate the issue. Now they are using disparaging, denigrating and untrue statements about why I was let go. *I wasn't let go...six of us were restructured out.* They are denying me what is due me according to their own manuals. They have totally abandoned any shred of integrity, so I will not sign."

What happened from there? Well, it was comical and like any fight when one is on top and suddenly the roles reverse and the other is on the top—a lot of fast backpedaling occurred.

My attorney told their attorney, "You are in trouble. I do not see this very often. She is standing for principle and is not going to sign the documents." My attorney informed me, "He about dropped his cookies and started freaking out, saying, 'You've got to help me. We've got to get her to sign.'"

I had them by the balls and the time was right to squeeze. In order to squeeze, *one must have a good grip, confidence in what one is doing and clarity on what one wants.* This is what the head of Human Resources from the parent company meant when she told me to get clear on what I wanted. That weekend I was clear on what I was to do—*I will not sign the papers.* From there, I had no direction, or more importantly, clarity on what I wanted, and I had no one to help me figure it out.

Boy, did I feel good about my decision not to sign, though.

[Without knowing, I was taking a stand coming from a spiritual place—doing what is right. However, like my attorney said, I was giving up a lot of money and, frankly, I needed the money, so—reenter the fear. I learned later that when we come from fear, our decisions are usually questionable at best.]

I had money set aside for my retirement and this action was severely cutting into its accrual. I was losing my position, and potentially, my career. I was losing the benefits I worked so hard to build up. I was being asked to start over, *again.* I no longer had time on my side to happily go to another company and start benefit accruals all over. I was 16 years away from full retirement. I was only five years away from having vested medical benefits until I reached 65.

[Notice that these are all security issues for me, evidence I was coming from fear. My Monkeys were in almost total control. Nope, they were in *complete* control.]

My decision not to sign the papers was a glimpse of the white light, a ray of truth among all of the Monkeys. For a brief moment, I was coming from making a stand for what was right and fair, not safe. At the same time, I was not clear on what I wanted to happen so, although this was a high point for me from a spiritual perspective, it also became the low point.

Why do I say that? In the end, because I did not have clarity about what I wanted. I did not have the courage or the trust in God to follow through on what should have been done. I should have sued. I got blamed for that anyway. What I really wanted was for them to investigate my claim and *help me*--a ridiculous expectation. They couldn't even fix what was dysfunctional in the company, and because they were one and the same, of course, I was not helped.

I will add to my mentor's statement, "It always boils down to personalities *and their Monkeys.*" He was right, when the chips were down, I would not go for the jugular even though I had the upper hand.

I cannot begin to tell you how furious I was, how filled with rage. If you get nothing else out of this part of the book, please understand how deep the rage went.

[And none of it had anything to do with my performance and everything to do with the Monkeys—mine and other people's Monkeys!]

In essence, the stock issue was settled. They did not give me the options but they did give me the financial equivalent, of course based on their valuation and not the stock markets. There was no more fight in me, so I let it go. I got what was due me financially, according to the manuals. *Nothing more.* We came to an agreement and I signed the documents. I signed because I was tired and emotionally drained. I did not sign because I got what I wanted, because I was not clear then that an investigation was what I wanted.

Blackballed. The mistreatment continued even after I left the company. Have you ever heard of being blackballed? That is illegal, you say? Still happens.

I remember being at the Corporate offices of Stars interviewing for an open position. As I was being ushered into an office, I saw Harold, the man Daman hired from Coke for Marketing Strategist. Harold, in my opinion, was no more a strategist than the man-in-the-moon, simply a yes-man to Daman, which was exactly opposite what the Corporation needed but exactly what Daman wanted. Quickly the company recognized this, so Harold was let go, not fired by Daman, who got him an interview with a friend, the President of Stars. As fate would have it, our interviews were on the same day. Go figure.

Our eyes met in the hall; it wasn't love at first sight. I assure you. I proceeded to my interview and was in the middle of a good interchange when the phone rang. The interviewer took the call. He stood up, saying, "I have to leave for a minute. I'll be right back."

Minutes later he returned and immediately asked, "Did you sue Cox?"

I thought, *Is that question legal?* I answered, "No, I filed a complaint that was dismissed." I was also thinking, If I had sued, I wouldn't be here right now. I would be on my own island sipping a pina colada.

That was the end of the interview and I did not get the job. Harold, however, did get a job with Stars.

[Thank you very much, Good-Ole-Boys Club, the purveyor of misinformation and our perpetual friend—fear, this time their fear.]

I called the head of Human Resources at Cox and told her what happened. Did she say she would address the misinformation? No, she said something to the effect of, "You started this." Did I? Seriously? Or was I responding to the accumulated treatment I had been receiving, and was ignored?

> *My mind popped back to the church as they wrapped up Jim's eulogy. I have so many feelings: sadness, wounded, but mostly anger. I wonder why I'm here paying respects to a man who recognized my value to the company and touted my job performance and yet would not protect me from those who were, in his words, slotting me. Where was the company's loyalty to me as a member of the so-called team? The wounds are way too fresh. And I still have no job. So why am I here?*

[I had no idea about Monkeys and how mine were in control of my life. Only the perspective of time would bring clarity to what had happened to me and why I was at Jim's funeral.]

CHAPTER 5
THE BRAND CONSULTANCY

By this time, I felt beaten down to such a low level, I no longer had any positive self-esteem but I did not know that. Keeping up my image was all I could do. I'd reached my low.

[Looking back, I see how I allowed other people to treat me. Little did I know the bottom was still not in sight.]

DOUBLE-CROSSED

I started working for the small consulting firm called The Brand Consultancy and a man named Arnold Cross. Arnold was a great guy, always in a good mood, laughing and bidding on EBay, a wonderful new platform where one could bid on products for sale. For Arnold, it seemed like a game—one he did not like to lose.

I had never worked for a consulting firm, so I was not familiar with their processes. You did not get *put on the payroll* until you brought in business. A few months in, two other consultants were hired. Shortly, I discovered they were getting paid a nominal sum so they could get benefits. Hello—what about me? I talked to Arnold about this. He gave me the same deal, but not until after he had taken advantage of me for several months.

[Essentially, they were using me for my contacts. I should have known then that the writing was already on the wall.]

I was there about a year when a lead I had developed was closed by Arnold. The agreement was that when one brought in business, one would be put on the project and be party to payment. Not only did he keep me off the project, he put everyone else in the office on it. No reason, no explanation was given except Arnold was the boss and could do whatever he wanted. This side of Arnold was new to me. He was no longer a nice man but a two-faced bastard.

I did something different this time--I left. This behavior was very different for me—a far cry from my usual fight-to-right things. No more fighting unfair behavior. I told them the reason I was leaving was to write this book.

Arnold asked, "Are you going to put me in the book?"

[Somewhere at a subconscious level, we know when we are doing harm. Arnold was frightened. I have no idea what his Monkeys were or why all of a sudden he turned on me, but he did. I was around long enough to see him lose his company while he mistreated his original partners. This story does not deserve any more time except to say, "He got his."]

This part of the story did nothing to start any healing for me; it did show me things were the same in companies big and small and, yes, boiled down to personalities and their Monkeys.

After the negative effects of working for The Brand Consultancy, I left to write my book, as I had told them. In reality, I was no longer going to stay where I was being victimized.

[I could not have articulated my victimization at that time because I did not recognize myself as a victim. I knew that I was not happy. What I did not know: I had to learn what to write about before the book could be written. Well, not the first part. Writing about being victimized was easy. When I looked back, I realized I needed to write that part while I was still extremely angry.]

So, the first part of the book was written years before the rest of the book. The next 18 years became my learning time and the time to heal, which was not a small undertaking. I lost my mother in 1998, so, except for my brother and his family, I was really alone. There was no one to fall back on. I was so ill from the issues of the past 25 plus years, I became my own worst enemy. Every time I attempted to look for another position in my chosen field, I would somehow sabotage my efforts.

[A friend of mine described me later as being paralyzed. My

subconscious Monkeys were driving me. So, poisoned, I subconsciously feared the same mistreatment would happen in a new position. Later I would learn—what you fear, you bring to you.]

I could not go through another damaging experience. I started to look for other things to do. That was in 1999.

[I did not realize I was about to step out onto a path of healing...a spiritual path of healing...The Twilight Zone.]

Part Two

The Twilight Zone

CHAPTER 6
VICTIMIZATION VS. VICTIMHOOD

*Until you heal the wounds of your past, you will continue to bleed
into the future.*
—Iyanla Vanzant

Well, if you haven't gathered by now, each Corporate situation of unfairness and discriminatory behavior added depth to my well of anger. To add insult to injury, each situation proved over and over that my parents' teachings were wrong. I was not rewarded for my successes as they said I would be if I worked hard and did a good job. And the more successful I was, the more threatening I became to some.

My best mentor told me, "When they can't take away the job you are doing, they will attack you personally." And they did.

[I do not know what their Monkeys were or what happened to them to create their mindsets but my Monkeys definitely threatened their Monkeys, and at this stage I still did not know I had Monkeys.]

Regardless of what each individual I encountered felt or did, my beliefs were challenged and my sense of fair play was uprooted, adding to the rage gathered over the decades. There was never a level playing field.

[Stay focused on this concept, as you will see this was the crux of the issue for me and many other victims. There were always two sets of rules and my ability to make a living was being negatively affected by that fact.]

My set of rules was one of severe disadvantage, at least *from my perspective.* There was a good ole boys club, and I was furious because I was not allowed "in." I think this is where my past lives were kicking in. Remember at the beginning of the book I said, "I was a male chauvinist pig in a past life and I had been more than a cad?" My experience, this time around: I had to come back as a woman in Corporate America, but somewhere in my psyche, I had not received the message I was now in a woman's body. My conscious self was functioning as a male. So, not being allowed into the clubs I surely worked to create *pissed me off.*

Because I wasn't allowed in, my ability to make a good living was being affected. That <u>really</u> pissed me off. I now was on the receiving end of the very behaviors I apparently engaged in during my lives as a male chauvinist. Whether you believe in reincarnation or not, work with me on this. When I first made that chauvinist statement, I was making a joke--it was a good way to start the book. However, the further down this path I went, maybe, just maybe, there was some truth to this so-called joke.

To say I was close to *going postal* was a mere understatement. (If you are too young to relate to that phrase, I'll explain. In Edmond, Oklahoma 1986, the first mass shooting of postal management and employees was carried out by a fellow employee. This was followed by several other postal shootings. The term is now slang for becoming extremely and uncontrollably angry, often to the point of violence, and usually in a workplace environment.)

I even had a list of people who, in my mind, deserved my wrath. The good news, I was smart enough to realize these people were not worth throwing my life away. Thank God, my mind was rational enough to keep me from the actual act of killing people. Hell, I did not even have a gun or know how to use one. I had only shot my uncle's shotgun and a Thompson submachine gun. I had a boyfriend who took me to shoot guns for my birthday one year and experienced Al Capone's favorite, the Tommy gun. Funny how it did not feel foreign. [Can you envision what might have happened had I had an assault rifle in my hands like killers do today?]

Being at the breaking point, I realized I had to do something. I noticed the years I was exposed to unfair practices had poisoned my mind, so rather than go to jail for misplaced anger, I put myself into therapy. (Besides, I would not have done well in jail and certainly would not have pulled the trigger on myself. Fortunately, or not, I had no courage to do that.)

Once one feels or is victimized, that victimization can become a way of life. It's like adding Alka Seltzer to a glass of water--the first couple of tablets do nothing to the water but make it fizz for a few minutes. However, as more and more is added to the water, suddenly a bump of the glass will cause it to fizz.

At this time, I was only aware I was very unhappy and I was doing a great job of blaming others for that unhappiness. I had no idea that, over time, I too had bought into the victim mentality and had plenty of Alka Seltzer in my glass.

[At this point I was not aware of my responsibility in all of this. The Monkeys kept me blind to those facts. I did not know about the Law of Attraction or Quantum Physics and had no idea how my thoughts about being victimized actually set up the very victimization I was trying to escape. In fact, if someone had used the words victim and blame to explain what was happening to me then, I would have defended victimhood and my state of blamelessness to the very end of time, which is the pattern of a victim. I did not know I had a choice in the matter and by changing my way of thinking, I could change my circumstances. After all, *they* were doing this *to me*. At this point in time, for me, there was absolutely no discerning the difference between **being victimized and choosing to stay in victimhood.** I was later to learn this discernment was the key to recovery.]

I put a stake in the ground. I was going to find the path to happiness if it killed me, not to mention killing those around me—ha! I wasn't going to physically move to another city anymore for any company, at least until I had a support group of people I could count on in my life–people who really cared for *my* wellbeing and not the needs of a Corporation. One of the reasons for my anger at Cox and the people in it was that I was alone and considered them to be my family. I was part of a team, and they were supposedly on it. So, when things happened the way they did and proved me wrong, I was devastated. There was no one helping me, no knight in shining armor. The closest thing to a knight in shining armor was President, Jim Robbins, for he was recognizing and praising the job I was doing. Unfortunately, all of that attention served to hurt me with those who were threatened and he did nothing to protect me from their unconscious wrath.

[I say unconscious here because those were *their* Monkeys at work. And, I had no idea what I had done to create this environment or why. My Monkeys ran my life. I was alone.]

My Fight with God

In 1999, after leaving The Brand Consultancy, I had my big fight with God. (Several more came later, but they were conversations more than fights.) Depression had me by the throat. Going postal was not an option, but the anger was still there and crying seemed to be my continuous state. I was totally directionless after losing my position with Cox, not only the loss of my position, but my career and what had become my family, the 20 plus years of friends I had accumulated. Because my job had me flying from Atlanta to the West coast, back and then to England, I spent a great deal of my so-called free time on an airplane.

One day I got on a flight to San Diego and the stewardess called me by name (way before the common use of computers). Bam! It hit me. Wow, she knows my name and I hardly know the names of my neighbors. What is wrong with this picture? For the first time, I became acutely aware that I had very few friends, no circle of support outside of my work.

At the same time, I was losing a relationship with a man I had come to care for deeply and who I thought cared for me. But he is not important here. What is important—this perceived loss was adding to my desperation for connection.

In the earlier days of my career, I had lost the two most important men in my life in the same year who were close business mentors, one being my soul mate. A similar experience happened at age 19, when I lost my father and uncle, who provided stability in my life. They may have been able to help me through my work frustrations with a bit more sanity and direction. Maybe, and maybe it needed to happen just as it did.

I had turned from a social drinker to a daily drinker to numb the pain. [I later learned the term *self-medication*.] Fortunately, I was not into drugs or even marijuana, so alcohol was my drug of choice. At least I stayed legal! I would get quite high simply to get to sleep. I drank all of the time to stay numb. My counselor and coach were hinting at the alcoholic label, but I would not take that on. [I think they call that denial—Ha.]

One night I was in bed crying, as usual, when I started screaming at God, "What do you want from me? You haven't blessed me with a family or children—and now you've taken away my job and career. What do you want from me? Tell me what you want me to do. Why am I here? I want to be like Jesus."

To ask to be like Jesus given where I was mentally—Whoa!

Remember the saying, "Be careful what you pray for, you just might get it?" I had no idea what a can of worms I was about to open, but at least I was able to fall asleep after my emotional outbreak. It felt good to yell at God!

God can take the scolding. Isn't that great -- He/She/It can take it. But when you ask for something out of desperation, you better be prepared. I had opened the flood gates--immediately things started to happen. I started to get instructions on things to do. No, they were not voices but thoughts would come into my head. (Maybe they were voices; who knows given all my drinking.) I was not having a discussion with myself.

First thing I was instructed to do—go buy a new Bible. I had Bibles in my house, and I had read parts of the Bible. Although I did not always understand what I read, I knew I felt better when I read it. Feeling better was all I could hope for given my state of mind, so off I went to buy a new Bible to read to *feel better*. I wanted to feel better by instinct, not because of any learned knowledge. I was not into the study of religion nor did I want anything to do with organized religion. That drive to feel better was paramount. I did not know where that knowing came from, nor did I care.

Yes, I had been brought up Christian but never liked the hypocrisy and judgment I saw in organized religion, so never joined any church. I would go to church once in a while, but as soon as people started approaching me to join, I was out of there. My parents did not push a certain dogma on my brother and me, instead they exposed us to many different Christian churches. There really was not much discussion about religion per se, but they made sure we were taught the teachings of Christ. I guess they wanted us to be able to choose our own path.

Dad was a Mason. Based on what I know about being a Mason, which isn't much, it is not a religion but a way of living. In researching Freemasonry, I found, it is not a religion but one must have faith in God or a Higher Power to belong. They profess high ethical standards with an emphasis on the brotherhood of man and are found to be heretical by many other religions, especially the Catholic Church. Well, that explained a lot.

Dad always appeared balanced and never took a position against others' beliefs. He would tease my Mom a lot about her Catholic religion, but I think I was observing a bit of comical play with my father.

Mom was not extremely devout to the Church but she was devout to her God and happened to be in the Catholic church. Things which happened to clearly affect her view of the Church were shared with me when I was old enough to understand. Mom and I had a great relationship and I could talk to her about anything. In the teen years, when my girlfriends and I started dating, we all came to her to get our questions answered. She was very nonjudgmental and fair toward us, which created a safe environment to talk about what was on our minds—sex.

She told me about the time a priest visited her after my brother and I were born. The priest said we were *bastards* and admonished her for living in sin because she married Dad (not a Catholic and a Mason to boot) and did not get married in the Church. She shared with me that was when she left the church, but not God. I remember her turning to me at my dad's funeral and saying, "Well, I guess I can go back to the Church now." I questioned the validity of any religion which would do that to another human being. Where was the love and acceptance Jesus taught? She didn't return to the Church.

***

Back at the bookstore, and not knowing much about Bibles, I deferred to the saleslady when she showed me a Bible many use who are doing a more in-depth study. So, I bought *The New Oxford Annotated Bible with Apocrypha*.[1]

[I later found out there are somewhere around 1300 different Christian Bibles, each with its own slant/interpretations to the writings. This is important to know for those looking for *the truth*.]

The year 2000 was approaching and all the end-of-days' stuff was in the air, so I started reading Revelations to find out what was going to happen. Ha! That was a joke. I had another...well, it wasn't a fight...more like a vehement conversation with God.

"So, what should I read? Where should I start?" Starting with Genesis was not in the cards. I did not care about who begot who and on and on.

The next day, (no lie, this really happened) Jehovah's Witnesses knocked on my door. I felt the love, so I let them in. Remember, *feeling better* at this point was all I wanted. It intuitively made sense. They had a little book for me called *Know Your Bible*. To say I was a little shocked and a little frightened was a small understatement. *What can of worms have I opened now?* I remember hearing the Twilight Zone theme in my head. (You will soon see why I called this section of the book The Twilight Zone!)

They had a nice conversation with me. They suggested I start a Bible study.

I got a very clear direction from the voice--"No Bible study with them now."

"You need help to understand what is written," they said.

I pointed up. "I do have help." I did feel the love, though. This was an important time for me to start learning to *feel* again. I was so ill and angry, I was numbed and could not feel.

So, with my new Bible and their little book, I started reading their book and the corresponding quotes from the Bible.

After a while, instructions started coming into my head loud and clear from the voice. "Don't read only what they tell you to read. Read the whole thing."

"The whole thing?"

"No, the whole New Testament, the teachings of Jesus," the voice answered.

THE SHIFT BEGINS

Anger and negativity did not make me feel good. Anything I could do to make me feel better was top priority. Reading the Bible made me feel better. So, I set out to read it. Understanding what I was reading was not relevant to me, only feeling better was applicable.

One day while out on my deck reading the New Testament, a feeling of complete and total *unconditional love* overcame me. The love feeling was so powerful I sat sobbing, this time with tears of joy. I felt a presence and started looking around to see who or what was there. Of course, nothing was visible but whatever it was I *FELT* it. Given my upbringing, I associated the feeling with Jesus and angels--that was all I knew.

[I believe this was one of the first times *vibrational frequency* came into my awareness.]

After that, not only did I feel good reading the Bible, but I was learning what the words meant. Questions I always had about religion were being answered. Because there are so many warnings in the Bible about false prophets and how one needs to be careful, I always had a question about what religion to follow. Which was the *right* religion, and more specifically, which was the *right* church?

There it was in the book, "He knows what is in your heart." All of a sudden, I realized, *this is not about what church you are in or what religion but what is in your heart. Are you coming from love or are you coming from hate?* (If you, reader, are not coming from love and you can't swallow the word hate, try the word judgment, which is nonacceptance and therefore hate energy.) There is _no right church_. It is what is in your heart and the energy you carry and put out. People are fools to think that God limits the ways one can get to Him/Her/It.

SYNCHRONICITY

I was in Barnes & Noble doing my favorite thing. I would get a cup of coffee and a few things to read, find a comfortable chair and relax. Once, when I had finished looking at those books, I looked around, relaxing, and on the table before me was another stack of more books. Reading the titles, I noticed each was about something on my mind. Three gentlemen sitting in the other chairs said the books were not theirs. I started looking closer at the titles.

One really jumped out, *A Spiritual Audit of Corporate America* by Ian I. Mitroff. Spirituality in Corporate America? None! Well, almost none. This book verified that very fact. Not that the people in Corporations weren't spiritual but they left their spirituality at the door when they went to work. The proof was all there in scientific studies concerning the soul of Corporate America. I couldn't believe it!

The book spends time delineating between spirituality, soul and religion.

"With few exceptions, most organizations do not acknowledge the concepts of spirituality and soul. If we can assume that they care in the first place, we can say that many organizations have lost sight of how to treat those who work for them as whole persons, as people with souls—and that they have lost sight of how to harness the tremendous energy that resides at the core of each of us. They have neglected to nourish this core, the source of all productivity and creativity in the workplace."[2]

"At the same time, it fails to recognize and acknowledge that *enthusiasm* (from the conjunction of two Latin roots—*ens*, meaning "within," and *spiritus*, meaning "god" or "spirit" —literally, "the god or spirit within") is fundamentally a spiritual concept."[3]

In other words, most organizations do not understand or focus on their employees as human beings, their most valuable asset. Rather they treat them as slaves for the complete benefit of the organization. They are unable to comprehend the tie between their employee's happiness and the organizations bottom line. Because the bean counters cannot grasp this correlation and more importantly show definitively how dollars spent on employees translate into higher productivity, which improves the bottom line, they spend their time showing definitively how much they can add to the bottom line by cutting salaries and benefits. This is the root of what happened to me at Cox.

"Chapter Three establishes unequivocally the existence of the divided soul of corporate America. Current organizations allow most people to bring only a tiny part of their entire selves to work, and, at the same time, the few parts that are allowed experience severe wounding. The need for healing is thus substantial."[4]

And that is where I found myself —in severe need of healing.

The other books piled there made me feel as if someone had picked them out specifically for me. I ended up buying all the books instead of the pile I had chosen. This was the beginning of the right books falling into my lap at the right time, an example of *synchronicity*, the state of being together, like synchronized swimmers.

Books were coming to me from all places and I was being instructed to read, read, read. I always knew which to read first because I would *feel* good about my choice. I became a voracious reader because I wanted to feel better, and in my negative, angry state, books lifted my mood.

At my neighbor's home having dinner one night, I was describing all the unusual things happening to me around the books and the Bible when my neighbor said, "I've got a book you need to read." See!

Here we go again! She returned from the other room, handed

me *The Celestine Prophecy,* by James Redfield, a fictional adventure wherein ancient manuscripts were discovered in Peru. These manuscripts described the nine key insights each human being needs to grasp as we all move to a completely spiritual culture on Earth. This became the next must-read. The book was describing a process, which turned out to be the road to Spiritual Awakening. I'm not going to give you all the insights here and spoil your journey. Although written as a fictional story, I thought, *this really isn't fiction. Wow, this is what has been happening to me.* Ah ha moments were coming so fast, my head would spin. I ended up reading all of Redfield's books in print at that time.

The Celestine Prophecy described the process of waking to one's spiritual growth. One of the important things you must learn in the process of waking up is to trust your intuition and allow those intuitive messages to come through.

[Doing that was one of the reasons my ventures in Corporate America resulted in business improvements and turnarounds, even though I was not aware I was listening to my intuition. Rather than touting the successes my intuition brought, I had one person in particular, who will go unnamed here, who went around bad-mouthing intuition as if its use would lead the company down the path of economic ruin. She made clear that I trusted my intuition, therefore I was not to be trusted and my business acumen could not be relied upon, despite my successes. This person was not a bad individual, but by choosing to degrade and put down *intuition* rather than supporting, promoting and celebrating the successes coming from its use was what a future Native American elder friend of mine called *speaking the dark language.* I was to learn later that what you speak manifests, so speaking the dark language was to be avoided if one wanted more positive results. At this stage, I spoke the dark language all the time, which is why I attracted others who also spoke it. There was no accident that this person was in my life speaking as she did. I did not know all of this then so I held a great deal of disrespect for her and her misplaced opinion.]

One day, looking for a book, a white cover with a picture attracted my attention from way across the aisle. I walked over to read the title and laughed—*Conversations with God* by Neale Donald Walsch. Well, I did not have the money to buy this book (dark language) and the one I came to buy. I started to leave but something would not let me leave. Three times I tried to exit the store without that publication. Finally, I gave up and pulled out my credit card. I ended up reading to book three in Neale's series. I stopped when Neale and Nancy married. I never picked up his books again.

[Being alone apparently was not a button I wanted to explore at that time. I was jealous he had found someone. This is what is called resistance. Resistance is always an indicator there is something you need to look at to get healed. It also may be an indicator that the time to deal with that particular issue might be later. Apparently, the time was too painful and not right for me then.]

I finally got used to things happening at Barnes & Noble. The preceding times were very humorous. However, I no longer thought I was crazy and went with the flow in the process. One day I took my coffee and the books I wanted to a table with a lady sitting in one chair, the other empty. On the table was a stack of books. *Well, I'll be!*

I sat down and asked the lady, "Are those your books?"

"No."

"Oh, someone must have picked them out for me."

One was *If the Buddha Dated* by Charlotte Kasl, Ph.D. Although I did not want to deal with being alone, dating was one of my issues and of interest to me. This book looks at dating from a spiritual level. The woman watched as I started gazing at the books.

Finally, she said with a quizzical look, "You are paying more attention to the books on the table than the ones you picked out."

"Yes, someone else must have picked them out for me and clearly knows better what I need than I do."

By this time, I was used to the phenomenon. The woman staring at me seemed quite perplexed. I never bothered to explain, assuming I could have.

THERE ARE NO COINCIDENCES

By now I was learning, "From a spiritual point of view, everything happens for a reason."[5] *The Celestine Prophecy* describes the awakening process to be: books falling off of the shelf when needed, people coming into one's life at the right time, leaving The Brand Consultancy *to write this book.*

[I had no idea that all the time I was spending was for me to learn what I was to write about. Chuckle.] I really thought I knew what I was to write about. For example, I believed the way to end the war between men and women was through the perspective of male vs. female. Clearly my experiences in Corporate America backed the male vs. female view. After The Brand Consultancy, I came to the conclusion everything happening to me was all about love vs. fear. So, when I saw love vs. fear as a way to end the war between men and women, I thought I had the answer. Ha! Little did I know I was only scratching the surface.

THE LANDMARK FORUM

By now I clearly understood via experience—there are no coincidences. After a year of therapy, I met someone who suggested I get a coach. At that time, professional life coaches were becoming more of a common idea, and because I did not have any direction on what I wanted to do next, I thought getting a coach would be a good idea. About two days later a coach walked into my life. Her name was Ruth Zanes.

I was starting to trust the flow and instructions I was receiving, so, when Ruth suggested I take the Landmark Forum, I signed up without question. I had no idea what Landmark was about nor did I care. I was out to fix myself and figure out where I was going with my life, and if doing Landmark would help, so be it.

Landmark Education is experiential education designed to help you be more effective in life by allowing you to observe how you are behaving in any situation. You cannot learn this from a book. If you read about these behaviors in a book and choose not to believe, there is no learning. But if you *experience something,* then your beliefs don't matter. From my perspective, experiential education helps you, as the Native Americans put it, *wake up*, spiritually and, as Landmark put it, see how one is *being in the world*. My focus was "Let's fix it and get on with life."

So, there I sat in a room with about 100 others facing a platform where the Leader stood. I wondered, *What the heck is this all about?* He talked about having a conversation and, if we participated in the conversation, things would move faster for us. Their mantra was—get out on the court and play the game.

Well, not me. I would sit with my arms folded, confused or angry all the time. I did not participate. I watched because I did not know what was happening. I felt as if I had been parachuted into Germany where the Germans were speaking English words but the meanings were in German, different meanings. My confusion brought up anger, which was always ready to make an appearance. This was to be my first true glimpse of the depth of anger I carried and how it was veiled with nothing more than a very thin layer of ice.

I did not participate nor did I change seats at the breaks like they asked. I sat listening and wondering *why am I here*. I knew I was supposed to be there—the *voice* made that clear. Why was another issue. After about a day and a half, I'd *had enough*. I went to one of the coaches. That was our agreement.

I confronted the coach and said, "I am outta here."

"Why do you want to leave?"

"Because I spent the last two years putting God back into my life and you are trying to take him out."

"Do you really believe that?"

"Hell no! I see his handiwork with miracles all over the place but you are not using the language."

She chuckled, "We do not use the language for a reason. Take a look around the room."

I turned around and the first person I saw was a man in a turban. Then it hit me as I saw every color, every religion, and all different cultures represented in the participants. There was no church I knew of with this kind of diversity and all of them expressing love for one another. Wow, I'm *watching God's kingdom coming right before my eyes*. How very eye opening. So, I went back and sat down. *I'm here for a reason. I might not know what it is but I know, beyond a shadow of a doubt, I need to be here.*

The third day sitting in the same chair probably with my arms folded I watched miracles that brought tears over and over. Then I noticed how everyone was hugging and making friends.

So, what is the matter with me? Am I Limburger cheese or something? For the first time I felt invisible, realized I was *being* invisible, recognized the kind of energy I was putting out, and noticed I was putting out no positive energy at all.

Imagine, arms folded, putting out looks that said, $&*@&^% *with me and I'll cut your head off.*

[No accident I used those words. Later, through past life regression, I discovered I was a guillotine operator during the French Revolution. *Now in this lifetime, I have the ability to cut one's head off with a look.* Karma?! Of course, I had no idea that was the body language or the energy I was putting out as I sat there.]

By some miracle, I finished the Forum. I still did not change my seat or uncross my arms.

[I had no idea how deep my need for security was and the fear I had about reaching out to people. That fear kept me from developing relationships. So, I started in the same chair and finished in the same chair.]

The breakthrough for me was to see I was not interacting with people. I did cry a lot seeing others have miracles happen. They were everywhere and very moving.

I stayed in the Landmark work for three years and finished the Curriculum for Living. Staying probably came from my need to meet goals. Somewhere in my subconscious, I believed I needed fixing and completing this work would fix me.

[What I did not know—there was no completing this work. Landmark calls it *peeling the onion*, the Native Americans *waking up*, Eastern Religions *enlightenment*. Later I was to call the resistance to change The Monkeys.]

After Landmark, three years of coaching and four years of therapy (running concurrently), I was barely coming out of my catatonic state. Drinking was still my form of numbing myself. If I had been ready to go postal when kicked out of Cox, by now I had put the guns aside and torn up my company list. I still was very angry and not capable of seeing the depth of my anger.

In the last stages of the Curriculum for Living, I showed up in class *very* angry one day. I had no idea why but I knew enough about the process to be in my chair with my anger. All I could do was sit through that class because the anger was so overwhelming. Interestingly, the only other person also exhibiting anger sat next to me.

[Remember, like energy is attracted to like energy.]

When it was almost time to leave, my group leader asked if he could coach me.

Like a snake ready to strike, I snarled, "No, I am leaving," and started to stalk out.

The leader of the class saw me leaving and called out to me. When I turned around, I can only imagine the look on my face as she literally recoiled. I guess I was about to cut her head off with that guillotine look—and she was trained to handle this behavior.

[We humans do not get to see what we look like when we interact with others. If we had videos of how we are being and show the body language we unconsciously use in our interactions with others, we might change and shift much faster. I suppose I looked a lot like Anakin in the Star Wars series, as he was evolving to the Dark side and becoming Darth Vadar. I was already on the dark side, so I can only guess how my face and body language looked to her.]

She made an appointment to talk to me on the phone the next day. By the time the call came, I had figured out what had triggered my anger. During this whole episode, I was far enough along in the work to recognize when I was *in my shit* or *in breakdown* as they called it. That meant one was about to have a breakthrough. I was able to stay in what they called the *observer role*, in awareness of my behavior but not able to change my behavior or how I was feeling in the moment. *Awareness is the first step in growth.*

I was just starting to *feel* again. Compassion was starting to show a smidgeon of a glimmer and I mean a smidgeon. My coach and counselor talked to me about how I felt. Ill and numb from my days in Corporate America, I really did not know how to feel. They would ask me, "How do you feel?" and "Where do you feel it in your body?"

Angrily, I would say, "What are you talking about, where in my body do I feel it? What does that mean?"

[I was so numbed to feelings. I had repressed my pain for so long, I had no idea where they were going or what they wanted from me. It was not an easy time. There was so much anger very little could bring it up. Unknowingly, I was also in a severe depression, which is anger turned inwards.]

Bible Study with Jehovah's Witnesses

One day I got another visit from the Jehovah's Witnesses, almost two years after their first visit. I had read the New Testament two and a half times, which did not make me an expert but it was eye opening. At the door, I heard the voice say, "Now you can do a Bible study with them." I hadn't even asked the question; the statement shot right into me from out of the blue. The voice no longer set off the old fear but it always surprised me. I had no idea why now it was okay and before it wasn't. So, I started a Bible study with the Jehovah's Witnesses.

During the two years of study, I noticed I was now at a level of understanding that allowed me to have a dialogue with them rather than allowing a dogma download from their perspective of things. They always started out trying to teach their dogma but the conversation quickly became a dialogue. We would start off on opposite sides of the conversation. I reduced everything to a discussion of words, their definitions, and the discussion of the energy behind everything. We would end up in agreement.

One day my friend asked me to join the church. I laughed. My answer of course was, "No."

"Why, after all of this time and study, won't you join the church?"

I smiled, "Because every church thinks it is the *right* church."

"Well, we are the *right* church."

I laughed again. "Thank you for proving my point but the Priest and Baptist minister down the street think the same thing about their churches. It is, however, the right church for you at this time."

From an energetic perspective, taking a position that your church is the right and only church simply sets up the energy for a fight. I am right, you are wrong. In this case, every other religion is wrong. Remember what I said in the beginning of the book about paying attention to the energy? So, answer the question...

Does the energy coming from any human interaction result in negative emotion, nonloving energy, such as separation, anxiety, fear, anger, secrecy, exclusion, special consideration for some, judgment, fighting and violence; OR does the energy from this interaction result in positive emotion, loving energy, such as acceptance, inclusion, unity, equal treatment, nonjudgment, joy and love?

The position of Jehovah's Witnesses was one of judgment and exclusion, setting up a positionality that would clearly lead to disagreement and possibly a fight by saying this is the right religion to the exclusion of all others. This position comes from the dark side in the name of God. Most every religion takes the same stance, except maybe Buddhism and a few others of which I may be unaware. However, each religion can be the *right* religion for those in it, at the time they are in it.

This is the reason I would not join any particular church. I am not sure she understood since she was so focused on being *right* and in the *right church*. [I hope you can see the point. It is a very important one.]

So those who choose one dogma over another, thinking they are in the right religion, are simply feeding the energy of separation and exclusion which is the language of the dark side. All religions can be stepping stones for a human's spiritual growth.

They can also become their spiritual prisons, the barrier to further growth. Or as the Bible warns, they become those false prophets who come in the name of God.

This time in my learning I was focusing on the energy behind everything. I studied energy in science in high school and college but now I was learning that everything was energy and, therefore, focused on the energy coming from words and actions. Is this fear-based or coming from love?

Once that revelation is identified, the false prophets are easy to see, especially those who come in the name of God. Maybe better put, it becomes easier to see the falsehood behind someone's actions, especially your own.

This study of energy was starting to give me a clearer view of the teachings in the Bible, their real meanings and how misguided most religions are. I was starting to understand the difference between the *intellectual understanding of the teachings or the words, which can be interpreted many different ways, and the heart-felt comprehension or the vibrational understanding of the teachings.* At that level, there is absolutely no interpretation. Love is love and when truly expressing it, one can act only one way. Period! This was only the beginning for me.

A BOAT CALLED INSATIABLE

During this time, I was lucky enough to have a best girlfriend, Ann, who had a boat, a nice 27-foot Bayliner on Lake Lanier, just north of Atlanta. At a moment's notice, we could call one another and be at the lake within an hour. What a great escape for both of us. Being on the lake meant party time, for her, to literally have a party with whoever was around. Unbeknownst to me, it meant reclusive drinking. I was not crazy about being around others but I would be if necessary. The real purpose for me was to be in nature. The drinking to get numb and avoid my feelings (all angry) was subconscious and part of my deep depression.

Much later, I understood the significance of the name on the boat and the irony it conveyed, given where I was in my awakening. Hell, I did not even know I was in a process. Before the market drop of 2000, I still had the money I worked all my life to accumulate. I was worth a couple of million and was told by my financial advisor I would never have to worry. (By the way, never hire someone younger than you to manage your money. They do not have enough life experience to realize things can happen they have never experienced and, with a few more years under their belt, would never have given that sage advice.)

I found myself taking a class on money from Landmark. But this money class had nothing to do with investments or how to accumulate money but how you behave with money or, as they would say, "It's how you are *being* with or without money."

When they asked me why I was taking the class, I said, "Because I am not happy with money and I am not happy without it." I wasn't happy no matter how much I had and I was always trying to get more. When I had it, I was afraid it would not be enough or, more importantly, I feared its loss.

Antarctica and Drake's Passage. I had started to realize this unhappiness when I was on the trip of a lifetime back in '97. I was on my way to Antarctica crossing the Drake Passage, which takes 48 hours from the tip of South America. The Drake's waters are the roughest waters in the world because there is no land mass to slow the seas down that go around Antarctica. We were on a converted 250' Russian research vessel. After the breakup of the Soviet Union, there were many of these so-called Russian research vessels with nothing to do, so many were converted into Antarctica tour ships.

I was sitting alone at the small bar talking with the bartender. I wasn't alone because I wanted to be alone but because everyone else, except our Russian crew and the bartender, were seasick. The water was pretty rough. Lucky for me, I do not get seasick or have trouble with motion. As I sat there, I realized *I am on this trip of a lifetime and am not happy or even excited. I am just experiencing everything. What is wrong with me? What is this all about?*

[What I was not facing—realization that money could not buy happiness. The situations led to unhappiness—not happy with money or without it and not happy on trips of a lifetime or without the travel. And little did I know I *really* did not understand what it was like *not to have money*.]

I only knew what it was like not to have *a lot of money*. Imagine that, Folks. I was worth a couple of million and I did not *feel* like I had a lot of money.

[What I did not know? My issue was not about money but rather *feeling secure*. There is that word *feeling* again. Even with the blessings I had, I did not feel secure. I had never experienced life without money or really being alone. Little did I know that in just a decade I would lose it all and get to experience what I had never experienced—no money. Well, it is all relative. Of course, at this time, all of this was very subconscious to me. My Monkeys were doing a great job of keeping me oblivious to my way of being and my dark language vocabulary.]

So here I was back on the boat called Insatiable, unable to have peace or be satisfied, so I drank.

The Difficulty of Speaking Up for Oneself. A couple of years later, Ann bought an even bigger boat, an older 38-foot Bayliner, two staterooms, two heads, nice galley and large living/eating area. We had great times on that boat.

One weekend Ann had invited her fiancée, another girlfriend named Clare and her date and me up on the boat for the day. Notice I am odd man out, no date. So, I asked her if I could bring Ken, a nice man I had met a couple of weeks prior and we had hit it off. Her reaction was what was of interest to me--*she totally ignored my request*. I went into the observer role and thought, *that is interesting. She is ignoring me.*

You would presume she would be curious to find out who this new man was. Wouldn't you think, being my friend, she would be all excited for me? Nope.

So off to the store I went to get stuff for that day on the boat. What happens? I took a really bad fall on cement. I did not pay any attention to it and went about my business not thinking it might be important. An hour or so later I arrived at the boat. Ann was already there. No one else had arrived, so I asked again," Do you mind if I invite Ken?"

For a second time, she ignored me.

I again went into observer role thinking, *that's interesting*, and did not say any more, just headed for the booze. I had no idea why I needed to get that first drink down fast and on an empty stomach to boot. The other couple came. Ann's fiancée was going to be late, so we went out on the lake to start the party.

Later when Billy called to say he was on his way, we started in to pick him up.

For a third time I asked, "Is it okay if I invite Ken?"

This time she started yelling at me. "It's too late to ask anyone else. I'm not going to wait for someone else."

Whoa. Where did that come from? Not only was there no interest in who Ken was, where he might be coming from, or how I felt about being alone when they were with dates but also, she was extremely angry. For the third time, I went into the observer role and did not say anything.

Off we went to enjoy beautiful Lake Lanier. By this time, we had already been into the alcohol for a while and enjoying the lake. Billy did not like the humidity. Rather than jumping into the water like the rest of us, he decided to close the cabin, start the compressor and run the air conditioning.

The compressor did not want to work, so off he went to fix it. What this meant was he had to open the engine compartment, which was the entire back of the boat. So now we had a 4x5′ hole into the engine compartment leaving about three inches to walk from the swim platform to the cabin—very dangerous, especially with us drinking. Billy did not seem to be aware of the danger even after I fell into the compartment on top of him. Fortunately for both of us, neither was hurt. You would think that would be enough warning to close the engine compartment. No, he kept working on what I do not know because by then he knew he could not fix the compressor without certain parts, which he did not have.

Yes, I know this sounds crazy but—I fell in a second time on top of Billy. This time I caught my little toe on something, dislocated it then fell. I know it's hard to believe but I was not sloppy drunk. I wasn't even drunk. Happy and impaired enough to catch my toe, but not drunk. (Or is that denial?) I was now scared to death to move and I was a smidgen angry that Billy had such little regard for our safety. Of course, he blamed it on *our* drinking. What he did not seem to get—we were there to enjoy the day and drink, not work on the boat.

I got home that night and would not go out of the house the next few days. I was really scared because I didn't know what was happening or what was going to happen to me next. I had taken three falls in one day, any of which could have been very damaging or even life threatening. Fear immobilized me.

The next day, I had a call with Ruth, my coach. As usual, I started off with what had been happening lately. I started telling the boat story and was glancing over the three falls when Ruth stopped me.

"Wait a minute. Back up. Tell me about these falls." So, I told her more.

"These accidents are no coincidence. I am a firm believer that accidents are nothing more than unspoken communication. Why were you angry?"

I insisted I was not angry. We were just partying at the lake. She pressed me and all of a sudden, I realized I was very angry at Ann for ignoring my requests about Ken.

Then Ruth asked, "Why do you have Ann in your life?"

I went into an extreme defensive posture and started babbling about how she was like a sister to me and we were *really* close and we were family. She was my best friend.

Then Ruth made the most profound statement probably of my life, **"We bring people into our lives to support our underlying beliefs about ourselves."**

That statement hit me like a Mac truck skidding on ice. I started hysterically crying as I realized, *I do not think much of myself to allow someone to treat me like I am allowing myself to be treated by Ann.*

A small thing—no—huge! So huge, in fact, about a week later I got sick. I rarely get sick and even rarer in July. It started out as laryngitis.

By this time, I was well into lots of different books falling into my lap. One of them was a book entitled *You Can Heal Your Life* by Louise Hay. The premise of the book—behind every disease is an emotional stress that disrupts your immune system leaving you vulnerable to the diseases you eventually get.

So, I looked up laryngitis. The emotion behind the disease— "So mad you can't speak. Fear of speaking up, resentment of authority."[6]

WOW! If that didn't fit, I don't know what did. At first, I did not get the resentment of authority part but, in time, it became abundantly clear. I had come from a home where children were to be seen and not heard. Given my strong personality, I could see the resentment was coming from someone taking an authority position over me.

Because I usually recover fast, I thought this bout with laryngitis would run its course in a couple days. Wrong! I did not realize how much emotional crap I was digging up for processing. My laryngitis developed into pneumonia and I was down for about four weeks. I couldn't get off the couch except for bed.

I looked up pneumonia in my trusty book—"Desperate. Tired of life. Emotional wounds that are not allowed to heal."[7]

Another big WOW! It was right on the money with what was happening. Ann did not call in all that time to see how I was, a significant departure from the almost daily mutual contact we had before.

That month was very sad because I started to realize I was going to have to pull away from the only friend I had who, in my mind, was like a sister to me, my family.

Well, you know that place in the Bible where it says, "He only gives you what you can handle?" 1Corinthians 10:13 Clearly, He/She/It knew I was not far enough along to be able to make this break without causing problems with my relationship, so guess what happened? One day shortly after my bout with pneumonia, Ann announced that after 22 years in Atlanta and with her business located here, she was moving to Florida. WOW...problem solved.

That move saved our relationship. My path and her path were taking different directions. As I started to stand up for myself, things were becoming—well, testy. She was not into looking at her behavior, so when I would mirror how she was treating me, she would get very angry. Understandably, the behavior was not very nice.

[Mirroring is a communication skill taught to help clarify understanding of an issue. My hurt little girl (Monkeys) had come out to use it to hurt Ann with the same behavior she was hurting me.]

So, Ann and Billy got married and basically, except for a yearly phone call, walked out of my life. Even though I was relieved, I did not have to push the envelope with Ann. What was I to do? They had been my family for years and I loved them both dearly.

[During that month of being sick, I did not realize I was in a form of mourning. I was processing a loss that I was having a great deal of difficulty giving up. But what was happening was necessary in order to save what was left of the relationship and my sanity.]

All along, both my therapist and coach had been warning me——as you move down this path, your friends will start to drop out of your life and new people will enter. They were so right but it still was hard, especially given the losses I had endured in my professional life.

By now, I began to trust the process. I may not have understood it, but I learned to go with the flow...unless I didn't.

CHAPTER 7
ENTER NATIVE AMERICAN TEACHINGS

A new friend, Deborah, had come into my life through my exposure to The Brain Garden, a multilevel marketing company that sold products focused on healing the body through all natural ways. Here I learned about sacred geometry, medicinal-grade essential oils and Don Tolman, one of the most brilliant men I have ever met, maybe because he has a photographic memory. He was the one I called who knows Hebrew, Aramaic, Greek, and other ancient languages to get answers about the Bible.

I still was not much for reaching out to others, so Deb had to take the lead with the relationship. We started doing a lot together and we were both on this path of self-discovery. She called. "Would you like to see a couple of Native American elders speak at a local cafe?"

"Of course." I always had an affinity for Native American Indians. As a kid, I always read books about horses, cowboys and Indians. I was always on the side of the natives. I believe I was a Native American in a past life. That must be the draw because I do not have any Native blood in this life, coming from a pure German background.

We saw the two elders speak, one named Robert John Knapp, the other Gary Adler Fourstar. I do not remember much of what they said but I do remember how impressed I was. That night Deb and I both expressed a desire to go to one of their *sweats*. I had read about these ceremonies when I was a kid but had never experienced any. So, without knowing it, we put having the experience out to the Universe and found ourselves attending a sweat a couple months later.

We both were learning the customs of this Native culture as we attended this ceremony. One of the customs was to offer tobacco in exchange for the water pourer to offer up prayers to the Creator on your behalf. So, as I entered the sweat lodge, I offered my tobacco to Gary, the water pourer, and requested, "I want to get rid of my anger and fear."

He challenged. "I do not see anger. I see rage."

That was reinforcement—I was way beyond anger. (And I already had been through three years of Landmark, four years of therapy and three years of coaching, all running concurrently) Wow. I had not been able to see the depth of the rage and I still couldn't, even though I was thinking about taking other humans to their grave.

[Truth is that when someone is in anger or rage, s/he is totally incapable of seeing it in themselves. There they are, the Monkeys with their invisible cloak again. Others can see them clearly, even if they are not awake at all. The only way the one who has the anger can see it is if there is a teacher to point it out in a safe way. Gary had pointed it out and that was enough then.]

I sat through the sweat with determination [coming from my Monkeys]. *I can do this. I can get through all four rounds without* going down. That means one gets closer to Mother Earth because it is cooler. In my mind that would have been a symbol of weakness or defeat. The water pourer pays attention to when you go down, which helps him identify what part of your life has unhealed issues. The first round is child, second adolescent, third adult and the fourth elder. I did sit up through all four rounds, though hot, my mind running the whole time. This was no pleasant sauna experience but sheer determination—*I'll show them!* (None of these people knew me, so I am not sure who I was out to show.)

I completed the rounds but no congratulations or acknowledgement of the accomplishment were offered. Not sure I was looking for that, regardless, it never came. I was really excited to be able to learn their ways. This was straight out of my childhood desire to be an Indian. WOW.

I got back to my life, which at that time was all wrapped up in

The Brain Garden. I was trying to make the business work. But then I got a shock, was hit hard. My closest cousin, who was only six months older than me, was killed unexpectedly in a snowmobile accident. I cared for him deeply and we were very close. He was there my whole life, when I had boy trouble and, more importantly, when my dad died.

I returned from my cousin's funeral when I was told two of my neighbors were moving to Hilton Head--one of them was a very close friend. Then I found myself going to another funeral as another friend passed. I was reeling from all the loss, so I decided to call my therapist to have a session, only to discover that my therapist, whom I had not seen in three months, had retired and moved to Florida. Wow, I was at a real loss. I was not sure where to turn.

One day soon after, I got an e-mail from someone named Debby telling me Gary did private sessions and what they cost. I was blown away—I received an e-mail out of the blue from someone I did not know about something so relevant. I was humming the Twilight Zone theme again. Then the thought popped into my head, *maybe I need to talk to a man about this.* So, I made an appointment.

And I can assure you, I did not even know what *this* was.

THE ANCIENT WAYS

Some people find their teachers in friends, therapists, clergy or others. Up to then I had my therapist, my coach, and the work in Landmark and I had barely cracked the nut. Now I was about to deal with a Native American shaman. A shaman is a person who has access to and influence in the world of good and evil spirits. Gary did not like to call himself that, but working in the ancient ways, he sure fit the bill. He was quite an imposing man, about 6'3" and well over 275 pounds but in fairly good shape. He was a former marine and a sharpshooter in the Vietnam War. I liked being around him because I felt very protected.

My first session with Gary lasted about three hours. Halfway through this session he stated, "So, you want to go to bed with me?"

I was horrified and immediately went into defense. "Of course not," I declared with great indignation.

He calmly stated, "You liar." I did not say anything and reflected on what he had said. He was right. That thought had crossed my mind when I first saw him back at the cafe.

So, I looked at him. "What? You can read my mind?"

He laughed. "No, but I can read the energy you put off and I am good at it. The sexual energy you exude is very potent. I learned about Kundalini energy from many years of study with my elders."

Well, that was the first real focused exposure I had to the study of energy outside of a science book. It shook me to the core and scared me at the same time. *What have I gotten myself into this time?*

After a couple more sessions and another sweat, along with Gary's first Animal Spirit Dance, I was hooked. There were a couple of things going on with me at this time. First, I was really questioning the direction in which I was being led. I was brought up Christian and Jesus was the force behind my journey, so why was Jesus bringing me to someone teaching the old Native ways? Why not a church or the right church? Not long after I would get those answers but, at this time, I knew it was *right* for me for it *felt* right. Remember, feeling good was of the utmost importance.

[I had no idea Native Americans were going to teach me about real love.]

I learned early on in this process when I read *The Celestine Prophecy*, I was to follow the intuitive feelings in order to pursue the right path.

People who typically join or are born into religions do not get that there is no *right* church or *right* way to seek connection with our Source. By declaring your way as the *right* way and others are wrong if they have chosen a different path is a bit arrogant, to limit God like that? To be sure, *that* thinking is pure Monkey business! Do you really think God would limit the number of pathways to get to Him? I guess I never understood that level of thinking. Besides the Bible says, "He knows what is in your heart." All of this was coming up for me because I was attempting to find my path, and the fact that Jesus had led me to a Native American was very perplexing.

[Well, enough of that for now. I wanted to express my understanding that any way one can learn to get closer to the Source is good. Everyone is on his or her own path in this spiritual growth process, so whatever works for you is good for you wherever you are on the path. We all have different things to learn. But don't ever tell me your path is better than or *righter* than mine or mine is wrong. That would be the Monkeys talking and that thinking simply tells me you are not coming from the light but rather from the dark side *in the name of the light*. That energy sets up a fight, the fight to be right.]

GOING UNDER TOBACCO

The second thing floating around in my subconscious and sending me into much confusion were my feelings for Gary. I was definitely attracted to him but at this stage nothing was clear. During one session, he told me to put the payment for that session toward *going under tobacco* with him. I had no idea what going under tobacco meant let alone what a commitment it would be. "What does this mean—to go under tobacco?"

"It means you have to present me with tobacco and a blanket then bring your prayers and what you want to accomplish to the Creator. I will then smoke some of the tobacco and pray to the Creator to see if it is appropriate to take you on as a tobacco student." (The tobacco smoke takes the prayers up to the Creator.) "If this is the right occasion for you to go under tobacco, you will then, in time, owe me an animal skin and later a horse." (The horse had to be fully trained and able to be ridden under fire. This simply established the value of the animal in ancient times. Same for today, a trained horse is much more valuable than a green one.) "Once I am given the go-ahead by the Creator, you will be under tobacco. This means you are asking me to do whatever it takes *to wake you up*."

My responsibility as someone under tobacco was to show up and go through the training.

The Native American term *to wake you up* is simply their way of describing a spiritual path to becoming a better human being. In Eastern religions, they call it the path to enlightenment. At this point, I was simply following the path I was being led to by my guide(s). Remember, all I wanted was to be happy again.

Gary often would ask me, "Are you here to learn these ways?" My pat answer was always, "No. I am here to change my patterns and rediscover happiness. If I need to learn these ways to do that, then I will learn these ways."

I didn't even know what my patterns were. I just knew I was not happy and changes needed to be made and I could not do it by myself.

As if it were yesterday, I remember the day I was to present him the blanket and tobacco. Confused and uncertain, I stopped and pulled off the road three times with questions going through my head like: *What am I getting into? Should I really do this? Is this right for me? Or is it him I really want?* I prayed and interestingly enough I started to feel the excitement of learning the Native ways. I remembered how much I loved reading about the different tribes and their different but similar traditions when I was a kid. So, I continued on to Gary's.

I presented my blanket and said my prayers to the Creator, which were to help me get rid of the accumulation of anger and fear as a result of my experiences in Corporate America. I then sat back and waited to see if I would be accepted into this spiritual school. The Creator, I suspected, looked into the heart of the student and the heart of the teacher to see if the time was right and if the teacher and student were well-suited to each other to learn what needed to be learned. Wow, *I won't be turned away because I am really out to learn and I don't think Gary turns anyone away.*

[I was wrong as, over the years I worked with him, I saw Gary turn several people away. Sometimes he would have them work with another teacher or sometimes he would let them hang around. He knew that water seeks its own level and whatever happened would be good for everyone…in the long run.]

As I attended his teachings, I became anxious to see if I would officially go under tobacco. Several weeks went by and finally one day he passed by me and whispered, "You are under tobacco." This meant I had now given Gary permission to do whatever it took to wake me up. I had no idea what that might entail. So, I was really excited and apprehensive at the same time, being very confused about the feelings coming up for me about Gary.

The reaction from my family was interesting as I shared what I was doing. My sister-in-law became very concerned about me, which made me feel cared for. She is Catholic and was ready to come down to save me from the devil himself. (See the emotions ignorance stirs up?) My sister-in-law is a wonderful person and her concern touched me deeply and instilled a sense of gratitude. She is, however, part of the Church that has villainized the Native population since Columbus first set foot on this continent. I believed they called them heathens and savages that needed to be saved or killed because, remember, in their eyes there is only one path to God—their path.

Back in the early years of this country, the Church and the authorities did nothing to try to understand the new culture. They judged it heretical and sought to convert or eradicate it.

[Fortunately, today, through cross-cultural education, we have overcome some of this misinformation, at least at the higher levels of the Catholic Church. Pope John Paul II in his speech in Phoenix on Sept. 14, 1987 finally recognized that the beliefs of the Native Americans did not contradict the teachings of Jesus. "The Gospel of Jesus Christ, which is the great gift of God's love, is never in contrast with what is noble and pure in the life of any tribe or nation, since all good things are his gifts."]

Once my sister-in-law got some information on Native Shamans, she became an apprehensive supporter of my path, even though she really did not understand it.

In the old Native tradition, when one is in the process of helping someone wake up, there are three rules:

1) *Do whatever it takes.* What does that mean? You can imagine where my thoughts were going with these feelings for Gary that were coming up for me.

2) *There are no rules.* Can you even imagine where my western mind went? Holy cow, what do you mean? Scared the ever liven' crap out of me.

[I did not realize then that my fear came from having no clear understandable boundaries on my part.]

3) *Do no harm.* How could you do no harm if there were no rules? What I did not understand is that these ways are all about learning to come from the heart, love and true caring. When you do that, there is no need for rules. The heart knows what is right and what is harmful.

[Because I was in my head all the time at this point and my Monkeys were in control, no wonder I was so confused. Someone else had always told me the rules—what was right and what was wrong. Can you even begin to see the subtleness of these teachings? When one is taught rules that are black and white, there will always be a time when the rules need to be broken to do what is good for all of those concerned. Often when the rules are not broken, innocent people get hurt or punished. With that black and white teaching, those who break the rules, even for the good of everyone concerned, have plenty of shame and guilt heaped on to them and there can even be legal repercussions.]

When you are taught these sayings, you must learn discernment, which can come only from the heart. Imagine if everyone, before taking action, would ask the question: If I do this, will I cause any harm to anyone? What a different world this would be. Sort of reminds me of Jesus' teaching "Love your neighbor as yourself." (Though I was corrected by my Jewish Psych-K instructor -- the true translation from Hebrew is: "Act lovingly toward your neighbor.")

The flaw in the translation *love your neighbor as yourself* is that most of us subconsciously do not love ourselves. We are only able under this translation to love our neighbor as much as we love ourselves, so we are capable of much mistreatment of our neighbors. *Act lovingly towards your neighbor* does not allow any misunderstanding, conscious or unconscious.

I was beginning to understand why Jesus led me to the teachings of the Ancients. They were teaching the same things he was trying to teach. Come from the heart. Regardless, I was in no way coming from the heart. I was in my head and learning intellectually what it meant to come from the heart.

During this time working with Gary, I was coming from confusion all the time. One thing I did learn in Landmark was that confusion was one of my *racquets*--a behavior pattern used by the subconscious to avoid looking at what one is really doing. Clearly, I was avoiding a lot. Avoid, avoid, avoid. I was avoiding everything. This is also called resistance.

I wanted to have sex with this guy. Not just sex, I wanted him to fall in love with me so we could have a real loving relationship and live happily ever after. Now where did that come from? I mean, isn't that what Disney sold me as a child—find love and live happily ever after? Did I care if the girl he was having a relationship with was hurt in the process? Well, you know the old adage, *all is fair in love and war*. (Being a male in past lives, I was probably one of the ones who made up this rule in order to give myself free reign to do whatever I wanted, despite the consequences, as many men and now women continue to do today.)

Besides, from my perspective, he wasn't treating her very well anyway. That told me he was still looking. Like the guys in Corporate America who were unhappily married. Rather than deal with the relationship they were in, they would stay in it because it was safe and then date on the side. They weren't dating in the true sense of the word but testing the ice—thick enough to proceed, they would. When the ice held and they found someone else, they would file for divorce and marry the new woman, often called the trophy wife. Gary, from my perspective, was doing the same thing. Remember, I was coming from the Corporate world where it was dog eat dog. No one really cared about the other guy, only getting ahead. If that meant hurting someone else, well, that was *just business*. (Now where have you heard that before?)

Given what was happening between Gary and me, I was getting very confused with the Kundalini energy with which he was working. There were a lot of sexual undertones and overtones and down-right flirting. Kundalini energy is creative energy and sexual energy is creative energy. I was dealing with a Shaman whom I was paying to wake me up but, at this stage, the waking-up process was nothing but confusion for me. I had never really, consciously, come from the heart, always the head. Hence the ease of believing it's all fair in love and war. Can you imagine how I felt when he told me that he had told Debby, the woman in relationship with him, he might have to go to bed with me? I was horrified--that is not how it works in white man's world. Everything is a secret there. At this time, he was not married to Debby, so he also had to deal with her and her white man's way of thinking. Of course, she was jealous and we had a few encounters. Me? I did not get what he was trying to teach both of us!

Gary had his own issues, as we all do. He was a product of a Jewish mother, who escaped from Nazi Germany between 1944-1945 through Siberia and across to Alaska. She met Jerome Fourstar, a full-blooded Assiniboine, who was living on one of the reservations. Gary was conceived out of wedlock and put up for adoption into the Jewish family line, for two reasons I was told. First, he was blond and blue-eyed and his father knew he would be severely discriminated against on the reservation. Secondly, part of the Jewish tradition was to adopt inside the Jewish family somewhere. His mother made the adoptive parents promise to expose him to his father's people and traditions. So, as Gary put it, he was this half-breed being raised by a traditional Jewish family going to Native powwows.

One day at about age five, his Grandmother, in apparently not so nice a way announced, "You are not of our blood." He went to his Aunt and asked her what that statement meant. "Oh, Honey, didn't you know you are adopted?"

From that point, I can only guess, he grew up thinking at some subconscious level that his mother had abandoned him. As a result, he developed issues with women. He seemed to need every female to fall in love with him, like trying to get Mom to love him over and over. Being around him for a while, the pattern became clear. And guess what? All of the women did fall in love with him. Well, maybe not all of them, but he always had an entourage.

When my brother visited me, I took him to a birthday party they were having for one of the other men. I had never discussed Gary with my brother. In the middle of the party, he asked, "Are all of those women in love with him?"

"Maybe." *If not, their little girl is in love with a representative of their dad.*

I was pretty impressed with my brother's observation. I decided later that all of them who had father issues fell in love, or at least infatuation. [Later, I would realize my little girl, who desperately wanted her father to love her the way *she wanted him to love her*, was really driving my feelings for Gary. I can't talk for the rest of them but they probably had similar issues, whether they recognized them or not.]

Gary once told me the tribal elders he studied under would laugh at him when he was learning, telling him that he always would have to be careful of the women. I guess this is true of most spiritual leaders. The energy they work with is attractive. All energy can be used for the good or for the bad. Jesus, too, was tempted. When they are tempted to do what in their heart they know will cause harm and their choice is incorrect, well, that is their karma.

WAX ON, WAX OFF/WAKING UP

I am sure many of you have seen the movie *The Karate Kid*.[1] Working with Gary was a lot like that. The teachings are through experiential learning as well as the history of ceremony, its

133

meanings and how the tribes lived. One day Gary had all of us under tobacco go outside and hug a tree. I had never hugged a tree before and had a western scorn for the process. I felt silly. Like the Karate kid who questioned the wax on and wax off process, I was wondering *why do we need to hug a tree?* Bottom line—I did not want to look stupid. What if someone drives by and sees me hugging a tree—s/he will think I am a little touched, if not crazy.

Coming from the dollar-hungry Corporate environment, those in the board room would say *those crazy tree huggers.* We had a cable system in Eureka, CA, so I heard that a lot—"How dare they get in the way of us making money by not letting us cut the trees." Never mind it would take 300 years to grow another tree like what they want to cut down. Never mind they would be taking and destroying something that cannot be replaced in our lifetime. Never mind they would be taking our children's legacy. Who cares? (OOPs, sorry for getting so far off track.)

Well, like in the movie, I did what I was told to do. Folks, the experience blew my mind. I put my arms around this big pine tree. I couldn't even get my arms all the way around her. (Yes, it was a her in spirit.) I felt the arms of a mother being wrapped around me, a warmth and comfort so significant I started crying. The feelings were incredibly intense. Coming out of Corporate America, I was so ill I couldn't feel anything, so these experiences, designed to wake me up and learn to feel the energy, were quite moving for me.

Then he would have us go outside and talk to the trees. The first time I did this, I was again blown away. I sat there in the woods and started talking, not verbally but mentally. You could talk out loud but it was not necessary. *Hello trees. I sure do thank you for all of the shade you are providing me today because it is really hot.*

Immediately, I saw the leaves on the trees around me start to move. There was not an ounce of air movement or the slightest hint of a breeze, yet the leaves were moving. I got goose bumps, a sign from the spirit world that you are on the right track or what you are speaking has great approval from the other side. Some people call them God bumps.

Gary had told us to be quiet after speaking, to listen to hear what the spirits of the trees have to say. My trees were really excited and said people rarely talked to them. I remember communing with the trees for a while. They said they were scared; later I found out where I was in the forest was slated to be cut for a new subdivision. I felt their fear. (I know you guys think I am nuts right now but I felt their fear.) I cry now and drop a piece of my hair every time I see a tree being cut. The practice is to offer prayers for the trees with tobacco or, if you have no tobacco, to pull a hair from your head and offer that. I do it all the time now because losing these big 100-200-year-old trees really saddens me. I cannot live long enough to see them that big again.

Depending on what issues a tobacco student had, Gary had a ceremony for that person to do to learn to feel the energy, trust the Creator and intuition, learn to come from the heart. No one knew where these ceremonies would lead, and neither did he.

He had me take my medicine (all of the things you would use to create ceremony, like drum, rattle, sage, sweet grass, matches, amulets that may have come to you, and flute if you played, etc.) to a stream where I could get away from everyone and be alone. My western mind would still get in my way when I did these things.

[I called the Monkeys my western mind because the Monkeys had not revealed themselves to me yet. I realized later these were my Monkeys, which grew up being programmed with the beliefs of the western white man. Given I was out to fix me, my unconscious belief was—*there is something wrong with me and I am unlovable.*]

By now I was starting to get a *small (very small)* glimmer that I really did not need fixing but I was in the process of learning to love myself.

Like the Karate Kid, I did what was *suggested* for me to do because I knew some new educational revelation would soon be thrown in my lap. Not doing it would say something, too. That was resistance, a road sign that you are fighting the lesson which was an indication that there was something there to be healed. So off to the stream I went. I had been scouting for a place for a while. I went to my stream during the week in the midmorning when I knew kids were in summer school or camp and most individuals were at work. This way I could avoid people. I hiked along the water for quite a while until I came to a place where a large rock on my side of the stream jutted out into the water. I was downstream away from everyone. In the middle of summer, the place was shady and cool—a good place for a ceremony.

I laid out my blanket and got out all of my medicine. I offered tobacco and said some prayers. I then used tobacco and cornmeal to create a perimeter around me for protection while I was in prayer. Once this was done, I drummed and sang some songs to call in the spirits and my spirit guides. I welcomed the spirits of the water and the trees. The trees again moved their leaves in response to my welcome, again no breeze. At this time, I had not been exposed to the spirit of the water.

I went into a meditative state as best I could. In this quiet time, I saw a Native American grandmother with gray hair in long braids with lots of beading, on her clothing as well. I took that to mean she was in some sort of ceremony herself. I heard her singing--the tune seemed to indicate a sad song. Then it hit me—she was crying for the water. Soon I found myself singing the same song. My whole ceremony started to center around this Native grandmother and her song. I literally started crying for the water. As I sat there singing and crying for the water, she turned to me (up to now she only stared into the water) and told me I could carry her song for the water. (All of this took place during the drought the South was experiencing prior to and including 2008. I am getting goose bumps writing about this.)

During the crying and singing, the thought came to me, *get into the water*.

It wasn't deep enough to swim but I could play and cool off.

There was no one around, so I stripped to my birthday suit and got into the cool, refreshing water. I laid there and let it do its dance around and over me, enjoying every minute. As I got out to dry off, I thought, *how sad if my stream dries up completely.* Then I knew I needed to keep singing her water song. In the Native tradition, there are many ways one can be given a song. What had happened was one of them.

Interestingly, when I left that sacred space, I was unable to remember the song. Maybe she wanted me to sing it in *our* sacred space, so "For now I respect that." What else was I going to do? The further away from the sacred space I got the less I could remember and I had been singing it all afternoon. Yes, I was getting older but this was not about memory.

As I hiked out along the stream and came closer to civilization, I ran into an older gentleman and a woman near the old mill, which originally had been in the stream.

I announced myself with, "Hello."

The man told me he was telling the woman about the history of the mill when he said, with a twinkle in his eye, "You wouldn't believe what I see in these woods."

I smiled. "Oh, I bet you do. I bet you do." Who was I to deprive him of any pleasure I may have brought him? Ha!

Several weeks later, I went back to the sacred rock to see if the grandmother would return with the song. This time I went prepared with a small recorder. Sure enough, she showed up and the song came right back to me. Wow! It blew my mind that I could go from total loss of the song to complete recall that quickly. Amazing! This time I recorded me singing the song so I could remember it and sing it at other times.

When I played the recording for a friend, she said, "That doesn't even sound like you." I replied "It wasn't me. It was the grandmother singing through me."

THE MESSAGE FROM THE HAWK

This story has to be told as it reflects one of the aha moments for me in this awareness process. In the Native ways, everything is alive and has spirit and we are all one. If you stop and stay open to the energetic messages, you will receive a great deal of information from nature, its plants and animals. So, in the process of waking us up, Gary would help us learn to do that. Those of us from a western programmed mentality had to learn to trust what was happening rather than second guess its validity. At least that was the case for me. I had a lot of that nontrust thinking going on. So, I had to be constantly attentive about keeping my mind open and not judging what was happening, a perpetual vigil that did not always work.

I was out to take my daily walk. Halfway down my street, I saw a hawk sitting in a tree about five feet from me on a lower branch, which put him at eye height with me. I knew this was unusual because hawks usually perch high in the trees. I stopped and we met eyes for what seemed like minutes but undoubtedly only several seconds. Finally, he flew north. I was so excited—he allowed us to be together for that length of time. I ran home to call Gary to tell him what had happened and ask what it meant.

Gary explained, "When a hawk allows you to get that close, usually it has a message for you. Sit quietly and go back in your mind to the moment you met eyes. Ask the hawk, 'What is the message you have for me?' Be quiet and see what pops into your mind first."

I did as I was told and the first word that popped into my mind was intimacy. I called Gary back and he had me write a page on whatever came to mind about intimacy. When done, the message was very clear. I could not be intimate with anyone else until I was able to be intimate with myself. Wow! That was powerful. I think there was an assumption one must learn to love oneself, at least that is how I read it. I was pretty far away from that kind of love.

I can remember Gary, during one of our sessions, dragging me into the bathroom and making me look into the mirror. "Tell yourself, I love you," he instructed. I could not do it. I could not even look at myself in the mirror, let alone say, "I love you." Very telling! How many of you can?

Singing to the Buffalo

On my way home from Gary's after having had a session, I was traveling down a road I had traveled for many years going to and from work when I lived in Woodstock, GA. As I rounded the bend, there in front of me were three huge buffalo. In Georgia? I couldn't believe my eyes. I turned around, pulled off the road and called Gary--I was so excited.

Gary asked, "Why don't you sing to them?"

"What will they do?"

"I do not know, so sing to them and see."

All three were grazing in the middle of the pasture, so I started singing the water song I had been given. I did not fancy myself as much of a singer, but as soon as I started singing, all three of those beautiful beasts popped up their heads and came over to me at the fence. They were less than three feet from me and there was only a double fence between us. I was blown away as I stood there admiring their magnificence while I sang to them. As soon as I stopped singing, they immediately went back to grazing, so I started singing again. Their heads popped up again. As long as I was singing, they stood there and stared at me (in all my magnificence, Ha!) When I stopped the second time, they again went back to grazing, paying absolutely no mind to me. I called Gary, all excited.

He asked, "Are they crying?"

I looked at the animal closest to me and, sure enough, there were tears coming down from the eyes. When I reported back to Gary, he said, "They cry for the people."

Maybe Gary knew that buffalos had naturally teary eyes. I do not know, and frankly do not care, if that is true or not. The experience was impactful on me and made me cry. I was beginning to learn to feel again. I was awakening a piece of humanity in me that had been buried and not allowed to come out for a long, long time.

Finding Our Animal Spirit

Gary took our group on another shamanic journey to find our

spirit animals. He would drum and lead us in guided imagery to the underworld. Once there, we were to take our medicine, tobacco and cornmeal and create a circle of protection. First a circle of tobacco was made asking for safety and then a circle of cornmeal with the asking of more prayers for security. The underworld has lots of spirits and they are not all good. The instructions were then to sit inside our circle and call out for our spirit guides. When an animal showed up, we were to send him back to the Creator. If the creature was not a good spirit, it would not come back. We had to send them back four times. If the animal came back all four times, that was our spirit guide.

The first animal to show up for me was a wolf--beautiful, stately and regal. I sent him away. Much to my dismay he never came back. The next was a ten-point deer buck, beautiful as he stood there in all of his magnificence. He did not come back either. Then a turtle lumbered in. It took him awhile to journey back to the Creator, never to return. A hawk showed up, same story.

Then a huge black buffalo arrived. "Go back to the Creator." He went lumbering off only to return a few seconds later. "Go back to the Creator." Off he went again. This happened two more times. On the fourth return, he plopped down on the ground in front of me and announced, "Well, I am glad that's over."

I cracked up laughing. The statement was not what I expected from my totem, a big, burly, black buffalo with a sense of humor. Thank God for that sense of humor because I had lost mine in the Corporate world. I would often later have visions with this black buffalo surrounded by five white buffalo and two bald eagles.

THE SPIRIT LED ME/GRAND CANYON

I was working at turning my financial situation around when I attended a real-estate workshop in Las Vegas. Yea, believe it or not, I was going deeper into real estate as a solution to my financial problems. After all, I had rental properties for over 20 years and a couple of them paid off. My reasoning was, a few more of these and I will have enough income to be set. Buying, fixing, and selling homes was also a lucrative way to make money, so getting into that was on the plate, too. That was going relatively well but it was somewhere around 2005-6.

[I didn't know it then but I was on my way to being humbled to a much greater degree than I even thought possible.]

Deciding to tie some vacation into the trip was something I had done all of the time while in Corporate America. My goal was to see all of the National Parks on the business' dime. Things were no different with my own company. I planned a several days excursion to the South rim of the Grand Canyon, making reservations to take the mule ride to the bottom of the Canyon and stay a night at Phantom Ranch--one of the things I wanted to check off my bucket list.

Arriving there, I spent the night in one of the cabins at the South Rim. I never get tired of that canyon—there are no words to describe it. The thing that most struck me on my first trip was the absolute silence. I was sitting on the edge drinking in all of the incredible beauty when a bird flew overhead, interrupting the perfect silence. The bird's flight sounded like a 747. I was in awe. Every time I go back I am hit with the same feelings of wonderment.

The next day I woke up with a touch of something that kept me close to the bathroom. (You know what I mean.) I was more than sick when I realized I would have to cancel my trip to Phantom Ranch. I certainly did not want to chance a ride on the mules with that condition. Even though I did not feel bad physically, I had no idea how long it would last. I went to bid farewell to the mules as they descended down the path to Phantom Ranch. Oddly enough, I got over my disappointment rather quickly, so went about figuring out how I was going to kill the two unplanned days now found in my possession. Mulling it over, I ran across a new curio shop full of rare, unusual and intriguing objects. Given the way I love to hunt for new artifacts, I thought I had been in all of these shops on my last trip.

As I entered the building, I was delighted to see a lot of Native

American art. I remembered how Gary would take us curio hunting and watch to see what drew our attention so he could detect what spirits were working with us. The first time he did it with me, we had come down from the mountain after doing my first *Hembleciya* *(ham-blay-che-ya).* This is a Lakota Sioux word for a Vision Quest or "Crying out for help." In the shop, he saw me eyeing a specific Kachina and came over to say he was not surprised that spirit was working with me. The Kachina is a spirit being in Pueblo (Hopi, Zuni, Tewa, Acoma Pueblo and Laguna Pueblo) religious beliefs. The Kachina concept has three different aspects: the supernatural spirit, the dancers who dress up as Kachinas during ceremonies and the Kachina dolls. Kachina dolls are figures carved, typically from cottonwood root, by Hopi and different Pueblo people, as well as some other tribes, to instruct young girls and new brides about the immortal beings that bring rain, control other aspects of the natural world and society, and act as messengers between humans and the spirit world (and now as sculptures for white man's consumption). This Kachina had to do with sexuality. As soon as Gary told me that, I dropped it like a hot potato and refused to have anything to do with it. My fear was evident. About two months later, I called the shop and bought the Kachina. Yes, the spirit was working with me.

At the curio shop, I was about three quarters around the store when a Kachina way up on a high shelf caught my eye. I stood there for a few minutes trying to make out what this particular Kachina was when the clerk came over and offered to take the piece down so I could see it more closely.

"Oh, no!" I knew where this action would lead and I did not want to spend money to buy another Kachina.

Down it came despite my protests. It was a blind Mudhead carrying a paralyzed Tuhavi. Legend has it that they worked together to hunt, travel, and accomplish tasks and are the true definition of teamwork.

That Kachina was a picture of exactly what was *not* happening in my life. It hit me like a brick. I was trying to find someone who would help and guide me in the real-estate ventures I was evaluating. I was the walking blind, looking for someone who would help me and I did not know how to ask for help. Already this Kachina was taking on some significance for me. Absolutely blown away, again! My needs were all about teamwork and I had no team. That was the same theme in Corporate America--I wanted to be part of the team but was continuously excluded. (By the way, in case you haven't noticed, there are NO coincidences on the spiritual path. Everything happens for a reason. And if you think this story is taking some surrealistic turns, just wait!)

For an hour, I stood talking to the two clerks about the significance of this Kachina, when we were suddenly joined by a Hopi Kachina carver, who happened to be in the shop. Yes, believe it or not, the very same Kachina carver who had carved the one I was admiring. When he told me that, the twilight zone music started playing in my head again. I couldn't believe the *coincidence*. Lester Crooke was a well-known carver in those parts. We talked for about another hour and, yes, now I *had to buy* this Kachina. (I have it here beside me as I write this, asking for the spirits' guidance.) After I had my new package wrapped and ready for my flight back home, we parted with each other's addresses. (Wow, now I could cut the middleman out and go to the source for Kachinas...always thinking like a White Man.)

As I left the little shop on the South rim, I wondered, *how could I possibly top this day.* I was floating on cloud nine, to say the least. I decided to drive to and stay in Flagstaff that night so I could take my time and not have to rush back to Las Vegas. Besides I was having so much fun seeing how the day would unfold.

THE WHITE BUFFALO

I took my time driving out of the park to stop and enjoy the beauty and silence. Once out of the park, I was doing what a dear friend called Gunkholing. He was a sailor and used this term when we went antiquing, stopping here and there for a drink or something to eat. It is technically a sailing term but I like to use it to describe what we did together, sort of free-floating through life with no particular place to be or place to go, an adventure.

So, I was tooling down the road when I suddenly burst out of the forest onto a huge valley. You could see from one end of the valley to the other and clear across to the other side. It was gorgeous. *What a beautiful painting this would make. I wish I had my paints with me.*

As I was driving, admiring the beauty, a thought popped into my head from the voice, *Stop and get a Coke.*

"I do not want a Coke."

Stop and get a Coke.

By now I knew not to question when I got these kinds of direct instructions. About then I saw a sign, *White Buffalo Cafe ahead 5 miles.*

The white buffalo for the Plains Indians are very sacred animals. Actually, all buffalo are sacred because they were the life blood of the tribes—every part of the animal was used for survival. The white ones were so rare, they held a very high significance among the people.

As I walked into the Cafe, I was pleasantly surprised to see all kinds of white buffalo information and all kinds of things one could buy to remind them of the white buffalo. I went over to the clerk and bought a Coke and we started up a conversation talking about the white buffalo and the Native prophecies around it.

Next thing she was asking, "Would you like to go see them?"

"Go see what?"

"Why, the white buffalo. We have six of them, including Miracle Moon out back."

I couldn't believe what I was hearing. She went on to say all six of them had been genetically tested and were all true bison. Apparently crossing beef with buffalo can produce a white version but they turn color over the years and are not technically real buffalo.

Well, I paid my $5 to see the buffalo and I was greeted with this long fence with all kinds of Native prayer ties attached. Actually, the sight was not only spiritually moving but also beautiful because of all of its colors. And around the corner from the prayer ties were the six white buffalo. Another huge WOW! I was marveling that I had stumbled onto these magnificent beasts out of the blue.

Or I should say, "I was directed to these magnificent animals."

I did not know there were white buffalo in the area. I moved over toward them and began singing my water song. Their reaction was the same as the three buffalo I had encountered at home. They came over to me with rapt attention. As I was singing to the buffalo, a man came out from one of the back buildings and started cleaning the pens. Jim Riley was his name, the caretaker of the buffalo. He and his wife, Dena, owned the ranch with the buffalo. When he got over near me, he stopped what he was doing and started a conversation (I was the only one out there). I told him how I was studying with a Native American. I also noticed there was one big black buffalo in the pens.

Jim proceeded to explain to me, "All of these buffalo are genetically true buffalo with no bovine inbreeding."

"Why do you have the black buffalo?"

"That male carries the gene to produce white offspring." The pairing of two whites, can produce a white, but it is more likely that black buffalo with the white gene will produce a white offspring. As he spoke, I thought about my vision of the white buffalo next to Blackie, which I had named my Animal Totem with a sense of humor. All of a sudden, I realized my vision was a prediction of this very moment. *I was on the right path.*

I was about to leave when he put his hand in his pocket and pulled out a big bunch of white buffalo hair. When he gave it to me, I was truly honored. In the Native tradition, this was a huge gift. Over the years, I have managed to give away most of it but still have some and carry some in my medicine pouch. It is reserved for special gifts because of its rarity.

When I returned to my car to carry on my trip, I could not

believe my good luck. Then I was reminded of the *voice* that had insisted I stop for a Coke. Thank God, I listened or I would have missed the most significant part of the trip. This was not luck but a sign. In the past I would have called it luck or coincidence. I marveled at their significance. I was definitely being given spiritual signs that could not be missed. For whatever reason, this was my path.

CALLING UP THE EAGLE

On a second trip to canyon country, I decided to take a trip around the north rim of the Grand Canyon, which took me into Zion National Park. As usual, I was blown away at the natural beauty all around me. I took the Zion Canton Scenic Drive for several miles. Of course, I was interested in seeing as much wildlife as I could, so I found a quiet place and got my drum out. I thought it would be really neat to see a bald eagle, so I sang our eagle song. I must have been there about an hour singing and meditating but, alas, no eagle showed his face. As I drove out of the park, I did see deer, hogs, turkey, horses and, believe it or not, buffalo. Wow, to see buffalo but no eagle after singing our eagle song was unusual.

I was lucky enough to find a place to stay that night right on a buffalo path, so I sat on the porch with a glass of wine watching the buffalo go down their trail against the setting sun. It was beautiful, peaceful and relaxing.

The next day I took off on my way to meet my friend, Lester Crook, the Hopi Kachina carver I had met on my previous trip to the Grand Canyon, a few hours trip but I was in no hurry. I wanted to take in all the beauty I could while I was there.

I drove along the highway out in the middle of nowhere, the scene as flat as could be with sage everywhere. Then all of a sudden, a white speck caught my eye way off in the distance. My immediate thought was *a bald eagle*. I was miles from any lakes or water that I knew of…probably a piece of white rag caught in a bush off in the distance. The voice, however, was very insistent in my turning around. So, I turned around and got out of my car to watch this spot of a white rag caught on a bush way off in the distance. As I watched this minute speck no bigger than half my little fingernail, I thought *how stupid of me to turn around for this.* Then right before my eyes this beautiful bald eagle rose into the air. "Oh, my God, it IS a bald eagle." I could not believe my luck. (Well, according to the natives, this was not luck.) I followed that bird for miles until he drifted away from the road I was on. I was blown away at my fortune in having an eagle show up.

When I reached my destination and found Lester, I told him and his friend about the eagle. They looked at each other, and I got a couple of raised eyebrows. He said that was very unusual. I was like a little kid skipping through life in glee. I had my native friend who took me on a private tour of the Hopi Mesas to visit his grandfather (medicine man), and I had a visit from a bald eagle. I was floating on cloud nine. What else could come into my life?

Until I was home telling Gary what had happened, I had no inkling that maybe I had done something wrong. We were all at one of our circle meetings and one of Gary's elders was visiting from California. Robert John Knapp was his name, and he was from the Ohlone tribe of California. As I sat there in my excitement, telling my story of the eagle, Robert John finally spoke up in a stern, forceful voice and said, "So why did you call up the eagle?"

I thought to myself, *I...me, myself and I called up an eagle? Can I really call up an eagle at will?* As I sat there thinking about how impossible I felt this could be, his forbidding voice again said, "So why did you call up the eagle? You called him up just to see him?" The next thing I knew I was having my hand gently slapped as he proceeded to say, "You only call the eagle up to carry your prayers to the Creator."

Hell, I had no idea I could call up an eagle or anything else for that matter. Then Gary got his hand slapped with, "Is this what you are teaching her?" I was a bit embarrassed at my lack of reverence for their ways...but I did not know. Gary later explained that I was not being irreverent because I was ignorant. Now I know you only call an eagle up to take your prayers to the Creator. The eagle is supposedly the only bird to be able to fly high enough to touch the face of the Creator.

Working with Gary was all about learning to open my mind to *feel* and to *trust* those feelings rather than reason or, as Gary would say, learning to come from the heart not the mind, to have the heart lead the mind, not the other way around. At this point in time, I was trading in my prove-it-to-me attitude to being open to experiencing things and energy that I could not necessarily explain. Why I had been led down this path rather than being shown what church to attend was becoming clearer. I was starting to trust the flow from the heart rather than *judging* what was *right* or *wrong* from the head. This was the *true* spiritual path, learning to come from the heart and not the mind—learning to come from intention (mind focus) to love (heart focus).

However nice that was, it was not paying the bills.

THE CAVE

Panic was starting to set in as my money was still outflowing, and there was basically no inflow. Seemed that no matter what I did, it was slipping out of my hands and that created an aurora of terror for me. I was in the early stages of fear and trying to do everything I could to turn my situation from outflow to inflow. I had lost a great deal in the stock market bust in 2000, not because I was in speculative dot coms but because I was in technology—Lucent, which went from $70 to $2, AT&T and a bunch of other up-til-now good stocks. When the Enron thing happened, I called my broker. "Sell it all. Get me into cash. I just came out of Corporate America, and this is the tip of the iceberg." Well, he talked me out of it, because I had *already lost too much money.* Good reason not to sell. Let's see how much money we can lose, all the way down to worthless, which is what I call $2 from $70.

I looked at all of my holdings and saw I was doing relatively well in real estate. I had four houses and two were paid off. I thought, *hmmmm, if I had a couple more of these rentals paid off, I would be sitting pretty good.* So, I decided to dive further into real estate and started going to all of the classes that taught you how to make money in real estate, thinking this will solve the outflow problem. (That would have been okay if it had been 1980; however, it was 2004-5.)

Meanwhile, I went to Gary for a spiritual solution to this problem. He said he was going to take me to the cave, another shamanic journey. As he prepared for the ceremony, he started to prep me for the mental journey. These trips are all in your mind. However, sometimes I really wonder.

"I will guide you with the drum. Do not get off the path or lose earshot of the drum." Wax on, wax off. Who was I to argue?

"Once at the cave, there will be three spirits waiting next to the fire. Each one will tell you what to do to turn around your situation." He went on to explain a fourth spirit would not come out unless he deemed my intentions worthy.

Gary described what was on the path, for example there are two rocks to your left, go to the right. So, as I traveled down this path in my mind, I was shocked to see things show themselves to me before Gary told me they were there. That kind of freaked me out. How could I see them in my mind's eye before he told me they were there? By this time, however, I was not questioning what was happening because I knew it could not be explained, at least on this plane.

I finally reached the cave, the fire burning brightly inside, and the shadows of the three spirits. The cave was a regular old cave, nothing special, except the walls seemed to glow red. I couldn't tell if it was from the fire or if the walls were made of red stone, or maybe both. I climbed the three steps into the cave and sat before the fire with the three spirits sitting on the other side, facing me. I started to talk first. (Actually, there was no real talking, just mental telepathy.)

"I need to turn around my financial situation and reverse the current outflow I am experiencing." Before I could explain my situation further, they started firing demands at me.

"You must become **humble**."

The second quickly followed. "You must show **gratitude.**"

The third, "You must be **generous**."

Creeping into my mind—*my generosity is a partial reason for the situation that brought me here.*

[I was still focused on the material things happening in my life. Everything was about losing *my stuff*. The problem was much deeper. I did not realize those things I called *my stuff* really represented *security in my old age.* I had no comprehension of the depth of what they were telling me. Humble, generous, gratitude. Frankly, I only understood those words from a purely intellectual level. I had not experienced those things at the spiritual level from where *they* were communicating. I did not know the level of teaching on which I was about to embark.]

I realized the fourth spirit had not made his appearance. So, I waited...and waited... and waited...and waited. No sign of the fourth spirit.

I started crying and begging, "Please come out, I really want to help. Please let me help." I wasn't clear on what I was to help *with*.

Finally, the fourth spirit made his entrance. He was more imposing than the other three, not that they were shrinking violets. His voice seemed to fill the whole cave. **"You must teach...teach many."**

What did that mean? And teach what? There were no explanations but the book popped into my mind (seven to eight years since I had started talking about writing this book). I had no idea how all of these things could or would manifest. These were not the quick remedies I wanted. I needed *something to turn my situation around now!*

Back in my living room with Gary drumming across from me, he asked, "It was moving for you?" I'm sure he was referring to my breaking down and crying as I said, "Yes."

Although a very powerful experience, it, like everything else, got relegated to the back of my mind—making money and turning my situation around were so driven by fear, I really could not think of anything else. The fear, actually terror is a more appropriate word here, was at a level I had never experienced before in my life. I needed concrete fast results. I had no idea what I was to do to accomplish what the spirits said I needed to do, other than writing the book. That was a longer-term process, especially because I was in the early stages of learning what I was to write. I needed immediate financial relief.

I also did not make the connection to gratitude when I started passing out my black gratitude stones (I have one in my pocket right now). My Assiniboine given name is Iya'saba Wiya (E Yah Sahbah Weyah) which means Black Stone Woman. When I was really down with no money, I gave these stones away, explaining they were gratitude stones to remind a person to be grateful for all they had even when losing everything.

[That was my first attempt to teach others (really me) how to refocus their energy, although I did not know that was what I was doing. Some understood the message behind the gesture, and some looked at me as if I were crazy. No mind, I was doing it for me, not them, even though I was really not aware. I was still very self-focused and I was doing anything I could to lift myself out of the depression and allow me to feel better.]

CHAPTER 8

REAL ESTATE BOOM OR BUST

A Sign from Heaven——Arbinet

About this time, I was at my lowest—on my couch during the waking hours contemplating suicide. I finally gave it all up to God. "I can't take anymore. I need a miracle. You are the man of miracles, so I put my life in your hands. Either you bring me a miracle or let me go."

I promptly fell asleep after my little self-pity romp through the It's-your-fault-God garden. I was throwing it all at His/Her/Its feet. None of this was anymore of my doing.

A day or two later, I received a call from my old boss, J. Curt Hockemeier, VP and General Manager at Cox, now President of Arbinet in New Jersey, a wholesale telecom exchange service. I read about him in the trades but we hadn't talked in about ten years.

After the usual niceties, Curt explained, "I have a situation here very similar to the rate situation you cleaned up in Oklahoma City and I need your help. I want *you* to do this for me. Just tell me when you can start and how much you want."

If that wasn't a miracle, then there is no such thing. I could not believe my ears. The self-esteem boost that provided was what I believe literally saved my life. The confidence in my ability was incredibly empowering. Finally, someone was rewarding me for the job I had done and the skills I had. He certainly was not threatened by me or my skills like the others had been. (I consider Curt to be the best boss I ever had. We did not always agree but there was always mutual respect, something I did not seem to share with any of my other bosses. Underlying the respect was his support and acknowledgement. Amazing what a little pat on the back will do for a human being. Today I credit Curt for saving my life in that moment and I will be eternally grateful.)

Back in the saddle again and loving every minute of the challenge. Rate realignments with customer value as a focus was one of my real talents. Seeing through the confusion seemed to be easy for me. Once into Arbinet's situation, the solution became evident.

At one of the meetings presenting my suggestions, the CFO remarked, "Wow, if we implement that, those people back there keeping track of the pricing will be like tumbleweeds blowing in the wind." I knew I had them then.

This consulting assignment lasted only a few months and was a significant reprieve for me not only monetarily but also it pulled me out of my depression temporarily. However, I still needed a more permanent solution to my outflow problem.

THE SPECTOR OF TERROR

After the consulting assignment, I buried myself in real estate, thinking *this could be the answer*. I signed up for another class from the Russ Whitney real-estate school. I invited a contractor friend because I could bring someone else for free. Besides, I was looking for a partner and his expertise fit the bill. We both got really excited at the seminar. He told me about two houses on the same street in Clarkston, GA. I still had some money, he had the expertise, so we became partners and I bought the two houses.

When I asked him to give me an estimate on the time to rehab the houses, he explained, "Because the two houses are next to each other, we can finish in about two months." Knowing that things happen even to the best-laid plans, I factored four months into the numbers. At month three, "Can you give me an estimate on the time left on the project?"

My questions made him angry. At month four, I realized I was dealing with a child who did not want to be held responsible for his commitments. I felt like a nagging mother rather than a partner. The man had no concept that time was money.

In eight months, we made about $27,000 each instead of the

projected $50,000. The good news: we did make money. Like I told him, $27,000 in four months was okay, but $27,000 in eight months was terrible, especially in the real estate business and when projections were $50,000 each in four months. He did not *get* it or was pretending not to, so he did not have to take responsibility for messing up the job (probably the latter).

What a huge lesson for me. Because I was used to working with Corporate level people, I assumed he would do his part of the job in a professional manner. I had run into a lot of different behaviors in Corporate America, mostly political and all intelligent. I had never experienced this little boy behavior. I certainly did not think I needed to babysit and I was not good at it. So, I found a professional contractor for my next projects. Time to make my next big mistake!

Consciously I was looking for a partner, someone with whom I could work and who would add to the effort rather than drain the partnership.

[I really did not realize how subconsciously I needed and was seeking support and help. I did not know my needs were grossly overshadowing my ability to evaluate the trustworthiness of an individual, coupled with the fact, like it or not, I was dealing with a different level of businessman. There seemed to be a focus on money rather than ethics with these people. I had absolutely no real concept of how much I was being driven by the fear Monkeys. When one makes decisions from fear, they are usually wrong or certainly not for the highest good of all concerned.]

ENTER THE SHYSTERS

I should have taken heed of the feelings I got when I walked into a real-estate club meeting—strong feelings of *shysterhood*. I felt it but paid no attention; I was a bit naïve in trusting some of these people. It wasn't so much a feeling of dishonesty, although that was there, too. I couldn't put my finger on it.

[I was feeling the lower energy levels. I did not know then that lower energy levels translate to nonintegrity, or maybe, better put here...greed, the looking out for oneself at the expense of another.]

After one real-estate meeting, an individual called who wanted to meet me to see if there was a business fit. I met him at Starbucks and we seemed to hit it off. He was beautifully playing to my need for support and said he would help me find the properties I required. He played me like a fiddle.

[I had no idea how fear drove my actions and drove me right into quicksand. I wanted someone to help me so badly, even though I was getting intuitive warnings, I paid no attention.]

He showed me several houses and explained how these houses were right on the line of the up-and-coming neighborhoods, and they were. At that time, everything in Atlanta was moving fast so being one street over from an improved area was a good thing. The other house was on the edge of Avondale Estates, an area in high demand.

[Little did I know both houses were on the *wrong side of the street* and the current movement had not yet jumped the street's demarcation line.]

I ran my numbers. Although these were not expected home runs like the last two houses could have been, I felt we could do it, so I purchased the two houses. As soon as the closings took place, my new *mentor* disappeared, took his money and ran. He apparently had an arranged cut from the sales; so much for helping me.

Turned out one house was in the *hood* (bad area of town) and the other was in a neighborhood where the houses were not bad but not moving. The home in the hood had the furnace stolen sometime after I inspected and closed before the renovation started. My first renovation for this house was an alarm system. With my new contractor, we renovated the two houses quickly and under budget with no personnel problems. I quickly had both houses on the market with them staged and decorated to look appealing. They showed very well, if I do say so myself. Then the fun began.

The contractor rehabbing a burned house across the street from my home in the hood called me one day, asking me about the cage I had installed around my air conditioner--he wanted to have one made for the house he was working on. He interrupted himself. "Oh, by the way, you do know there is no air conditioner in this cage, don't you?"

I about had a heart attack. "No, are you kidding? How the heck did they get it out of the cage?" He exclaimed, "You mean there was one in there?"

That began my war with the thieves. They disconnected the electric meter, so the house had no electricity, which allowed the alarm batteries to run down. They broke in and stole the stove and all my staging material. Clearly the neighbors were allowing all of this to happen without calling the police--probably the neighbors were doing the stealing. I never did find out how they got it out of the cage.

While my fight with the thieves was going on, I had a couple of investors offer to buy my house at my full asking price as long as I did not have an issue with them making some money on the deal. I went to the same workshops these people went to and said fine but I had the house priced at retail with no lookers. To make a long story shorter, I sold the house to the investors. Imagine my surprise when they got funding for $80,000 over my asking price. All smelled fishy to me but the comps supported their price. Needless to say, my mentor and I worked through four rewrites of the contract to make sure my side of the deal was clean.

As everything around me was falling apart, I forgot about the words from the Spirits in the cave--*generous, grateful and humble and, teach many.* Could this be what they meant by being humbled--that I had to lose everything? Terror was taking over the fear.

Clearly my scientific western mind was right—this spiritual stuff was all a bunch of hocus-pocus. Nothing I was doing was working to turn things around monetarily. I was being told to sell the houses and get into cash. A crash was coming and I had been moving my efforts in that direction. My efforts to get my houses on the market and sold were being foiled left and right.

The things happening that kept me from selling my houses were so unusual they were almost comical. However, nothing was comical to me as I watched everything slip away, all which I had worked to accumulate to keep me happy and secure in my later years.

The Florida House

At one of my seminars, I was given a great opportunity to buy and build a house in Florida, where prices (and profits) were climbing and climbing fast, so I bought. By the time the house was finished a year later, it was appraising over $100,000 more than the purchase price. By the time I went to sell a year after that, the bottom had dropped out of the market. I ended up selling the house that appraised for $274,000 for $122,000. I was lucky to sell it at a short sale. (A **short sale** is a **sale** of real estate in which the net proceeds from selling the property will fall **short** of the debts secured by liens against the property. In this case, if all lien holders agree to accept less than the amount owed on the debt, a sale of the property can be accomplished.) Yeah, if I had been in a saner frame of mind and could have covered my costs with rents, the prudent thing to do would have been to keep it rented. By now my pockets were not what one would call deep anymore and too much was going on. I was, slowly, mentally losing it.

I remember being at a Millionaire's Mind Weekend with my girlfriend doing everything I could to turn things around both mentally and physically. By now I was in varying degrees of unloading six houses, all mortgages mine. No renters, only expenses. By then I had been to so many of these seminars and nothing they told me to do was working. I was in such a negative state of mind––I wanted to run up on stage, grab the mike and yell out, "You are all liars. This does not work."

[There was no real understanding of the energy I was putting out at this time. I was coming from such terror, I had no concept of how I was negatively affecting or creating what was happening to me.]

I had a house in Oklahoma City I was in the process of selling to my tenant, who had expressed a concern about a crack in one of the living room walls. I told the management company, "Give him a copy of the pier report we got last year." (A pier report is a study of the foundation of a building to determine its stability and whether it has been undermined by, say, water.) I had it done because they had built another house next to mine *literally* three feet away with absolutely no drainage provision, so all of the rain water from that house's roof, with no gutters, was emptying right at the base of my house. All the ducting for my house was in the slab and my house started to flood through the duct work, so I had to move the furnace to the attic and reduct the whole house, hence the act of getting a pier report. All of that was nonrecoupable expense.

I met with the builder of the house next door, to no avail. Of course, he said it wasn't his fault because he was issued a permit by the city to build. I visited the city only to be told there was nothing they could do and they were not responsible.

I hired two attorneys to sue the builder and the city for issuing the permits. The first was only focused on getting paid by me. The second one said I had a case but would not win—they had just had a similar case, went to court, and lost. How could that be? I no longer had the money to fight the bastards.

Much to my dismay, when I asked the management company to give the tenant a copy of the pier report, I found out they did not actually *get* a pier report. They had the pier company come out to inspect the house and had given it an OK status. After reading the management company the riot act, I told them, "Go get an actual pier report so we can give it to the tenant."

My girlfriend, attending the seminar with me, and I went to lunch. I was in a real panicked state of mind and crying in my soup. I sat at lunch trying to deal with my terror around the losses I was experiencing when I received a phone call from my management company calling from OKC.

"Your pier report has come back and you need to put eleven piers under that house before you can sell it." That translated to about $15,000 in unrecoverable costs just to sell the house.

I lost it and all I could say between tears was, "I'll call you back later." To say I was broken was a slight understatement. What made things really unbearable? I was going through all of this alone. No spouse. No partners. No mentors. And I was so defeated. [I never thought to call any of those people I paid to teach me the ins and outs of the business, besides, subconsciously, I was blaming them for getting me into everything.]

By now I luckily realized how bad a condition I was in mentally and went to my M.D. I was in a very deep depression and losing hope by the minute. I had a very spiritual doctor and she was very comforting. However, this time she said, "Well, maybe you have to lose it all."

I felt so defeated. Although her comment made me want to jump out of my chair and strangle her, I sat in complete paralysis and disbelief. That was the last thing I needed to hear. Fortunately for her, I was too numb to do anything. She talked to me for a while, wrote me a prescription for Zoloft and wrote a bunch of different quotes on her prescription pad for me to tape to my bathroom mirror. They said, "The next step is always easy. If it is not easy, it is not the next step." "What would love do now?" And my favorite, "The only way to the resurrection is straight through the crucifixion." Because I sure felt I was being crucified.

Then she sent me to a psychiatrist to get an opinion on whether this was circumstantial depression or something more serious. Fortunately, it was diagnosed circumstantial, but, at this rate, the circumstances would far outlast my ability to cope.

Everything I am sharing with you now was not happening chronologically, but overlapping each other. I felt like I was in a boxing match with five guys taking turns landing blows.

The Coup de Grace

If all of what was happening to me wasn't enough to get the message across that I was not supposed to be in real estate, God decided to send me one more lightning bolt.

I met Cindy when she posted a sign *Horse for Lease*. I had

always loved horses and took riding lessons but never had a horse or even one near me. Cindy had a farm right around the corner from my house, so I leased Baron, a tri-colored (black, chestnut, and white) ovaro paint, a beauty with an almost total white face. Several months into the lease, Cindy sold Baron with a first right to buy back if the new owner decided to sell him. About a year later, Baron was going up for sale. Cindy and I drove to see him with the intention of buying him back.

When we got there, we discovered Baron and the girl who now owned him did not get along. When she got on him to ride, he acted up, throwing his head and generally misbehaving. She was *in his mouth* which he hated and had a tight rein on him. I told Cindy, "She is afraid of him. I think he has thrown her." To make a long story short, I bought him, feeling more like I was rescuing. He actually tried to bite this girl as we left.

Even though my money was still outflowing, I took on this horse. I rationalized, if *I don't do it now at almost 60, when am I going to do it—at 70?*

Cindy had Kevin training her horse Lilly. Several of us, Lin, Cindy and Kathy, were also taking riding lessons from Kevin. Everyone had their own horses, except me, until I bought Baron. Kevin worked Baron for six months before he would let me back on him because of the damage the last owner did. Baron had to learn to trust again. After that, Kevin would work Baron once a week and I would take lessons on Baron once a week. It was fun. Kevin would teach the horse and the horse would teach me. If I did things right, Baron would perform perfectly.

On a beautiful summer day, Cindy, Lin and I had our horses at Kevin's for a lesson. We were busy doing our thing with the horses when I noticed the sky. As I yelled out for them to see how black the sky was, the tornado sirens went off, as did Cindy's and Lin's phones--their husbands calling to warn us about the weather and to get home ASAP. We had the tack off, loaded the horses in the trailer and were on our way home in about five minutes, getting home in time to put the horses up, fed and for me to get home around the corner. As I pulled into the garage, the sky opened—not just rain, but pea-sized hail. Having lived in Oklahoma, I was very familiar with the precursors of a tornado and hail is one. On the TV, all the stations were covering the weather and our sirens started to go off. I headed to the basement and waited for the worst to pass.

The next day, I was preparing to go out to check my houses. I had two of them next door to each other that I had finished rehabbing, one on the market, one about to go on the market. Four days earlier my landscaper had come out to pretty-up the two properties, readying them for the public--cutting the grass, putting down pine straw and trimming bushes.

As I was walking out the door, I got a call from my friend Montana. "Have you been to your houses yet?"

"No, I was just walking out the door to do that."

"You better prepare yourself—the media is saying the tornado hit right at the corner of your subdivision."

My subdivision was small—that was not good news. As the 20-minute ride got me closer, I could see all the trees that were down. When I turned down my street, it looked like a war zone. All you could hear were buzz saws--the electric company was out in force cutting down trees in an effort to get the power back on to the homeowners. I could barely get down the street, driving around downed limbs and debris. When I got to my houses, I went into shock.

I stood in front with a rake in my hand and a blank stare like the painting "American Gothic" by Grant Wood. *I was out of it* was a gross understatement. Everyone else had chain saws and front loaders. "God, I know you want me out of real estate, so why won't you let me get out?"

Standing there overwhelmed at the devastation, I saw the press show up and a limo being driven down the street (with the State Insurance Commissioner). He interviewed me, basically telling me about my insurance rights, the information falling on deaf ears, because I wasn't functioning at full capacity. Frankly, I'm not sure I had any capacity. The big media focus was the house next to mine, which had a four-foot diameter tree right through the middle of the house. There had been seven people in that house. All made it out without a scratch. Amazing!

I had ten trees down and two of them hit structures. The insurance company only covers removal of trees that hit structures. My first quote to remove the rest of the trees was $10,000. Georgia declared the area a disaster area, which meant I could move all of the tree debris to the front of the houses near the street and the county would remove it. Great! I did not have to pay to haul it away, but where was I going to get the money to cut them up and move them to the street?

The repairs, two new roofs, removal of broken fences, hail damage, and leak repairs, to mention a few issues, plus tree removal kept the houses off the market for another six months. Now we were full force into the burst of the housing bubble. The timing was such that I no longer was able to sell the houses.

That was the last straw. I was on the verge of bankruptcy. I tried to save it all but nothing seemed to work. Two times I had one of the houses sold by almost giving it away but the bankruptcy court stopped the sale, *twice*. Once it was because they were afraid the sale would cause a taxable event for me and I wouldn't have the money to pay the taxes. The other time I don't remember why. No matter what I did, I hit a brick wall. So much happened I can't remember half of it nor do I want to regurgitate more of it here.

In an effort to be a good citizen, I kept the houses and the company afloat with my retirement, thinking things would turn around. (Wrong move.) Bankruptcy can't touch any monies in retirement accounts. If only I had Donald Trump's advisors—I would have put everything into the company and bankrupted the company instead of me personally. At least then I would still have my good credit (which is why he can start over right away without personal repercussions).

I ended up declaring bankruptcy in 2009 and lost all six of the houses I was unable to sell at a short sale. Three went into foreclosure. Funny how my doctor's words were so prophetic. I lost everything but my own house. The Spirits had been right—I needed to be humble, but I had not known how that would happen. I had been significantly humbled or so I thought. (Little did I know there was more to come.)

CHAPTER 9
MOVING ON

Yesterday I was clever, so I wanted to change the world.
Today I am wise, so I am changing myself.
—Rumi

THE UNHEALED INNER CHILD

While the disasters with my houses were going on, I still was working with Gary. Nothing I did was turning my situation around. I was starting to learn about The Law of Attraction from *The Secret* and teachings of Abraham-Hicks in the book *Ask and It Is Given—Learning How to Manifest Your Desires* by Jerry and Ester Hicks. That was not working either. None of those books seemed to give any direction on what was stopping the *good abundance* from coming to me. Instead, everything I had worked all my life to accumulate was falling through my fingers. I thought I was doing what they said to do to bring abundance to myself but, alas, there was no reversal of my situation. I was very discouraged to say the least.

Working with Gary was testing me because he was bringing out a lot of pain I had around my father, particularly my not being acknowledged by him.

[I had no idea the energy of my absolute terror kept the disasters coming or that my Monkeys were being programmed, and the programming I chose to infuse into them unconsciously was *something is wrong with me and I am unlovable.* That is what I made the rejection mean. Because Gary, like it or not, became a representative of my dad, I was unconsciously looking for the same acknowledgement from him that I sought from my dad. And, no surprise, I wasn't getting it. Given I had underlying beliefs of my invisibility and felt unacknowledged, I brought more people into my life to prove me *right*. Of course, all of this is unconscious until one wakes up to the fact.]

IT'S NOT ABOUT THE EAGLE FEATHERS

For me, the waking up about this issue was all about eagle feathers. Gary had already kicked me out of the nest, so to speak. As a friend said to me when I was discussing what was going on, "You pushed his abandonment button."

I actually did not *do* anything. We were at a conference for a multilevel marketing company, World Leadership Group (WLG). Gary was in my downline (I had brought him into the business), which he did not like. My upline wanted to talk to me alone. Gary followed us and my upline respectfully told him that he wanted to speak to me alone. Gary walked away and came back as we ended our conversation. I caught Gary saying to the man (who seemed two feet shorter than Gary), "There can be only one bull in a pasture."

I was appalled at Gary's disrespectful behavior toward the man, who protested that he had no interest in being a bull in any pasture. Given my Corporate background, I was horrified again but this time at the lack of respect for me being put forth by my teacher.

Our relationship took a dramatic turn and never recovered. He blamed me for whatever he thought had happened. From that point forward, all I got from him were hot pokers in the side. My little girl, who loved and wanted her daddy, was devastated. His unhealed little boy was very mean and unleashed a level of cruelty I had not experienced before. After one particularly devastating exchange in which he turned the energy of the group against me, I ran out absolutely destroyed. I went to my girlfriend's house in a state of crying destruction. She informed me there were much easier ways to deal with these issues and asked why I kept going back.

"I got on this horse to cross the finish line and I intend to do that, whatever that means."

Those days were not easy for me. He would acknowledge everyone in the group but when my turn came, he acted like I wasn't there. Sound familiar? My roommate at the time, who was also in the group, couldn't believe he was ignoring me the way he did.

"Do you think he knows he is ignoring you?"

"No, but the Creator knows and there is something I am supposed to learn from his behavior. When I point this behavior out to him, he will use it against me, so for now I need to keep quiet and observe."

[What I did not understand was the energetic alignment had not been shifted, so the results in my life would continue unchanged. My subconscious energetic expectation was—"I am not worthy enough to be acknowledged." Remember what my coach said, "We bring people into our lives to support our underlying beliefs about ourselves." Because this issue, which started back with my father, had not yet been healed, I kept bringing people into my life who kept bringing the issue up for me. This nonacknowledgment would not stop until I became aware of the issue, healed it and realigned my subconscious thinking with being acknowledged. All of this understanding came much later in the process and, I might add, after many years of internal work. So, at this time, I was still deeply in the dark, under the Monkeys' invisible cloak.]

In the traditional tribal ways, when people were to be recognized, they were often given eagle feathers, which was quite an honor. Eagles are protected in the USA and only Native Americans can own, or give away, their parts. As usual, when Gary started to give out eagle feathers, I was somehow forgotten. There seemed to be no real reason for the awards. *Does one get recognized because they learn the ceremonies, or because they are given songs, or because they complete a vision quest or because they come to the functions all of the time or because they are working diligently looking inside to change themselves? What were the criteria*--a typical white man thought. Even though I was doing all of those things, I was still passed over. Everyone would get something but me (that is how it felt to me, and my inner child got hurt and angry every time).

Then something started to happen way beyond my control. Every time he gave away eagle feathers, that night I would have a dream. The eagle would come to me in the dream, fly over or land in my vicinity and proceed to pluck some of his feathers and drop them at my feet. After the third or fourth time I had this dream, I started to realize the message—I did not need Gary for eagle feathers. Acknowledgement came from inside me not outside me. Until I was able to acknowledge myself, I would not be acknowledged by others. Remember how I told you that in Corporate America I would win awards and the acknowledgement would slip away?

[What was happening before my eyes was the healing process all around not being acknowledged as a child.]

By this time, I had shared with Gary that he constantly left me out. I could tell by his body language he, until that moment, was not consciously aware of it. I can assure you he would be aware from then on and I was right. I laughed the last time Gary gave away eagle feathers. It was after the first big Inipi Ceremony in Virginia where Gary's group was invited to bring his Animal Spirit Dance to the Natives in Virginia. Gary, in a vision, had been directed to bring back the Animal Spirit Dance because it had been lost over the years. By now, his reputation around the ceremony had traveled to other parts of the country.

Cindy, my girlfriend with the horses, wanted to go to the dance and sweat lodge. She was starting to acknowledge her Native roots and wanted to learn. We had to leave before the ceremony actually took place because her stepfather had to go to the hospital with heart trouble. As a result, I had her go to the meeting a week after the ceremony. Much could be learned from the experience of the dancers at that meeting. I was always amazed at the healing I witnessed at these functions. Things happened which were unexplainable, at least from a western perspective.

As we sat in the meeting, Gary proceeded to announce he was giving eagle feathers to two of the men. As he proceeded with the ceremony, he turned and asked the woman to my left--"So, Linda, when did you get your first eagle feather?" Before she could respond, he turned to the woman on my right and said, "So, Ann, when did you get your first eagle feather?" He was deliberately trying to deliver a hot poker to my side. Something different happened for me though--instead of being hurt or angry, I was laughing inside. The cute little antics had no effect on me anymore--I was happy for the boys, but no longer in need of eagle feathers from Gary. I had become self-reliant. The damage done, as a child, was healed. I was free...free as an eagle.

WALK FOR THE WATER AND DR. MASARU EMOTO

A year before I declared bankruptcy, while still trying to sell my houses and stop my financial bleeding, I was working with Gary on the Board of his 501-C3, Many Horses Foundation (www.manyhorses.org). Georgia was in a significant drought and Gary wanted to do a Walk for the Water. This would be a huge ceremony to help break the drought. Much of the planning started a year or maybe even two earlier. I had received a commitment from Dr. Masaru Emoto to be part of the ceremonies, which was a huge coup for us.

Dr. Masaru Emoto was a Japanese scientist who studied water over his lifetime and developed a way to photograph water as it was freezing.[1] During that development, he noticed water responded to the beautiful music he was playing while he photographed the water as it was freezing. His photographs showed beautiful snowflake-like crystals when exposed to the music. So, he started experimenting and discovered that if water was exposed to noise, or words of hate, no crystals were formed—the pictures looked more like boiling water. He went on from there. Exposed to the word love or similar words, beautiful crystals formed. Please review the following photos, one entitled *Love and Gratitude* and the other *You Disgust Me*. As you can see the Love and Gratitude photograph shows a beautiful crystal has developed while the You Disgust Me photograph shows no crystal but instead looks like boiling water.

© Office Masaru Emoto

Love and Gratitude

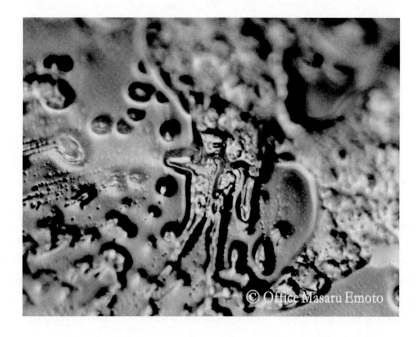

© Office Masaru Emoto

You Disgust Me

Along with this study, he carried out a different experiment. He took three jars, put cooked rice in each jar and added water. He exposed one jar to the word *love*, the second to the word *hate*, and the third was ignored. After several weeks, the experiment showed the rice in the water exposed to the word *love* did not spoil and smelled fresh. The rice in the water exposed to the word *hate* spoiled and smelled poorly. The rice in the water that was ignored putrefied and smelled terrible.[2]

(Why is this important?) The human body is made up of about 70% water, so our psyche responds the same way as in this experiment. A human needs love. Given love in the form of positive feedback, a person tends to develop a positive loving self-image whereas given attention via negative feedback, s/he could develop a poor self-image and being ignored creates much anger.

Of course, these statements are to bring out a point, not to prove a scientific fact. Many other factors are involved. The point––the danger of ignoring a human being can be more damaging than hateful exposure.

[In my opinion, this is why the kids of today are killing themselves and their school chums or a mall full of strangers. With TVs, computers, and iPhones as baby sitters, there is less and less human contact and communication, good or bad, and that is not good. Communication and contact show a child someone cares. We no longer allow touching in our schools out of fear of improper touching, but kids in school need the hugs the most. The movie *Doubt* with Philip Seymour Hoffman and Meryl Streep[3] brings out this type of fear in spades.]

Water seems to be definitely affected by vibrations emitted by each word's energetic pattern. In my opinion, his work supports the indigenous people's belief that everything has spirit, including water. Clearly, it is affected by the energy to which it is being exposed. So, Dr. Emoto's work around the study of water is an example of the effects of vibrational energy. His work was represented in the movie *What the Bleep Do We know!?*[4]

While his work is an interesting hypothesis, the scientific

community does not support it because Dr. Emoto has not used a rigorous scientific method to prove his findings, or so they say. Well, scientists have not been able to prove there is a God either. Nothing spiritual can be proven, at least with the science we currently understand. Moving from the paradigm of reason and intellect to the realm of love requires an ability to let go of the need to prove anything, for love cannot be proven any more than the existence of God can be proven. And yet most feel His/Her/Its existence.

For the Native Americans, Dr. Emoto's work seemed to substantiate their belief that *everything has spirit including water*. The more I learned and the more I experienced, the more I, too, believed we were all one and all have spirit.

The people involved did a great job of putting on the Walk for the Water. There were great venues and great programs and the walk took place but it was like a great party that no one attended, except the promoting group and their extended Native reach. Because they did not lead with Dr. Emoto and instead let their egos create a forum for their Native pontifications, the Emoto part of the program got lost in the mix and failed to bring in its customary draw. Dr. Emoto was not happy because he had never had such a small turnout and our opportunity to create a lucrative funding platform was lost.

By now, I was realizing my time studying with Gary was coming to an end.

BLUE THUNDER

With everything going on in my life, the stress was taking its toll on my body. My chiropractor at the time was desperate to get me stress relief as she said my adrenals were shot. All the things I was doing from a health perspective were not enough to turn the situation around. Everything in my life was causing stress—the real estate business going down the tubes, the damage to my houses causing an inability to sell, the dysfunction on the Many Horses Board, etc., etc.

At my chiropractor's insistence, I contacted Blue Thunder,

a.k.a. Bennie LeBeau, (Bavado) Rainbow Thunder Heart (in Eastern Shoshone) formerly known as Bavado, of the Eastern Shoshone Nation, located on the Wind River Indian Reservation, in Ft. Washakie, Wyoming. He was another Native American elder who happened to be in the area and I set an appointment to get some help to break the energy drain or cord, as they call it, with Gary because the energy was quickly turning negative.

I had met him once at a circle meeting at Gary's. I told Blue Thunder about the things happening to me and that I needed to change the energy or I was going to have a physical collapse. He did a ceremony that consisted of drumming and guided imagery not unlike many practitioners today.

Once in ceremony he said, "Call up your little girl."

An immediate picture popped into my head of a little brunette girl about two or three years' old running through a field where the things normally green were yellow, all kinds of brightly colored flowers grew and I was chasing a butterfly.

Blue Thunder directed, "Call her home." When I called her home, she morphed into a small baby that entered my body on the left side (the left side represents the feminine) near my womb. After entering my body, she then grew up on my left side. The experience was all very powerful, emotional and significant.

When the ceremony was over, I told Blue Thunder what happened. "What color was the butterfly?"

"Blue."

"Oh, the color of truth. You are chasing truth." He went on to explain that this ceremony ended up being a soul retrieval.

Everything made sense to me. Gary had always said I suppressed my femininity. This could have been a symbol of the retrieval of that female part of me.

[Remember, I was a male chauvinist pig in past lives. I had no idea I was only starting to crack that nut and there was more to come.]

Gary always said he was a bridge. (I think that is true of every teacher whether they are your pastor, priest, minister, therapist, guru, shaman, or any individual who crosses your path. Everyone is a student and a teacher at the same time. One learns from what we label as the good and the bad in others. How you react toward those teachers and their teachings is the important observation. They tell you where you are in the process, that is, if you are awake enough to be able to see yourself and your behavior in the process. Most don't see themselves because they are too busy projecting onto others what they don't like about themselves.)

I watched as people approached Gary, the bridge--some stopped, others approached then ran away, some walked onto the bridge, some stayed on the bridge, some jumped off the bridge and some crossed it. Those who crossed the bridge learned what they needed and moved on with their life, having healed that part of themselves this teacher had the power to heal.

The learning of the old traditional Native ways was a way to open my mind to three important things I needed to learn:

1. how to *feel again;*
2. there is a reason for everything and no coincidences; and
3. the nature of caring love.

People who say, "Oh, it is just a coincidence," have not experienced what I was learning and are not at a level where they can comprehend. Mysticism is nothing more than lack of experience and/or education. I needed to learn not about romantic love but caring love for all my relations, the plants, animals, creepy crawlies and the needs of all human beings.

I learned a lot from Gary and will always be grateful for the time with him. I learned to set my own boundaries. I learned my teachers are not Gods and are human and make mistakes, too, and my job is to learn from those so-called mistakes. I learned about issues I had around my father. And I learned *the time had come to move on.*

PSYCH-K

Once you are aware that you are on a spiritual path, people and circumstances interestingly come into your life at the right time. As an insatiable reader, I stumbled on the book *The Biology of Belief* by Bruce Lipton, Ph.D.[5] I do not remember how I stumbled upon it but here it was in my life. For you western-minded thinking or scientific-minded people, I highly recommend this fascinating read. Bruce is a cellular biologist and ends up coming to a spiritual realization through the study of cells.

I remember commenting to myself on how many books were being written about the spiritual journey people were having but all were coming from different perspectives. *That's so cool to see—people from such diverse places coming to the same conclusions.* That is why I liked Bruce's book so much. I never thought one would come to spiritual conclusions from the study of the cells. Wow! The real benefit I got from reading his book was my introduction to Psych-K.

I immediately googled Psych-K and found a couple, Yonie and Bernice Werzberger, who were husband and wife practitioners and instructors of Psych-K here in Atlanta. Wow! I called and talked to Yoni and found myself signed up for the Basic class that weekend.

Psych-K: The Missing Piece--Peace in your Life! by Robert M. Williams[6] describes a process to identify subconscious beliefs that are incorrect and become blocks to the advancement of the individual. Once identified and corrected, the blocks are removed and the individual can move on with his/her life.

I was perplexed about what to write in my book for advice on what others could do to make shifts in their lives. My path had been hard and very painful at times. I certainly did not feel I could suggest people follow my path and relive any suffering they may have had. Well, I could have, but I was sure others would not want to dredge up agony. Although it became easier and easier for me and almost fun, later in the process. I knew I was pretty strong and certainly committed to this course where others might not be.

There has to be an easier way for everyone else. Because I did not have an easier way to suggest, I felt I had no conclusion to my book. Taught in Corporate America to come in with solutions and not problems, I thought *how can I have no ending to the book?* I finally realized I was in no position to recommend anything to anybody. I only could tell my story and let people take from it what they felt. What a relief to realize I did not have to fix or help anyone. Their guides would do that job. However, a new modality did fall into my lap thanks to Bruce.

Psych-K is a plus-25-year-old technology based on using Applied Kinesiology. The practitioner muscle tests a belief statement. If one's muscles go weak, that particular statement is false; if one's muscles stay strong, then that statement is true.

In my first class, I tested the statement: "Painting is easy and fun for me." The results were strong, which meant that was true. Perplexed by this outcome, I blurted out, "If that is so, why am I not painting?"

The practitioner I was working with suggested a two-word change to the statement. "*I believe* painting is easy and fun for me." Sure enough, I tested weak for that statement. As long as I had a subconscious belief that painting was not easy and fun for me, it would not be easy and fun. So, we did some exercises to reprogram the subconscious, and now I am painting and having fun doing it. With some things, people see immediate shifts. With other things, time is needed for the transformation to take place and for one to notice a difference.

I embarked upon six years of Psych-K study. I took the beginning class and the advanced class four to five times over a period of three years. Privately, I also was going to Bernice, my practitioner, who has an uncanny ability to get to the real issues quickly. The practitioner is a guide—a very educated guide.

The whole process is a permission protocol. The practitioner is constantly asking the Higher Self of the individual being worked with for permission, direction and which methods to use for the transmutation of the belief.

During my first advanced class, we were learning about the relationship balance. I had a list of people with whom I thought I needed a relationship balance. In cases like this, we muscle test to prioritize the list. I was a little surprised—the first person on my list after that prioritization was the Past President of Cox, Jim Robbins, not my father, mother, past bosses or God. That was interesting and perplexing at the same time, until I completed the balance process. Since Jim was deceased, we had another participant surrogate for him. During the process, we came to the point where we had to muscle test to see which of us, Jim or I, was out of balance in the relationship--both parties tested strong which meant neither person was out of balance. We did not know what to do, so we called Bernice over and told her what had happened. "This does not happen very often and when it does, usually the two people in question had some sort of karmic agreement to behave in this lifetime as they did thus they are not out of balance."

Woah! All of a sudden, why Jim did not protect me from my slotters at Cox was clear--if he had protected me from the discrimination I was experiencing, I may not have lost my position; if I did not lose my position, I may never have gone down this path, never written this book. Any anger I still had around Jim not protecting me at Cox totally disappeared. This was a soul agreement. He, at a soul level, was helping me to travel the path I had chosen to take in order to turn around some of my (and other's) negative karma.

For the first time, I understood why I had to be at his funeral, even though I did not understand when I was there. At some subconscious level, I was paying respects to the man who helped me follow the path I was here to follow. What a very profound moment of realization for me.

[As I write this, I am still unaware of what this book might set in motion *out there* but I do know that this writing is not my conscious choice but a subconscious drive to set things straight. What things? I am not sure but then I do not need to know everything.]

Enter the Weight Fairy. As I continued my work in Psych-K, I started to notice some subtle changes taking place. I always had an eating compulsion. After many years of diets, weight loss and gains, I simply quit worrying. I was attempting to love me, however I looked. I knew decades before the doctors and their counsel that a calorie was a calorie no matter the kind of food; I also knew different body types metabolized foods differently. How? I just knew--I didn't know where the knowing came from. [Well, now I do.]

Several months into the Psych-K work, I started to notice a lessening of the pull to binge eat. During the six years working with Gary, I gained 30 pounds. His method was to use a *hot poker* in an attempt to get me to react and then hold the mirror up to show me my behavior, a very confrontational style. My response to the hot poker was reactive binge eating. Every time I *chose* to be hurt by his behaviors, I went running for the Big Mac, ice cream or a bottle, all a substitute for the love I needed and was not feeling.

Yes, I said CHOSE. Being hurt is a CHOICE. *The other person is not responsible for hurting you. You are responsible for allowing the hurt.* Being reactive or hurt is simply a road sign to show you there is something unhealed in your psyche. Same with being offended. Being offended is a CHOICE. Because you are responsible for how you react or respond to life does not mean others are not hurtful or insensitive. When some of my teachers would say to me, "You are giving your power away," I had no idea what they were talking about. It is very clear to me now.

I remember when Gary was poking me with the hot poker and another woman working with him said to me, "Do you think he really knows what he is doing when he does these things?"

I responded, "I don't know. Sometimes I think he does and sometimes I know he doesn't. But I do know one thing—the Creator knows. So, whatever he is doing and however he is behaving, whether conscious or not, is exactly what I need to have happen to wake me up to the things I need to learn."

Always keeping this in mind allowed me to work with him and

not blame him for how I was feeling. I can assure you there were times when the hurt I was dredging up was devastating. The victim mentality blames others for the pain. It is your reaction that is a choice.

In the early stages of working with him, he made me buy a refrigerator magnet that said, "I never met a man I couldn't blame." When I came out of Corporate America, the man vs. woman thing was a real issue for me.

[Fortunately, much later, I came to realize *love vs. fear* was the real issue.]

Most people working with him never got to this stage in their growth. Most ran away. They couldn't handle taking the deep responsibility looking in the mirror requires. The good news here is that there were many paths to the peace and happiness I was seeking. Not everyone needs to take the same route I did and one can take a much slower pace. I remember a particular time when I was absolutely devastated by Gary's behavior and was at another tobacco student's house crying my eyes out. She was a psychologist and said nothing much in the two hours I carried on and on. Finally, she said, "Oh, I see—he must have you on a fast track."

I remembered him asking me in the first or second session, "Do you want to do this fast or slow?" I blurted out, "I need to do this fast; I don't have much time." Obviously, I did not understand what the choice I had made actually meant. For the most part, I had finished this road with Gary. I believe the hot poker method was absolutely necessary for me to wake up and learn quickly.

[I found out later, for me, this lifetime, was/is all about transforming some significantly unpleasant karma. All of this had been necessary for me to be able to write this book.]

Starting Psych-K and transforming hidden beliefs that were road blocks on my road to happiness and joy, I began losing weight. I was not doing anything differently—no diets or workouts, just Psych-K, but I was dropping weight at a regular rate. I ended up dropping 43 pounds. [*The more false beliefs I transformed the more weight dropped off.*]

I noticed my reactive behavior gradually changing. First, a lot more energy was needed to push my buttons and, when they did get pushed, I did not automatically run to the store for my then-favorite food. When I did buy something formerly forbidden, I could keep it in the house a lot longer. My point: Psych-K was responsible for the dissipation of my reactive binge-eating behavior and I was not even working on losing weight. It just happened.

Many people doing this work report similar results. They also report the disappearance of disease, aches and pains. As you raise your consciousness level, you will move into more healing energy. But then life happens--it kicks you in the butt, which is why this work many times feels like two steps forward and one step back.

An Equal Playing Field. Recently I had a session with my Psych-K instructor who took issue with my continual statement of *"there is no equal playing field."* She said there is an equal playing field. A better statement would be: *"Below the level of enlightenment (600), there is no equal playing field."* I found this unequal playing field true in Corporate America. (VTK) VTK= *Verified as True with Kinesiology*

Notes: VTK = *Verified as True with Kinesiology* (by muscle testing). Enlightenment level/spirituality of 600 out of 1000 will be discussed further on in the Mystery Schools.

I was not privy to the JOR University that Duffy referred to in his eulogy for Jim. I was never asked to join Skull and Bones or any other exclusive club. I was not part of the good-ole-boy network that gives a helping hand to its members.

Well, I clearly totally disagree with her assessment that there is an equal playing field. If there were an equal playing field, then there would be no victims. Everyone would have the *exact* same opportunities. Notice the emphasis on exact. You see, I have had this discussion with many white males who think there is a level playing field, everyone has the same opportunity here in the good ole USA, you just need to work hard. They are completely unaware of the fact many doors open to them simply because they are white and male but do not open to black or Latino males nor women.

My Psych-K instructor was talking from a much higher level of Mystery School understanding because she knows through the same study I do that everything emanates from the thoughts one has in his or her mind. *So, at the <u>higher levels of spirituality (above 600), there is a level playing field</u> because each of us creates what comes into our life via our thoughts about ourselves so we can learn our lessons. (VTK)* In the upcoming chapter on energy, you'll read that the energy you put out in your thoughts, both conscious and unconscious, attract the same energy back to you. *So, if you think people are victimizing you, you will attract victimizers into your life to prove you are right. (VTK)*

Once we can grasp this truth, we can more easily understand, from an energetic point of view, that each of us is totally responsible for what manifests in our lives. This perspective comes from a very high spiritual place and is incomprehensible to those who calibrate at lower consciousness levels.

Let me be clear, I am not saying that there are no people who victimize because there are. The energy you put out, however, determines whether they come into your life experience. Thinking victim thoughts has the same energy (vibrational frequency) as someone who victimizes; therefore, you are very likely to meet up with victimizers on your life stage.

I was quickly transitioning to the Psych-K method and the study of Dr. David Hawkins' Map of Consciousness. These methods were much easier on my psyche. Or the work I did with Gary had significantly healed my psyche so I no longer had the sensitivity charge. When emotions would come up, I no longer reacted at the same *intensity.* And if I did, the process described in Dr. Hawkins' book *Letting Go* helped to move me through the issues.[7]

Psych-K tames the Monkeys at a subconscious level, calms them down and allows change to happen. All of this could be done with or without a conscious level change, although I would find it hard to believe that utilizing Psych-K would not help a consciousness shift.

In the context of religion, all of the different positionalities, religions or dogmas simply represent different pathways to God. They represent the fact that we all live on different facets of the diamond and are at different consciousness levels. All of them are blessed by God/Universe or, if you prefer, the energy of love. None of them are the one and only way. Love and life enhancement is the one and only way to the Source/God.

PART THREE

THE MONKEYS

CHAPTER 10

THE MONKEYS ARE BORN

Just cause you got the Monkey off your back doesn't mean the circus has left.
—George Carlin

WHY MONKEYS?

I guess it is time to give you an in-depth explanation of the Monkeys. I am sure many of you have figured out basically what they are. I did not explain this earlier because I wanted you to discover them the way I did, slowly and with little awareness.

Q. So what are the Monkeys?

A. They are those thoughts, feelings and behaviors that keep you from growing spiritually and consciously. They are the part of you that says, "I can't," "You're not good enough," "No one likes me," "I am better than you" or any other comments that keep you from being in relationships, limiting your potential, or living your life—I mean REALLY living your life. We are afraid of everything that the Monkeys say and represent and we believe them!

Q. Why did I choose to use Monkeys to represent our behaviors?

A. Because monkeys are cute, mischievous, fun-loving, lovable, rambunctious, excitable, reactive, amusing, make mistakes and are teachable. They are loving, caring, innocent, pure beings and are teachable. They can be angry, mean, vengeful, self-righteous, closedminded, judgmental, opinionated, greedy, always right, in resistance, scary, blind projectionists. They can blame others for their life's circumstances, and display sometimes downright evil manners and, did I say, they are teachable? Yes, the

Monkeys can be taught and tamed. *They are not in any way bad.* They can do bad, evil things but they in themselves are not bad or evil. We have used them in our culture to add humor to situations and to get across lessons and concepts that otherwise could be rejected and certainly resisted. "Monkey see, monkey do," "hear no evil, see no evil, speak no evil," etc.

I used and continue to use the humor of the Monkeys to make the journey of inner discovery easier for me. I could look at the Monkeys and laugh, whereas, if I pictured a devil—well, there is nothing funny about the devil. When I started this journey of awakening, my main underlying belief was, "There is something wrong with me and, therefore, I am unlovable, need fixing, am bad and broken."

[Of course, all of that was totally unconscious for me and *untrue.* I did not know what beliefs were driving my behavior.] I knew I was alone and did not want to be alone. I wanted to be successful but could not get past a certain level of success. My conscious mind could not handle the thought that I was bad, so resistance became commonplace. Looking at anything I could interpret as implying I was bad was not going to happen. Of course, I was not bad. Only my personal Monkeys said so. When the Monkeys were in control of my thoughts, there was no humor about my behavior. I needed to add humor to my process because I did not see anything to laugh at. After all, I could not possibly be responsible for my situation; it was all *their* fault (whoever *they* were).

What I call the Monkeys, some people use shadow self, inner child, that evil part of us, dragons, etc. I chose Monkeys to describe these states of mind as a replacement for what many call their demons, for several reasons. First, the word demon implies something or someone who is really bad or even evil, hence they need to be exorcised or saved. This wording comes directly from Judeo-Christian teachings. This interpretation causes people to avoid taking personal responsibility for what happens in their lives. They don't want to think of themselves as bad, so avoid looking at themselves. Blaming the devil or others is easier. *The devil made me do it.* Using the word demon to describe this phenomenon may not allow a person to see themselves as anything but bad. The Monkeys (their behaviors) are benign, sometimes good, and sometimes labeled as bad.

Unfortunately, in my opinion, the Church has damaged a lot of people with the programming that we were born with sin. Sin, properly translated, simply means error or mistake, not bad or born bad. So, I chose the Monkeys because I like to look at myself and others as lovable creatures, full of mischief, who make mistakes, have misapplied perceptions, often do not have the whole story, create prejudices based on past experiences, always seem to assume they are right no matter the facts, make things up about what is happening with no basis in truth, live as if it is all true, fight to the death if someone counters their belief or position--a *creature, who simply needs to be acknowledged and loved as it learns the real truth about itself.*

The second reason I use the word Monkeys is because the Buddhists call our ordinary state of mind the Monkey Mind. Chatter, chatter, chatter. The voices never abandon the owner. A Buddhist friend of mine told me the Monkeys were the *bad* Monkeys (there is that word *bad* again). They are the voices in your head that say, "I am not good enough," "I can't do something," or, in my case, "I am not lovable," etc. I do not want to label the Monkeys with the term *good* or *bad*. They just exist.

This is the first of many distinctions I learned. There is a huge difference between *bad behavior* and *bad people*. There are *no* bad people, only people in pain, some a great deal of pain.

Eckhart Tolle calls it one's *pain body*.[1] The Monkeys have been allowed to run around for so long ignored, mistreated and in control of one's life, (for most) to look at them as anything other than bad or even evil is impossible. This is so because *mankind has not reached the collective consciousness level that lets us see the innocent person beyond the behavior. (VTK)* For the most part, only God and maybe a mother can see this innocence. We have not learned that bad behavior is a cry for help and, or more importantly, a cry for love. Unless you have raised your consciousness level, and are able to have the compassion to see the innocent person behind all of the pain in *you,* you will never be able to see the innocent person behind the behavior in *others. People can only love someone else to the level that they are capable of loving themselves* (VTK).

If we accept that making mistakes is OK, we are much more likely to take responsibility, really look at the Monkeys we have, love them and tame them, so our lives can take a more positive, joyful, balanced, peaceful, productive and loving path.

Another reason I am writing this book is the fact that *the Monkeys are why the Law of Attraction does not seem to work for some people.* Well, it works but because the Monkeys, unbeknownst to you, are subconsciously the ones putting out the prayer energy, your life's manifestations are subject to Monkey beliefs unknown to you. If your Monkey thoughts are focused on the fact you are being victimized, then more and more victimizers will come into your life. So, the law works but not in a way you consciously may like.

THE KNOWING MIND

"The intuitive mind is a sacred gift and the rational mind is a faithful servant. We have created a society that honors the servant and has forgotten the gift."[2]

I want to reemphasize that everything I am writing are my opinions based solely on a lifetime of over 70 years personal experience, extensive study through reading, observation of myself and other's behavior, study through the application of consumer behavior, advertising, marketing and intuitive talent, as Einstein calls the *sacred gift.* I am an insatiable reader--I read to learn, watch TV to learn, attend seminars, lectures, courses and travel to learn.

Although my successes in Corporate America came from my intuitive side, I saw it as common sense. I had an ability to see what others could not see. I remember a counselor in my Corporate years once saying, "Trust me when I tell you, you can see what others can't see." I did not understand they could not see what I thought was obvious.

Seeing such was a gift and the basis for my successes. At the same time, that gift also felt like a curse because this innate ability threatened many of my colleagues. I was actually put down because my knowing did not come from existing facts or reading the research, at least as they saw it. Of course, the fact that I more often than not had correct evaluations of the situations made me even more threatening to them. So, most of my credibility comes from the side Einstein calls a sacred gift. I have spent my life studying what makes people do what they do from my years of training in advertising, the visual arts and marketing to my natural talent to be able to observe and recognize what motivates people and consumers. Most of this study has to do with the subconscious mind. And now with the works from Dr. David Hawkins, M.D. PhD, and Robert M. Williams, we are able to muscle test for the truth in these evaluations and statements.

PROGRAMMING THE COMPUTER

We are like a brand-new computer before any software is loaded. As we grow physically, we start to learn, and what we learn is programming us, like a computer. Unlike the computer, the human mind is programmed in two different ways: 1) conscious learning; and 2) subconscious learning. Conscious learning is that which takes place when you are aware of what is being taught. This includes experiential learning and book learning. Subconscious learning is all experiential and observational learning that we are unaware is taking place every minute of our lives. The subconscious is 40,000 times faster than the conscious mind, at least that is what I was taught in school when learning about subliminal advertising. Of course, much more has been understood since I was in school and there apparently is no real consensus as to how much faster the subconscious is than the conscious mind. Dr. Bruce Lipton, author of *The Biology of Belief* indicated the subconscious mind processes 500,000 times faster than the conscious mind. Regardless of the correct speed, the subconscious mind processes faster than one's awareness, which simply means we are learning things we do not even know we are learning. And they say we use only <u>10%</u> of our brains.

Science has shown we exhibit different brain waves at different ages. These brain waves allow learning at super speeds at the younger years.[3]

Birth - 2 years	Delta Wavesup to 4 HZinstantaneous learning
2- 6 years	Theta Waves 4-8 HZ1-2 repetitions to learn
5-8 years	Alpha Waves 8-13 HZ21 repetitions
8-12+ years	Beta Waves 13-30 HZthousands of repetitions

The Delta waves allow a complete download into the brain without any discernment of truth or falsehood. This programming becomes the individual's truth. The Theta waves allow almost the same downloading without discernment. Young children are in Theta waves a good part of the time; we often describe them as *sponges*, which is happening mostly through observation—this is why the teaching method of *do as I say, not as I do* does not work for kids (or anyone for that matter). They learn from what they observe [so watch what you are doing, parents]. They are like little computers subconsciously being programmed by the actions of parents, peers and society. They mirror the behavior we model for them. As one is programmed with these beliefs and experiences, no one is checking to see if what we are taught and the beliefs we develop through experience and what we made them mean are: a) accurate, or b) true.

A recent way of programming is via television and computer games. Through some of these computer games, children are being programmed to be nonthinking killers. *Parents allow this programming under the false belief that the child knows it is a game. The child may know but the subconscious mind is incapable of distinguishing real from not real. Therein lies the danger. (VTK)*

The computer is subject to *garbage in garbage out* in terms of the software being programmed into it. If the operator programs the computer with faulty information, then the computer will function and put out faulty results until it is reprogrammed with correct information. The human mind is similar—taught falsehood, it will *believe* falsehood until it is taught, learns or experiences something different. The Nazi movement in Germany understood this all too well with the Hitler Youth programs.

The critical difference between humans and the computer— humans *think*, humans *judge* and humans *make things up*.

In fact, humans are meaning-making machines. In the subconscious mind, the Monkeys are born and develop. *That making up of things empowers and allows the Monkeys to develop and grow. (VTK)*

If we program the computer that 2 + 2 = 5, we have programmed an error, which is neither good nor bad, just an error. That an error was made does not mean anything about the computer or the programmer, only that an error needs to be corrected. Nothing happens to the programmer or the computer when the error is acknowledged. If, on the other hand, we program the human mind that 2 + 2 = 5, we have again programmed an error. That is where the similarity stops. Depending on how the human is treated (its exposure to energy) when the error is made, the Monkeys can and will take root. Let's say a parent or adult says, "You're stupid," (belief system programming) rather than "You made an error." The human mind receiving the statement can create all kinds of meanings about itself (e.g., *I am stupid, therefore, I am not worthy, I am not lovable*). What we make it mean about ourselves may not be true but we live the rest of our lives as if it is true. **This is how the Monkeys are born.**

If you are ready to look into the mirror and see a cute innocent part of you that has made errors which need to be corrected rather than demons to be exorcised, the path can become easier, less painful and with less resistance.

So, in a nut shell, the Monkeys I refer to are a combination of the ego, the unhealed inner child, our belief systems, imaginations and our consciousness level and energetic exposure. Some would probably say this is an oversimplification of what is a very complicated subject. I am here to do that…simplify, if I can.

THE INVISIBLE CLOAK

The Monkeys have an invisible cloak, which is similar to Harry Potter's. When Harry put on his cloak, he could see everything and everyone around him but he was invisible to those outside.

The Monkey's cloak is different. When the Monkeys put it over their owner, everyone can see that person and his behavior for what it is but the owner cannot see himself or what he is doing-- his Monkey behaviors are invisible to him. Interestingly, he can see the same behavior or way of being in others, who also have that behavior, and he is quite quick to point it out, but he is totally blind to the fact he also has the same behavior or attribute. So, the invisible cloak, simply put, makes the person who has it on totally blind to himself and his own behaviors. If he gets a glimpse of his behavior, he can and will justify it in some manner and even defend it to the death, *until he wakes up.*

In case you are already judging yourself or others, I must caution you…**everyone has Monkeys.** If you are human, you have Monkeys. The key is to **become aware of them.** You cannot tame them until you can see they are there. So, the first part of the healing process is becoming aware you have Monkeys. The second part to learn is that "anger without projection is impossible"[4]

The Native Americans call this process *waking up.* In their world, one is either awake, asleep or waking up. Dr. David Hawkins, in all of his books, describes the asleep state as anything unaware of the truth. The level 200 is the demarcation line between the ability to be truthful and not. Anyone who calibrates below 200 lacks integrity or the ability to be truthful to themselves, are completely asleep, and the cloak is on. Once one crosses over the demarcation line of 200, s/he is *now* **capable** *of courage*, which is needed to start looking at oneself in the mirror, being honest, and understanding the waking-up process. Because one might calibrate above 200 does not necessarily mean one is awake, but one has the *courage* to start the journey of waking up. Each level has its Monkeys to tame and truths to uncover.

RESISTANCE TO SEEING THE MONKEYS

On paper, there is an actual demarcation line. In reality, there is no line. One moves up and down the consciousness levels. Where one is at any given time depends upon the **resistance** one puts up and, believe me, most of us do put up resistance, especially in the early part of the process. Those who are awakening understand that resistance is simply a road marker. They know when it comes up, there is something for them to learn and not to judge it.

When you ignore the resistance and continue to resist, it simply means you are not ready to learn the lesson at hand or to move to the next level, the lesson needs to be repeated until learned. My coach Ruth Zanes always would say, "What you resist persists." Resistance is a very powerful form of energy and leads to confrontation not peace.

The Monkeys like to keep you right where you are. They really do not want you to grow or get closer to your Source. Growth means change, especially in one's thinking, and change is scary. In the Judeo-Christian language, growth takes you closer to God and the dark entities do not want you to get closer. In *The Exhaustive Concordance of the Bible,* one of the definitions of Satan is resistor.[5] Interesting, huh?

Here's a cute story on resistance and the creativity of the Monkeys. The girl who got me a part-time job with a dentist did it under her subconscious need to learn what another of her friends was learning from me. I knew this was happening even if she did not, but I was a little surprised she hit me with this desire the very first day I started.

She told me she wanted to learn why she was having relationship problems with some of her friends. I started with an explanation of resistance, what it looked like and how it manifests. I did this so that, hopefully, when the resistance Monkeys showed their heads, which they certainly would, she might recognize the resistance and make coaching a little easier for me. A nice dream.

Later she started to explain to me that she thought there were *two* kinds of resistance—*good* resistance and *bad* resistance. See what was happening? She had already determined resistance was *bad* and, at some level, she knew she was in resistance. In order not to be bad, she, or I should say her Monkeys, created these two levels of resistance. All this was an attempt for her to declare she was in *good* resistance, therefore not *bad*. It was comical to me. The Monkeys are so creative.

I let her talk and explain her view, then laughed, "There is only one resistance," I said, "and you are in it."

I explained that resistance was not bad, just a road sign to indicate something needed to be learned. Unfortunately, she was not ready for the learning, at least not from me. She was in that place of *being right* and was not in a place to start giving up that positionality and her subconscious truth that everything happening to her was someone else's fault. Her intent was not to learn to change herself. Her subconscious intent was to change others because, of course, she was right about everything. Also, her subconscious intent was to compete with her friend, who did have the intent to change herself. When she determined I was not going to agree with her, I became a negative force for her. At some subconscious level, she knew she was not facing her issues and I was a constant reminder of that reality.

For me, that situation was a lesson in how quickly one can be pulled back into the negative energy. Even though I recognized the environment was not a positive one for me and I was getting ill again, I stayed. My accumulated anger was resurfacing and I was becoming more and more foul. Because of my fear around money, I allowed myself to stay. One Saturday, I declared to a friend that I was going to leave the dentist. This person knew my financial situation and asked why.

"It is too negative an environment."

Did I resign? No. I talked myself out of that thinking, *if I stay one more week, I can pay this off and that off.* This was fear talking. Little did I know I had already communicated my desire to leave to the Universe/God, who heard me. That Thursday, the dentist let me go for no real reason. Best thing that happened for everyone as my energy and the collective energies of the office were very different and, therefore, not compatible. Any more time there would have been very detrimental for my recovery, because I was being sucked back into that low energy.

You can see her resistance and then my resistance. You also can see that if you are in the process of waking up and are learning about the Monkeys, they still will work to keep you in the dark. How amusing that I am teaching her about resistance and then find myself smack dab in the middle of it, yet again. This, I think, is why they say one must teach what one needs to learn.

What matters is how active and in control the Monkeys are over you. The lower on the consciousness ladder you resonate, the more in control your Monkeys tend to be. Different things trigger their release. For those of you who read this and say to yourself, "I don't have Monkeys" or "My Monkeys are under control," beware. You are probably the very ones whose Monkeys have you under their invisible cloak and you can't see them. That cloak makes them invisible to only you, the owner. All the rest of us have the ability to see them in you.

People at all conscious levels can and do experience what we, who study Dr. Hawkins' work, call consciousness storms. No matter where you are on the ladder of consciousness, you can experience a storm that takes you back to old lower consciousness behaviors or to higher ones.

I had a roommate who demonstrated this beautifully, a 52-year-old woman who was kind, gracious, fun-loving and a hardworking graphic artist. According to my Hawkins' study group, she calibrated in the low 400s. (A good pick for a roommate for me because that is where I calibrated at the time.) As we got to know each other, she indicated to me how she loathed her mother. I would say, "You need to heal those feelings," and suggested all different modalities to help her do that. (No one can push some-one down his or her path, and the effort taken or not taken by each on that path needs to be respected.) To my knowledge, she was doing nothing to heal her pain around her mother because, of course, she had no responsibility in the matter. Of no surprise to me later, when I did something that reminded her of her mother's control, she reverted to her reactive behavior and let all of her Monkeys out for the attack. Her Monkeys exhibited the behavior of a disrespectful, rebellious, blaming, finger-pointing, screaming, tantrum-throwing 12-year-old. *Her behavior was calibrating well below 200 in this storm. These storms are what we see in road rage and happen to everyone at most all levels, except maybe those who calibrate over 540 (unconditional love). (VTK)*

Your underlying beliefs keep you where you are and the more emotion (pain) attached to those beliefs the more likely you will resist discovering the understanding around them. My roommate had too much pain around her mother and she could not handle taking responsibility for her part in the matter. Her Monkeys kept her in the dark about her behavior when confronted by a control situation. Needless to say, our roommate days were over--I had no interest in taking on her wrath around mother.

"When one disagrees with truth, one is in resistance." When I made that statement, my Psych-K instructor took exception and argued the point. She argued that one could disagree with opinion or position and not be in resistance. That interaction helped me understand a key distinction which most are unable to make. So here is the distinction.

When one disagrees with truth without knowing its context, one is in resistance to seeing the whole truth or diamond. (I use a diamond here as an analogy, with the whole diamond representing the complete context of truth and each facet of the diamond as a different perspective of that truth. This will be clarified later.)

When one disagrees with position, one disagrees with a perspective or only one facet of the truth. This focus is on content and argument. Most who are in resistance see the truth as opinion or perspective, which is why they cannot see they are in resistance to the total truth because their view of the truth is only one facet or perspective. Both views of a position can be truthful but when one stays focused on his or her perspective of that truth without taking the other perspective into consideration, s/he is in resistance to seeing the whole context of the truth. The Monkey puts the invisible cloak over us.

To Cage or Tame the Monkeys

When dealing with the Monkeys, you have two choices: 1) cage the Monkeys, or 2) tame the Monkeys.

This choice is unconscious until people start the waking-up process. In the unconscious state, the Monkeys run free because people do not know they have them. As people get older, they suppress their Monkeys—they know what *bad* behavior looks like. This is what I call caging the Monkeys. Caged Monkeys are what is responsible for most road rage or any hate rage for that matter. As a person goes through life, injustices happen to the person that bring up anger or rage, which, if not dealt with in a loving, fair way, the anger gets suppressed to, what I call, the *well of anger*. The Monkeys get put in their cages.

As the Monkeys sit in their cages ignored and unloved, the anger builds. This causes people to blow when the pressure gets too high. Once built up, little is needed to rattle the Monkey's cage. An automatic release button allows all the cages to open at one time and causes people to *go off*.

Remember the Alka Seltzer analogy? As one adds the Alka Seltzer (representing mistreatments to the individual) to the water, over time, the additional Alka Seltzer causes a flare-up with just a slight bump of the glass.

I had a friend who had been planning to walk part of the Appalachian Trail and I was going to be her contact. She was going to drive from her Houston home to my house in Atlanta, pick me up, go to the trail head, spend the night to make sure she had everything she needed, then hike her planned part of the trail. After her walk, I was to pick her up and take her to my house to recuperate for a couple days before driving back to Houston. I was so looking forward to this because I had not seen her in two years and the adventure would be fun, even though I was not going with her.

She also was helping me with an Indiegogo campaign to get funds to help me with this book. Because she was on my team, she was able to access the website. I asked her to go onto the site to read what I had written and give me pointers or make comments.

When she came back with her input, she announced, "Well, that is not how I would do it."

I was a little shocked and was thinking, "*Of course not. It is my book, not yours.*" But I remained quiet because I had asked for her input.

She then volunteered, "Well, you sound like a victim."

I said, "Yes, people must know I was victimized, trapped in victimhood and how I overcame it. That is part of the purpose of the book."

Her tone had a distinct disgust and anger in it when she blurted, "Well, then it is perfect as it is and you do not need my help."

I thought to myself, *where did all that anger come from?* I encouraged her to cut and paste and tell me how she would do it which ended the conversation.

The next day I received a call from her when I was not feeling well.

She exclaimed in her usual exuberant tone, "Well, you are off the hook. I just got my cousin in Cleveland, GA, to take me to the trail head and pick me up. Besides he has several people who know the trail."

I was so sick, all I could say was, "This is not a good time. I'll call you tomorrow."

When I called her the next day, I started out by telling her, "I never considered myself being *on the hook* for helping you with this adventure. I love you and am looking forward to seeing you because I haven't seen you in two years."

She informed me in a somewhat cold tone, "Well, I don't think I am coming to Atlanta." (She meant she would go directly to the trail and skip my house and me helping her.)

She was driving all the way from Houston and would only be 50 miles from my house!

Those calls were the beginning of the end of a ten-year relationship. She systematically cut off communication until she totally walked out of my life. [What I figured out was, at some level, she was dealing with unhealed anger toward her mother who, by her own words, apparently never supported her for doing what *she* wanted to do with her life. What she had done was to treat me like her mother treated her with nonsupport because I wasn't doing my things her way. So now I became a reminder of the pain she had around her mother for not supporting her the way she wanted. Rather than healing the pain, she chose to remove the reminder of her pain, me, from her life.]

I tell you this story to show how the Monkeys can run your life if they are kept in cages. Because she did nothing to heal and love the Monkeys she had around the pain regarding her mother, I am no longer in her life and who knows how many others had the same fate. The Monkeys will continue to resurrect their heads as long as they are ignored and caged. I am sad about this, however, I must respect where she is on her path. One must be ready to heal the pain, but it may be so great that it cannot be healed in this lifetime.

Unfortunately, my girlfriend confused the word *approval* for the word *love* in her interactions with her mother. Many of us do the same thing. Because our parents do not approve of what we want or are doing with our lives, we think they do not love us. See how the Monkeys make things up?

So, it is always better to tame your Monkeys rather than cage them. They desperately need your love, acknowledgement and understanding.

This, my friends, is how the Monkeys are born and grow. Other people's Monkeys are a lot easier to see while your own are very difficult to recognize. One thing I learned: **What I react to and see in others exists in me somewhere.** *This is true for everyone.* (VTK)

Other people's Monkeys are mirrors for our Monkeys.

RECOGNIZING THE MONKEYS

If we all have these Monkeys, what are some of the signs:

1. Anger (expressed or repressed)
2. Resistance
3. Needing to be RIGHT
4. Refusing to allow dialogue (a form of being "right")
5. Not listening to understand another's point of view, instead listening to manipulate
6. Reacting as opposed to responding
7. Projecting one's behavior onto others (pointing fingers)
8. Defensiveness
9. Justification of one's own behavior
10. Talking over others
11. Attacking others verbally or physically

These are only a small part of the list but they are the big ones. Some of this list includes communication tactics.

When a person is exhibiting these behaviors, the person is in resistance to how they are being. They are in reaction and are completely unaware. The Monkeys rule in their life. News talk shows are good examples of these behaviors and, recently (2016), the Democratic and especially the Republican primary debates.

CULTURAL/ANCESTRAL MONKEYS

One additional element to the Monkeys which some of us have and some do not is the influence of cultural/ancestral Monkeys, what some people call baggage. These are beliefs that some carry around which are left over from previous generations or family members. These Monkeys are usually carried around with much pride and martyrdom associated with them. Once a group or family of people are victimized, victimhood and martyrdom sets into becoming a way of life and then carries on for generation after generation. The bigger the group of people victimized, the more difficult for an individual to break out of the victimhood/martyrdom state.

Some obvious groups that come to mind in describing this state are black Americans, people of the Jewish faith and Native Americans. Each of these groups of people have been victimized in the past and many continue to be victimized today in some form or other. As a member of any of these groups, one has a choice to carry the cultural Monkey on their back or not to carry it. Remember, once victimized, one has a choice to live in victimhood/martyrdom or not, or better put, one can carry the victimhood Monkey around or not. The victim has a difficult time seeing the energy s/he puts out that perpetuates the victimization. There is a sense of entitlement that victims seem to adopt. When victims adopt the entitlement attitude, they unknowingly put out the very energy that brings the victimizers into their life.

RECOGNIZING THEY ARE IN CONTROL

So, how do we tell if the Monkeys are in control of our life? Once I became aware of the existence of the Monkeys, I figured out that they do not necessarily work in our best interest. They do seek to preserve the status quo, protect the organism (me or you), keep one from being hurt or facing pain. On the surface, some of those things sound like good things. As I progressed through my transformation, I realized that, basically, the Monkeys are there to keep me functioning from some form of fear. I learned that when I function from fear, I exclude possibility. I can see no possibility of a different outcome. When I function from fear, I have no faith.

Where possibility exists, there is no fear. There is only possibility or, using a different word, there is only faith. Faith and possibility are driven by love and trust. Where there is fear, there is no love. The two cannot exist at the same time. So, where fear exists, love does not. Where love exists, fear is banished and can't exist.

So, to recap, the Monkeys are all of the things a person has been taught, all the experiences one has had in one's life, the beliefs one has developed, an individual's truths, the protectors of the status quo, defenders of an individual's truths to the death—the death of a friendship—the death of a relationship—the death of a country, one's own death. When one chooses to follow the fear Monkeys, one chooses death.

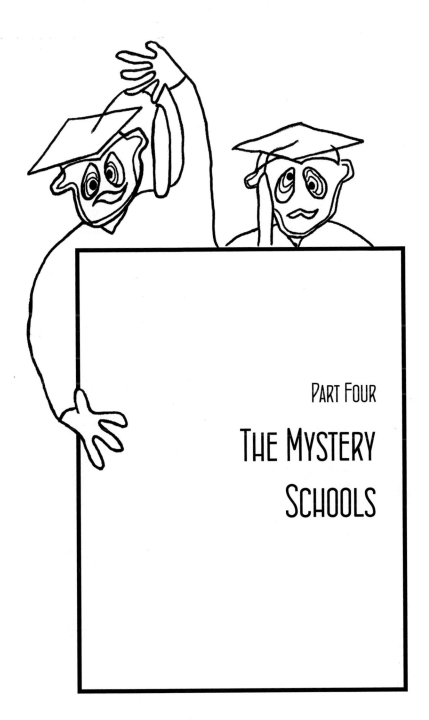

PART FOUR

THE MYSTERY
SCHOOLS

Chapter 11
So Much to Learn

If you want to find the secrets of the universe, think in terms of energy, frequency and vibration.
—Nikola Tesla

The following chapters are the things that I have been learning on this journey and, frankly, am still learning. Each day there are more and more distinctions, clarifications and new concepts that seem to crop up. What I find different is the level of joy and happiness that I am experiencing. Several years ago, I sat on my couch contemplating suicide. Now I find myself smiling and laughing at things on TV that before I would scoff at thinking *what the hell is so damn funny?* I realized for the first time that the purpose for doing all of this work for me was to reach that place of joy and happiness again. I had no idea that doing all of these things was actually seeking enlightenment. Now, the road to enlightenment never seems to stop.

While contemplating this and the things I was learning, a thought hit me—*these things I am learning seem like the Mystery Schools talked about by the ancients.* I did not give the thought much more consideration at the time. [Of course, I had no idea what I was thinking because I knew nothing about the Mystery Schools that had been mentioned in my study of religions.]

Several months later at a Psych-K class, the name Psych-K came up because the creators were contemplating a name change. Someone in the class, who was versed in numerology, ran the name and told them not to change it. *The name, apparently, was a beacon to call together all those people who had studied the Mystery Schools in ancient times to again study them now. (VTK)* I was a bit blown away at that revelation because those of us in the classes all seemed to be on paths to heal people, ourselves, Earth, or to help shift the course that human consciousness seemed to be taking. Wow!

As I study more about energy and get more into the understanding of Quantum Physics, I realize *the Mystery Schools are nothing more than understanding the laws of the universe at higher consciousness levels (VTK)*, which, back in Jesus' day, were not common concerns. Shelter, feeding oneself and staying alive were more paramount issues then. People had no idea how natural laws affected their everyday lives nor did they care, (actually much like today.) Most people today go through their lives oblivious to the natural laws and how those facts affect people. *In the Bible, Jesus seemed to refer to the Mystery Schools and consciousness levels, without using those actual words, of course (VTK)*. In Matthew 13.10-13:

"10 Then the disciples came and asked him, 'Why do you speak to them in parables?'

"11 He answered, 'To you it has been given to know the secrets (mysteries) of heaven but to them it has not been given.'

"12 'For those who have, more will be given, and they will have an abundance; but from those who have nothing, even what they have will be taken away.'

"13 'The reason I speak to them in parables is that seeing they do not perceive, and hearing they do not listen, nor do they understand.'"[1]

The words "from those who have nothing, even what they have will be taken away" is what today I would describe as cognitive dissonance. Cognitive dissonance occurs when an individual is confronted by new information that conflicts with existing beliefs, ideas, or values and refuses to incorporate the new learning. This keeps people at the lower levels of consciousness and the lower levels of understanding and at risk of losing what understanding they have. Yes, we can go backwards on the consciousness scale. (VTK) "Both Hitler and Napoleon calibrated in the mid400's during the early constructive phases of their reigns but later fell to very low calibration levels, which led to their defeat due to grandiosity (ignoring counsel of seasoned generals, etc.)"[2]

The Mystery Schools were only for those with the capability to grasp concepts at more advanced levels, like being in first grade where the concepts of arithmetic must be learned first then the more advanced algebra can be grasped. Humanity in general calibrated at about 100 in Jesus' time, which is in the survival consciousness level.

The teachings of the Mystery Schools, from my perspective, include but are not limited to: consciousness, truth, energy, communication, and how they intertwine. Because they intertwine, talking about each individually is difficult. I tried to pull them out as best I could. I have been actively studying all of these elements for decades and I still have questions and seek distinctions. Like peeling an onion--you think you understand at a more profound level, more distinctions arise that take you to another level, so you never seem to get to understanding from a total context perspective. A newer understanding from a different perspective is always to be had. Later you will see that I compare Truth to a diamond with the entire Diamond representing the total context of Truth. Humans rarely get to a level to see the whole diamond. But, as we add different facets to our perspectives, we are able to see things from a completely different view, which enables us to do as the Bible asks us to do—"Walk in another man's shoes."

So, 2000 years later, some of us still do not understand at the parable levels, often consider the Mystery Schools woo-woo, or are simply totally unaware that these schools or different levels of understanding exist. Right now, almost 80% of the world's population still calibrates below 200 (over 50% in the USA) which means they are totally unable to understand at any level above parable teaching or even at this level. *They still lack the knowledge to understand from perspectives other than their own. (VTK) The good news is that only a small number of people need to calibrate at higher levels of consciousness in order to balance the whole of mankind and offset the lower conscious vibrational thinking. (VTK)* If not, mankind would surely destroy itself, because levels below 200 are life depleting and based on falsehood.

Like the Bible says, all will be revealed in the end times. The words *the end times* do not necessarily mean the end of the world but the end of the current cycle or your personal cycle. What the Ancients called *The Mystery Schools* is what is being revealed today. Well, I should say, *is being revealed for me today*, as these teachings have been around for millennia but only understood by the few because only a few have reached the higher consciousness levels.

THE MOST IMPORTANT LESSON OF THE BOOK

The next four sections are an attempt to clarify the two different levels of communication--the linear (words) where most of the world resides and nonlinear (energy). The nonlinear or energetic level is where most of us are unfamiliar and because what happens at this level cannot be proven or often believed (until experienced), most of us roll our eyes and consider this woo-woo. This is where you start to tell truth from falsehood, which makes this a very important level.

The section on Consciousness represents the two different levels of communication at all of the different levels of consciousness. The section on Truth represents the linear world of words. The section on Energy represents the nonlinear world of energy. The section on Communication represents the two different levels together. As one moves up the consciousness ladder, the ability to feel what is truthful and what is not improves.

I will discuss these levels in this order for clarification, knowing that in the world there is no real order.

Chapter 12

Consciousness— The Shift from Linear (Words) to Nonlinear (Energy/Feelings)

It was easy to love God in all that was beautiful. The lesson of deeper knowledge, though, instructed me to embrace God in ALL things.
—St. Francis of Assisi

Maslow's Hierarchy of Needs

Many people know about Maslow's Hierarchy of Needs. There is another hierarchy most people are not familiar with--Dr. David Hawkins' Map of Consciousness. If you have not already done so, please look up The Map of Consciousness on the Internet and print it or get one of Dr. Hawkins' books for a reference. I would reprint it here but was not given permission to do so. The best book by Dr. Hawkins that explains these levels is *Transcending the Levels of Consciousness*. Please review the different levels, words and behaviors so you get an understanding of the distinctions.

Besides the fact we are human and judge everything, the way we communicate, which is linear, automatically makes you think there is a bad side to the Map (below 200) and a good side (above 200). Below 200 seem to indicate bad, negative, low vibration, low frequency, etc.; *above* seems to represent the good. There are no good or bad positions on the Map of Consciousness, simply different levels of understanding.

The lower levels represent the animal survival view of life, survival of the individual(s) at the expense of the others, which is why the Monkeys live and develop here. The lower levels are life depleting and fallacious. The behaviors at the lower levels can be viewed as selfish hence the label *bad*.

"At the lower consciousness levels, the ego (Monkeys) dominates life based primarily on the techniques and emotions of animal survival, which are aligned with pleasure, predation, and gain." ... "It's (spiritual energy's) influence is accompanied by progressive awareness and responsiveness to the energy of love..." "The energy of love is also aligned with progressive awareness of truth..."[1]

As humanity evolves consciously and reaches above 200, spiritual energy has increasing power. The focus on love energy and amplification of vibrations permit more and more spiritual energy to come in. Evolving in this direction allows one to increasingly rely on feeling the love energy and moving away from the linear/word level.

It is important to note here that, "...it's uncommon for people to move from one level to another during their lifetimes. The energy field that is calibrated for an individual at birth only increases, on average, by about five points."[2] However, it is possible to make big leaps in growth.

The only thing you must be vigilant about is: understanding whether the beliefs in which you find yourself involved deplete or enhance life—are they aligned with love or hate, positive or negative? Do you find yourself attacking others to be right? If those actions deplete life, yours or anyone else's, in any way, especially energetically, then your beliefs represent the antithesis of God or moving away from the Source. If they enhance life, yours or anyone else's, you represent love and are moving toward the Source. Which direction you are traveling is not important—some people must go closer to the dark side to understand what the dark side represents for them. Often you hear people say, "He hasn't hit bottom yet." Most of us must hit our own personal bottom in order to choose a different direction. I did.

Diagram I shows Maslow's Hierarchy of Needs[3] with the numbers from the Map of Consciousness overlaid on the left of the diagram. You can see that the levels of the map of consciousness extend beyond the top level of Maslow's hierarchy of needs. Transcendence is being added by more recent scholars of Maslow to the Maslow chart. Some even include it in the triangle. If you study the complete Map of Consciousness, you will see that both Maslow's hierarchy of needs and Hawkins' Map of Consciousness dovetail nicely.

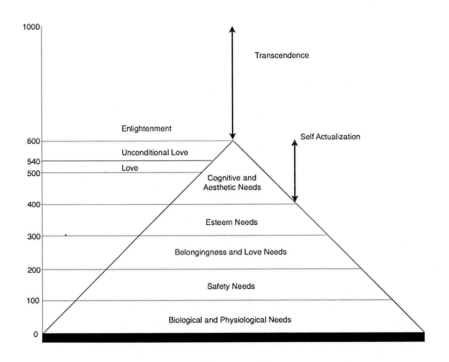

Diagram I—Maslow's Hierarchy of Needs
Maslow, Abraham H.; Frager Robert D. .; Fadiman, James, Motivation and Personality, 3rdED., C1987. Reprinted by permission of Pearson Education, Inc., New York, New York.

Maslow, whether he knew it or not, was describing the needs of the lower levels of consciousness, the levels of needs that have to be met before one can have the spare time and feel safe enough to study and begin to transcend to enlightenment. However, because so few of us ever reach enlightenment (less than .04%), it is of little relevance to most—only the few focused on raising their consciousness level.

I put self-actualization on the right side of the chart because the process of becoming self-actualized actually starts once one is above 200. It can be, and usually is, a slow process. Only those who stay committed move more quickly.

THE FIELD

The Consciousness field does exist and everything in it affects everything else in it. (VTK) We are all connected, we are all one.

I was affected by this field in the use of the term Monkeys in the writing and titling this book. When I picked the title, I had no conscious understanding of the Buddha concept of the monkey mind nor any of the countless other references to monkeys in relation to our mind's folly.

So, the consciousness level you are at affects your ability to understand these laws of the universe or as Jesus put it, "…know the secrets (mysteries) of the kingdom of heaven." *Raising your level of consciousness or your vibrational frequency is the best thing you can do for yourself and the whole of humanity.* (VTK) The more people who are waking up and raising their vibrational levels, the more people are offset at the lower vibrational levels, thus, better for humanity.

This is true because the vibration of love is exponentially more powerful than the vibration of hate. The energy of love (power) will always overpower the energy of hate (force). A recent good example of this was when virtually the whole world refused to support (love energy) Trump and his policy to take children away from their parents (hate energy) who crossed the border. So much so that he finally had to reverse his policy. When the water rises, all the boats on it rise. *This rising consciousness shift is happening right now* (VTK) and it is very exciting for those aware of the transformation taking place. Because most people are focused on the actions of the 80%, they only see the negative and the bad happening in the world.

Because we all tend to judge ourselves and others, I must state *there is no correlation between IQ and consciousness levels.* (VTK) I know there are people who will think they have high IQs and must be at a higher consciousness level. Sorry folks—**not so**. You can be very smart and calibrate very low or vice versa. *Our tendency to need to be viewed as **good** rather than **bad** will give the Monkeys permission to throw the invisible cloak over us and allow our judgment of ourselves to blind us to our actual behavior.* (VTK) This was true for me as I went down this path, always pointing fingers at the people who were doing whatever to me.

To show yourself that you are good, you will project onto others those things you do that you do not like about yourself. You view them as bad, undeserving or unworthy in your eyes because that is how you see yourself subconsciously. *The reality is that it is yourself that you are judging.* (VTK) What you see in others is really a mirror of what you subconsciously think of yourself. Being under the invisible cloak keeps you from understanding—it is yourself you are judging, and not the one out there you are pointing at and projecting onto. Projection onto others simply strengthens that in you. My Native friends always said don't point fingers because there are always three pointing back at you.

Well, if you haven't guessed by now, there are no coincidences. Just as I sat down to write a little more on consciousness, an article popped up on my Facebook feed from a year ago entitled, Leading Neuroscientists and Buddhists agree: "Consciousness is Everywhere" by Sam Littlefair.[4] One line--"New theories in neuroscience suggest consciousness is an intrinsic property of everything, just like gravity."[5] Wow! I love when science starts to merge with ancient beliefs instead of refuting or resisting them.

For millennia, Buddhists and Native Americans have believed that all things have consciousness (spirit). Probably all indigenous peoples around the world have similar beliefs but I have not studied them. The Native Americans say all things are alive and have spirit, which is why they pray to protect *all my relations*. This is why being in balance with all creatures and things in nature is very important. You are either awake, asleep or, in my case as I came out of Corporate America, catatonic. They are not describing a physical state but an *awareness of spiritual concepts* state. I was totally unaware of any of this—thus, I was totally self-focused and completely unaware of how I might be affecting those around me.

Without getting into all of the science around this theory, the real point is that all of the beliefs are merging. Buddhists teachings, Native people's beliefs, contemporary scientific theories, i.e., Dr. Masaur Emoto's studies of water, Dr. David Hawkins' Map of Consciousness and the science in Littlefair's article--are all coming together in their views of consciousness.

Dr. Hawkins' Map of Consciousness simply gives one a more concrete road map of the path to higher consciousness levels--the same thing the Buddhists have been studying and ancient peoples have known for millennium.

Dr. Emoto's work has proven that human consciousness has an effect on the molecular structure of water and we are made up of about 70% water. So, our thoughts and words affect our physiology and our own well-being.

Conscientiousness is the awareness of energy in all things and actions. Each minute is a choice between negative energy or positive energy. My view of God is that He/She/It is energy and, with free will, we choose minute by minute whether we follow love or nonlove energy, God or the Dark Side. God does not judge at some later date--He forgives all sins. With our choices, we are the ones doing the judging and there are always consequences for those choices.

KARMA

Our karma is the accumulation of those choices, positive or negative and whatever energy we choose comes back to us. We all come into this world with a clean slate purely from the perspective of what is in our minds. Another element is karma which carries over from past lives. Dr. David Hawkins explains karma this way:

"At every instant, one is really making a choice between heaven or hell. The cumulative effect of all these choices determines the calibrated level of consciousness and one's karmic and spiritual fate."[6]

Notice rather than using the words love or nonlove, or positive and negative, he uses heaven or hell. Same difference. Wikipedia defines it this way:

"**Karma** (Sanskrit: कर्म; IPA: [ˈkərmə] (listen); Pali: kamma) means action, work or deed; it also refers to the spiritual principle of cause and effect where intent and actions of an individual (cause) influence the future of that individual (effect)."[7]

Many Christians do not think that Christianity supports karma as a concept because the Bible does not mention the word karma in its teachings. This posture is incorrect--simply because the word karma which is Sanskrit and not used in the Bible does not mean the belief is not supported. The concept of *reap what you sow* is actually a definition of karma. When researching the statement on Google, I found 67 different Bible references for *reap what you sow*.

Both definitions are relatively the same but have a distinction of their own that makes them very different. The definition given by Wikipedia is one from a Newtonian perspective, that is, coming from the scientific theory of Newton. Newtonian theory is one of cause and effect and exists at the linear level. For every effect, there is a cause. With this basis in thinking, blame is easy to establish in any given situation. The cause of whatever happens is to blame for what happens.

Dr. Hawkins' definition comes from the theory of nonduality. He often explains this theory in his books and lectures by showing there are no opposites. In other words, there is no such thing as cold, only the absence of heat, the lack of which we describe as cold. Or there is no dark, only the absence of light. One does not go into a room and turn on darkness.

Karma, in a world of nonduality, is simply the accumulation of positive or negative energies that, over time, result in one's consciousness level and what can be expected in the future. If one is constantly adding negative energy to life, more negative energy will come into that life. If one, on the other hand, is constantly putting out positive energy (love), one receives that same energy back in their future.

After I filed bankruptcy, I found myself constantly lamenting my lack of resources to pay my bills, travel, or buy things that I wanted. I was poor financially. I did not realize that those words and thoughts brought me more of the same...no money. Then I was taught by Blue Thunder that I was speaking the dark language (my reality). He taught me to speak <u>as if</u> I already had the abundance I needed. That shift was slow and took practice for me because I was in the habit of talking about the current negative state. I now always have the resources I need to pay the bills and get what I want. The best news is that I do not experience the fear anymore at least not to the degree I did. In fact, I get excited to see where the next thing I need will come from.

Each person's karmic propensities (probabilities) are different and have a connection to what level of consciousness one has when coming into this life. The only thing that one comes into this world with is one's Consciousness Level, which also can be called karma (VTK).

My personal journey is all about being happy again. I am, will and have studied whatever I need to in order to recover that happiness.

CHAPTER 13

TRUTH—
THE LINEAR WORLD OF WORDS

Truth is like a diamond—the facet you focus on becomes the perception that colors your life.
—Victoria Barkan

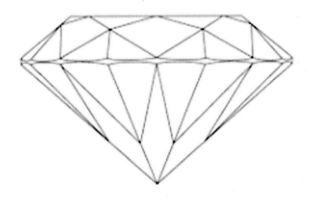

Diagram II—Drawing of a Diamond

If the diamond represents total spiritual truth or the context of the truth, then the facet of the diamond represents the content or the level of understanding any particular individual has achieved. Persons at the facet level have a myopic view of what they think is the truth, which in total context of the diamond may indeed be falsehood. (VTK)

You can see in the drawing of the diamond that it has many facets--each facet represents a different perspective of total truth.

The chapter on Truth represents the linear/words level. At this level of understanding, each facet has a different view and each facet has different words or languages to describe the view from that perspective. So, if you stand on a different facet than the person you are trying to communicate with, the same words being used may have different meanings and, therefore, much misunderstanding is created. Additionally, at this level there is the interpretation of the words being used.

Those in victimhood will receive the words with their own personal charge. In other words, they choose to be offended and then apply misplaced meaning to the words and further complicate the interchange by blaming the other person. At this level, nothing is ever their responsibility.

There are so many facets and so many different languages and so many different words, thus you can see why the diamond and Truth can be so convoluted. This is why a billionaire white man cannot possibly understand a black man's perspective of growing up in the ghetto. They are not only on different facets but they are on different sides of the diamond.

The mistake all humans make, to a greater or lesser degree, is believing everyone else is on the same facet of the diamond and understands from the same perspective as they do. A billionaire white man can rarely understand that a black man does not have the same playing field, and, because the white man thinks he does, the white man will come up with another reason that the black man did not make the same billionaire status. A common false belief is--he must be lazy and doesn't work hard.

Discerning Truth from Falsehood

Most of the time one cannot distinguish the difference. Today, distinguishing is becoming harder and harder as those in advertising know *repetition of a falsehood will eventually turn to truth in the mind*. Dr. Hawkins discusses in one of his lectures how repetitive advertising has reduced by about 40% a person's ability to distinguish the truth. Coming from the advertising field, I can assure you the marketers know this and are constantly using it against you.

A recent good example—Direct to Consumer (DTC) advertising for pharmaceutical companies, which was against the law until 1997 and for good reason--a consumer has virtually no education in medicine. Only two other countries allow DTC—New Zealand since 1981, and Brazil 2009.[1] The pharmaceutical companies know that when you see their ads enough, you will go to the doctors and demand the products. If the doctor refuses to give it to you, you can go to another doctor. [Pharmaceutical companies are not in the healing business, although they justify their actions by believing and acting like they are—they're in the money making business! Do not ever forget that! They are not doing a good deed by telling you about possible reactions but to protect themselves in potential future lawsuits.]

The point is--repetition sells. Repetition can transform truth into falsehood or falsehood into truth. It allows the Monkeys to pull their invisible cloak over you and blind you.

Let's look at this repetition of falsehood in relation to the phenomena of traditions.

TRADITION AS A FACET OF THE DIAMOND

"The very traditions that ground us can also serve to impede our growth." Victoria Barkan

Tradition, aaaah, is a wonderful thing! We have all kinds of traditions--some good, some maybe not so good. Traditions can turn into hard, fast beliefs and most of the time do. This is where traditions can turn less than supportive for a person's or humanity's growth, both spiritually and progressively.

Here's a joke told to me by my brother's father-in-law. After several years of marriage watching his wife cut off the end of the ham before she cooked it, he finally asked her one day, "Why do you cut off the end of the ham before you cook it?"

"Because that is how my mother taught me."

The next time they were at her mother's house, he asked her, "Why do you cut off the end of the ham before you cook it?"

"That is how my mother taught me."

And the next time they were at the great-grandmother's house, he asked her, "Why do you cut off the end of the ham before you cook it?"

"Because my pan is not big enough."

I laughed so hard when I heard this.

Have you noticed as the traditions pass through time, people lose all understanding about why they are doing what they are doing? This is true about everything. If the information behind why one is doing what one is instructed to do is not carried forth, then all reason for doing what one is doing is lost or misunderstood.

Traditions that fall into more important categories than a ham can hold generations or whole cultures of people back and keep them from growing. Many of the examples of traditions I have fall into the humorous category, at least to those of us who do not take part in the tradition. The people who take part in these traditions are very serious about them and that they should not be broken. Therein lies the roadblock.

Mali, West Africa. Around the year 2000, I was floating down the Niger River in Mali, the main river for movement of trade goods from Timbuktu through the south of Mali, stretching all the way to the Gulf of Guinea, south of West Africa. Our group had its own boat, called a pinasse, which measured about 40-feet long and about ten-feet wide, pretty nice considering we were in Africa. Ours had a roof over a section of the boat for shade or sun bathing and a bathroom in the back, if you consider a hole in the upraised portion of the boat with curtains for privacy to be one. We did not do comfort stops, so it was a welcome addition. Of course, the makings of the bathroom made clear you would not like to end up in the water for any reason.

As I was relaxing under the shade of the sunbather's paradise reading my book on West Africa, I noticed a young man near the back of the boat with the captain, who was steering the outboard motor, which was at the base of where the boat started its climb out of the water to provide a place for our toilet accommodations. While the captain steered the boat, the young man bailed water from the boat.

I thought, *Hmmmm, this boat is leaking.* So, I asked the captain, "Why don't you fix the leak in the boat so he doesn't have to bail?" You'd have thought I had suggested throwing the young man overboard.

The captain replied, "Oh, no! He must bail to learn how to be a captain."

Seriously, that makes no sense, I thought.

As we continued down the river, I started to notice the other boats traveling the river--*all the boats had a young man bailing, so all the boats must be leaking. Wow. This is crazy. No wonder they (Africans) can't climb out of the third-world status.*

Later that day we were taken to a place located alongside the river where they made the boats. If this situation wasn't already a bit absurd from my perspective, we were told, yes, *they made the boats leak,* all in the name of teaching young men to be captains. Like the joke about the ham, I can only imagine what started this *tradition* and *well-developed belief.*

My coach, Ruth Zanes, in the early years of my transition urged me once, "You need to reflect on why you pluck yourself up out of your life and plop yourself down in third-world countries."

"I was going on vacation."

"People do not go to third-world countries on vacation. They go to the beach or the mountains or the lake to relax."

She intimated there was more of a reason than going on vacation; after all, I had a choice of where I could go. As I traveled, I became more open to the differences in each of us as well as the sameness. *This was experiential learning at its best.* There was much to learn from what most would call less-civilized cultures. I began to see that the word *civilized* warranted examination, which brings me to my next example.

Sepik River Region, New Guinea. Why did I go there? Well, at the time, I considered this to be one of the least civilized and more dangerous places to go. My game plan was to go to the dangerous places first and save the safer places for my elder years. Besides I had just seen a Jacque Cousteau special on New Guinea and how *uncivilized* (by our standards) it was, which appealed to me. I laugh at that term now as New Guinea ended up being one of the more *civilized* places I went. (I will explain later.)

While on the way to one of the villages in the Sepik River region of New Guinea, our guide told the story of the orator's stool. Each village has its own Spirit House where the men of the village go to have discussions, sort of like going to the local pub only there are no drinks, just Betel nut chewing—the local marijuana. Unfortunately, years of chewing the nut causes one's teeth to turn red, which is why you rarely see the older folks showing their teeth when they smile.

Women and children are not allowed in the spirit houses, only men who had gone through the rite of passage. The many villages not only had different languages but also varying rites of passage. Each Spirit House has an orator's stool, a basic three-legged stool to distinguish who has the right to speak. Each person who has something to say will sit on the stool while speaking. The men believe the spirits of all their ancestors live in the orator's stool--it is very sacred to them and is not allowed to be photographed.

One day some tourists visited this village and one had a Polaroid camera. Not many white people came to this place, so a Polaroid camera had never been seen. This person started to take a picture of the orator's stool. One of the natives saw him and grabbed the camera. A picture was taken and, of course, because of the movement, it came out with a double image of the stool. The natives felt this was proof positive that the spirits lived in the stool. *A nice story*, I thought.

After about an hour of negotiation with the men of the village, we were allowed to enter the Spirit House. They even let us women in because we were *not of their culture*—pretty civilized, don't you think? In I walked and, by gosh, right there, tacked to one of the poles holding up the Spirit House was a Polaroid photo of the orator's stool with a double image.

It hit me, "*Wow, they really believe this,*" and, why wouldn't they? They have not been *educated* on the *science* of photography. I began to think about my beliefs and what more education on an issue would change them.

Why All This Talk About Tradition? Well, it hit me that maybe, because of my educational level, these seemed funny to me. I wondered, what traditions do we have that someone of a different educational level would find amusing. What if we were visited by extraterrestrials that had superior knowledge to us? What beliefs and traditions of ours would they find comical? What are our beliefs and traditions that hold us back simply because we do not have all of the facts or refuse to leave our facet of the diamond?

We can look back in time at some of the beliefs and traditions humans had that were not true—the sun revolves around the earth. And there is the keyword, *truth*. We can examine the lengths some people went to keep the beliefs alive even with new evidence to the contrary. Study the Catholic church's history, the Inquisition and the murders committed to keep beliefs alive that were not believed to be true or had no tie to the truth. To challenge these traditional beliefs was considered heretical. This is the height of *cognitive dissonance.*

Cognitive Dissonance. The refusal to accept evidence that works against a strong core belief and protects the core belief. People will rationalize, ignore and even deny anything that doesn't fit in with the core belief.

Analyze the behaviors of scientists when new scientific theory or even evidence becomes available. Depending on whose reputation and Monkeys are at stake, the scientific community tends to discredit or ignore the new information and those presenting it until years go by and they can get used to the new idea or the old people (beliefs) die.

The point is, human nature protects belief systems and traditions regardless of the new emerging facts. Humans who calibrate at the lower levels need to be right and are willing to do whatever it takes to prove their rightness, even kill. This is the main behavior that keeps individuals from moving to different consciousness levels and keeps whole communities or cultures from changing and growing into more loving human beings. As one climbs the levels of consciousness, the need to be right evolves into a more compassionate understanding and ability to walk in another's shoes. I use the word evolves because *each consciousness level has its Monkeys and traditions to overcome. (VTK)*

Your job is to look at all of your traditions and beliefs, including religious dogma, and question why? Does this still serve me or us? Is this really true or just *my* truth? Is this coming from love energy or nonlove energy?

This leads to a deeper discussion of truth. How do people of different traditions look at the word truth?

"The truth is rarely pure and never simple."[2]

Have you ever given any thought as to how often the word *truth* is bandied around? We hear it in religion, politics, and everyday life. Most of the time, the person or entity is using it in its most rigid, absolute form or meaning—something is either true or false, leaving no room for perception, interpretation, missing information, or context. The reason—most of us exist at one level or on only one facet of the diamond. That is because most of humanity exists at the linear/word level of understanding.

I believed perception was reality because we were taught that in advertising. We, the advertisers, were the manipulators of perception, manipulators of what you think, and if you think it, it is the truth for you. We know if we repeat a statement enough times, whether it is true or false, you, the public, will begin to believe what we tell you to believe. So, let's explore the diamond as a representation of the truth. From the advertisers' perspective, the viewing public is very malleable. In one study, people were asked if they were susceptible to advertising—92% replied no. So not only are people malleable but they are completely oblivious to the fact they are—a very dangerous combination.

CONTENT VS. CONTEXT

If the facet of the diamond is the content (partial information), then the whole diamond is the context (total information). Most of us live on only one facet of the diamond, which, in the context of the whole diamond, is content, a part of the diamond and part of the whole truth. Our facet, the one we live on, is simply our perception of what we think the truth is. Perception is not reality or the whole truth. At best, it is partial truth which in the context of the whole truth could indeed be falsehood. I know this sounds a bit confusing but observe a diamond to see my analogy.

Unfortunately, some of the media is no longer reporting the news objectively. With opinion stated as fact, they are <u>indoctrinating</u> those who listen *to their way of thinking,* like the advertisers. In countries run by dictators this is called propaganda. We, in the USA, are a free country so propaganda couldn't happen here, right? People are sheep and follow this indoctrination right over the cliff. They have no clue how powerful advertising/repetition is to the subconscious mind.

The subconscious mind operates many thousands of times faster than the conscious mind so the subconscious mind is taking in the information being viewed faster than a person is aware. To add to the situation, the subconscious mind is <u>incapable</u> of discerning the difference between falsehood and reality.

This is why visualization is a very effective training tool. Here's a story. A man was a prisoner of war in Viet Nam. To keep sane while going through his ordeal, every day he played golf in his mind. Prior to the war, he was not a particularly great golfer; however, once back from Viet Nam, his first time on the golf course, he shot below par. The only difference was his mind's visualization during captivity. This is why computer games with killing and violence are so dangerous—they are teaching the player to become an unconscious killer. One mother said, "My son knows it is a game." *Yes, but his subconscious mind does not!* Why do you think the military uses simulators to train? Because they know they are training a person to be an automatic reactor, to kill without thinking. Could this be a partial explanation of all of the school shootings today?

Repetition distorts the truth. This is being played out today in our political environment.

The reality is that only the all-seeing God/Universe can observe the total context of the diamond, which is why humans (for the most part) are totally incapable of distinguishing the difference between truth and falsehood because each of us live on a single or collection of the facets and are not exposed to the whole context or the whole diamond. *Seeking enlightenment and climbing the consciousness ladder allows one to escape the facets of perception. (VTK)*

Most, when they use the word truth, are using it in absolution and are taking a position of I am right and you are wrong. They stubbornly defend that position seemingly to the death, while thinking they have the corner on what they think is the real truth—and the only truth—so help me God!

Nothing could be further from the—no pun intended—truth. When people use the word truth, most of the time what they are really talking about is their perception of what they think the truth is which may or may not really have any truth to it at all. A diamond has many facets and truth also has many facets. Many people confuse what they think, what they want, or how they feel with truth. You see this in politics as well as religion to mention the top two.

So, the truth is like a diamond. There are many facets. The more facets you are able to acknowledge and comprehend, the more you as an individual will be able to understand other people, because you will be able to see through their eyes not just yours. This ability typically indicates a higher level of consciousness. At the facet level or the level of perception, one is incapable of knowing the full truth. *Enlightenment is transcending perception. (VTK)* The lower consciousness levels seem to be stuck on one facet and can only see things from one perspective–theirs. Not only that, they also carry a great deal of subconscious fear, which translates to killing those who disagree with them, literally or figuratively.

Remember Jack Nicholson's, "The truth, the truth, you can't handle the truth."-- in *A Few Good Men*[3] A truer statement was never made.

When I went online to get a definition of the word truth, I was blown away at the proliferation of information on that one word. Etymologically, the word truth comes from the Greek word Alétheia and means *nonconcealment*. Other basic definitions found are:

- the quality or state of being true;
- that which is true or in accordance with fact or reality; and
- a fact or belief that is accepted as true.

From the perspective of self-awareness, I like the translation from the Greek: nonconcealment, which allows all to be seen, there are no secrets. Everyone is on the same playing field and has the same information. Where there are secrets, there is deception and power which can be misused.

I often heard business people say, "Information is power." Let's take my experience in Corporate America. Why do you suppose some corporations do not allow employees to talk about their salaries? Simple—salaries discriminate. If they didn't, there would be no need for secrecy. Ranges, if used, could be published. A range would accommodate individual accomplishment as one could move up or down in the range. Mostly they are not published. If they were, women and men would be making the same salaries for the same work.

I remember talking to my new boss, J. Curt Hockemeier, when I joined Cox Communications in Oklahoma City in 1986. Somehow, we got on the subject of salary discussions. I shared with him that each time I was interviewing and was asked what salary I was receiving, I replied with the amount I knew the job was worth. I was never questioned because it was within reason. Of course, it was not my true salary because I was always grossly underpaid, at least compared to males in equal positions. (I was simply right-ing a wrong. Women still only made $.77 on the dollar in 2015 largely *because of secrecy*.)[4]

He was horrified. "I never lied about what I made."

I replied, "Aren't you lucky you never had to."

THE THREE LEVELS OF TRUTH

There seem to be three basic levels of truth. I have categorized them in my own way: (1) Individual Truth; (2) Collective Truth; and (3) The Unassailable Truth.

Level One: Individual Truth. Each human being has his or her own individual truth. Any self-help book today will discuss the fact that if one believes something, then it is truth—for that per-son, that person's perspective of what s/he thinks is the truth. It is the facet of the diamond with which they have chosen to be asso-ciated. An example is *I cannot speak in front of people*. Everyone can speak in front of people--some are terrified to do it. I was--but my jobs required me to do it, so I had to get a great deal of training and had to practice a lot. Because I believed I was a poor speaker—I was. I was focused on doing it right rather than getting comfortable with what I was to say. I could have easily believed I could be a great speaker and then become one. "Whatever the mind of man can conceive and believe, it can achieve."[5]

Level Two: Collective Truth. A collective truth is a common fact or belief that is accepted as true and which many people share. An old collective truth was *the world is flat*. Back in the 14th century, everyone knew the world was flat and believed that to be the truth, until it was proven differently. At our current level of understanding, the concept of a flat earth is almost comical. But back when those were common beliefs controlled by the Church, to offer evidence to the contrary could cost you your life. Beliefs which people think are true die hard, hence the leaking boats in Africa.

Level Three: *THE* Unassailable Truth. This is the realm of natural laws and the context of the whole diamond. These truths cannot be changed, which is why we usually use the word law to describe them. They can be ignored, not believed, challenged and argued but they cannot be refuted. Gravity is an example of one of these truths. Our understanding of these universal truths may evolve with new knowledge but the laws themselves and how they behave do not change.

The trouble is all of us who are not aware, conscious, or awake, or on a spiritual path to awakening, think their individual truth is *the* one and only truth. What's more important to understand is that we each live our life as if our *individual* truth is *the* truth for everyone, and we live as if our *collective* truths are *the* truth.

These *individual* and *collective* truths are just different levels of understanding and different collections of facets on the diamond, not necessarily *the* complete truth. What we must understand—as human beings, we are all unaware in some area of our lives. *We do not know what we do not know.* The act of scientific discovery every day uncovers new information challenging current collective truths, which have become entwined with our beliefs or our individual truth or, worse yet, our traditions. In the early stages of an individual's awakening process, the truth about oneself is often the most difficult to face. Just remember, *the truth isn't distorted; our view of the truth is distorted.*

Around in 1990, but popularized in 1998 by Gloria Steinem, is the Bible's John 8:32 statement, so succinctly put by her as, *"The truth will set you free, but first it will piss you off."*

People really get pissed when faced with looking at themselves in the mirror. I do not mean literally here, although that might piss you off, too. I mean figuratively looking in the mirror at your behaviors. I read that most people incarcerated today do not believe they are guilty and most of these people are incapable of looking at their behavior as the possible cause of their incarceration.

Imagine that you are holding a mirror. Be prepared because the Monkeys of the person looking into the mirror will project, defend, justify, make faces, go into denial, argue and fight to keep from seeing the truth about their Monkeys. Why? Because that person is in resistance. At a subconscious level that person is judging him or herself to be bad. S/he at this stage, projects on to you, the mirror holder, that you are judging them to be bad. S/he has not learned to take responsibility for their own Monkeys yet. Hey, at this stage S/he can't even acknowledge that they even have Monkeys. At the lower levels of each stage, the Monkeys have virtual free reign. Yes, each stage at the transition levels has Monkeys which need to be tamed.

I told you about my roommate who, after several months of living with me, had a significant disagreement about a very insignificant issue. I was in my usual place of doing everything I thought I could do to save the relationship, so I asked her if she would be willing to participate in a session with someone who teaches nonviolent communication. Her screaming and yelling is what took the insignificant issue to one of high charge because I did not know how to deal with someone who screams and yells.

She replied, "I would be willing to do that if *you* think *you* could learn something." I had to laugh.

The whole interchange was an example of someone whose Monkeys are in total control. Her answer told me she was not in a place to acknowledge any responsibility in the matter, so, in my world, the meeting would be a waste of time. Notice I use the word *responsibility* and not *blame*. The relationship was not savable because she was not ready to look in the mirror and take responsibility for her part. She was in the place of blaming everyone else for what was happening to her. Her untamed Monkeys were in total control.

Truth is never absolute except when one is dealing with one of Nature's laws.

From a spiritual perspective, once people evolve higher on the Map of Consciousness, they are more capable of seeing the different facets of the diamond of truth. They start to see that truth is a matter of perspective and there is no black and white, I am right, you are wrong absolute interpretation. Once these realizations occur, the tendency to judge starts to subside.

So, remember, truth is like a diamond with many facets. Each facet has a somewhat different take of an absolute truth and each is as valid as the other. We call this perspective.

The lower on the Map of Consciousness you currently function, the more prone to positionality you are and the tendency to believe *your understanding of things* as the only true and right point of view; additionally, the more prone you are to villainize other people's points of view in an overt effort to be right.

Truth in this chapter represents the linear/words level of understanding.

CHAPTER 14

ENERGY — THE QUANTUM OF PHYSICS

It's all about energy.
—Cesar Millan, The Dog Whisperer

EVERYTHING, EVERYTHING, EVERYTHING IS ENERGY...E = MC2

This is the nonlinear world of energy...no words just feelings. I studied energy in science class in high school and college. One tuning fork set vibrating would set the rest of the tuning forks in the room on the same frequency to vibrating. There were countless experiments with electricity and other forms of energy. That is the Western way of thinking—scientific. I, like most of us, had never studied energy in relation to the thoughts I put out or how the thought energy made me *feel*. My life as a marketer and artist, flying around the world, did not leave me time to contemplate quantum physics, physics or any other science.

I felt I was about to enter the land of what some call woo-woo, the land of the unexplained, the twilight zone. When I started to study with the Native American, Gary Adler Fourstar, the study of thought energy began. How would it feel to me at first? When I began to study with this Native American and his other students, there were many things I experienced that could not be explained. He would encourage us to *be with the experience because the answer to why was simply the booby prize*. This was difficult for me—my life's work was about understanding what made people behave the way they did, so the answer to the question why was a fundamental pursuit for me.

This ability to read energy is similar to Cesar Millan and his ability to rehabilitate even the most incorrigible dog. Cesar reads the animal's energy and, more importantly, the owner's energy, which usually falls into the arena of fear, anxiety or aggression causing the dogs, who feel that energy, to act up. All of these feelings put out their own vibration but the owners do not know they are putting them out. The average person says, *dogs can smell fear*. I would say they <u>feel</u> it.

Animals are great teachers about the subtleties of the energy we unknowingly put out. Humans have the same ability but it has been ignored in our modern world. Most of us are *asleep* to our abilities. With television, computers, computer games, smart phones and constant attention on those products, there is no time to *experience* the subtleties of our energetic messages. In order to reawaken these abilities, we must be taught and experience what we once knew.

HORSES AS AN ENERGY INDICATOR

I am now many years into the study of vibration in everything, so my ability to read the energy behind communications is getting much, much easier and comes faster.

How subtle this is, was demonstrated when we were about to have a sweat later on in my work with Gary. I was in the pasture clearing the grounds for a ceremonial dance that night when all five horses came to me and nuzzled me, even the young colt, usually very shy and standoffish. I was basking in the love being given by these animals when I turned to get a rake and saw Gary coming down from the house to the sweat lodge.

He yelled out, "Well, you never know who will show up at these things."

We were having some head butting in our sessions, so I decided I would not engage. I got the rake and started back toward the horses. Interestingly, they were moving away from me. I stopped. They stopped and started grazing. I walked toward them again. Every one of those animals started moving away from me. I thought, *Whoa, what is happening?* I started again. The horse I usually rode was closest to me, laid his ears back and turned his head toward me as if to say, "One step closer and I am going to let you have it." Those of you who know horse body language know the laidback ears is a distinct warning that he is not happy about something. I was blown away to say the least. I suddenly realized, *these horses are picking up on a subtle shift of energy coming from me. Wow, they are sensing something in me they do not like and of which I am consciously unaware.* I did not feel angry or any other negativity.

I tell you this to impress how subtle this vibrational stuff can be. Animals are very sensitive to energy, especially prey animals because they have to keep their senses focused all of the time or be eaten. We are also animals and have the same ability to feel the energy though we are not aware or awake to it, being too busy to develop this ability. For example, when you first meet someone and take an instant dislike or liking to them, that simply means you are resonating with their energetic vibration or you are not.

Many of us believe it is a lot of woo-woo anyway. That's OK––people who don't believe are less educated and experienced at *really* feeling. Many of us won't truly believe the subtleness or the power of this force until we learn to relax, open our minds and experience it. At first, especially if you have a western-thinking mind and were brought up in the world of science, your Monkey mind will try to talk you out of believing what you are experiencing. Some people's Monkey minds are very powerful. Nothing is wrong with that because it is an indicator of the level of resistance one is experiencing.

THE PHYSICS OF ENERGY

There are two different definitions of the word *alive*. Most western-thinking people think something is alive if it eats, defecates, grows, moves and is capable of dying or, in the case of plants, have the ability to photosynthesize. In the chapter on Communication, I state this to be the linear/words level.

At the higher/energetic level, a deeper definition is that energetic movement is in everything, even in things we see as solid--all matter is made up of atoms and all atoms and subatomic particles have vibrational movement at the subatomic level--everything is connected and communicates. From that perspective and my study of quantum physics, the Native American beliefs seem true—all things are alive from a vibrational subatomic perspective, connected, have Spirit and can interrelate through that frequency. This distinction is not to be argued because it is simply two different perspectives, both correct by the use of the different definitions of the word alive. However, it requires thinking differently, which is difficult for some.

The Dark Language

In the course of study with my Native American friends, I told you about one elder named Blue Thunder. When I worked with him, he came to stay at my house many times. I remember the very first time--he had been in my house about an hour when he spoke, "Now I know why I am here."

"And that reason is?"

"I am here to take you to the next level and teach you about the dark language that you speak."

"Dark language, what is that?"

"You speak it all of the time."

"OK, explain."

"You constantly speak about where you are, not about what you want."

"I speak my reality."

"Yes, and your reality will not change until you shift to a focus on what you want and away from where you are. This must begin in your thoughts. By the time your thoughts become words, your reality is set."

I remember my native teacher, Gary Fourstar, always saying, "Form follows thought." At the time, I paid little attention to the depth of the statement.

What they were teaching and what I just taught you is nothing more than Quantum Physics. I know, I am over simplifying.

THE LAW OF ATTRACTION

The Law of Attraction is a name applied to this physics principle. From an energetic position, the scientific Law of Attraction always works no matter how you may interpret what is happening, like gravity. *The Law of Attraction is how prayer works. It is Quantum Physics. (VTK)* Don't let the words Quantum Physics scare you. It is easier than you may think to understand, at least at the superficial level.

Most of us were taught about Newtonian physics in the lower grades and high school, particularly, everything in the physical world is made up of atoms and molecules. Quantum Physics takes the study to the subatomic level and has discovered particles even smaller at this level and beyond.

In 1925 Albert Einstein discovered the equation E=MC2. Prior to that, based on Newtonian Physics, things were believed to be created as a result of gravity and that all things in the Universe were solid objects made up of atoms. Einstein discovered these atoms, broken down into subatomic particles, were pure energy. He believed this energy was in the form of particles and had the appearance of being solid.

Another physicist, Thomas Young (1773-1829), believed this energy existed in the form of waves and resurrected the century-old wave theory of light.[2]

Enter another scientist Niels Bohr. In 1927, he and many other quantum physicists got together for what came to be known as the Copenhagen Interpretation, which revealed that both scientists' beliefs were true.[3] The subatomic particles were *both wave and particles but not at the same time.* They determined that energy is in wave form until *attention* is focused on it. In other words, waves were all of the possibilities that existed and, as soon as focus was placed on one possibility, that possibility manifested, and all other possibilities collapsed. *The thoughts and beliefs of the observing scientist* determined which it was—waves or particles. (One focused on waves and the other on particles.)

I want to demonstrate how this energetic law works in relation to your Monkeys, your thoughts both conscious and unconscious. *The Monkeys are why the Law of Attraction does not seem to work for some people. (VTK)*

The name is given to the maxim *like attracts like* which, in New Thought Philosophy, is used to sum up the idea that by focusing on positive or negative thoughts, a person brings positive or negative experiences into one's life. So, the dark language, the law of attraction and this part of quantum physics are all one-in-the-same. The Bible says *you reap what you sow.* All of these expressions are describing the same law of the universe.

When *The Secret*, by Rhonda Byrne[4] came out, which talks about the law of attraction, many naysayers said the principles espoused were woo-woo, that applying the scientific process, nothing could be replicated--if the law worked, then if we focus on winning the lottery, it should manifest. There was never any consideration given to the barrier forces in play that could keep the manifestation from happening or slowing it down. Because the manifestation did not happen immediately, the conclusion was that the so-called law did not work--classic thinking coming from an immediate gratification society.

What does this mean to you? *It means that all things in your life manifest based on your thoughts, beliefs <u>and your focus.</u>* "If that is the case, why can't I get the money or car I want?" When our intent is not being focused using the conscious mind, the intent is left to the subconscious mind and the subconscious mind is where the Monkeys live. *Subconscious intent may be counter-productive to conscious intent. (VTK)*

Think of a car with a gas pedal and a brake pedal. As soon as you think about something you want, it starts down the energy road toward you. What determines whether this desire manifests and in what time frame is determined solely by your Monkeys and their subconscious intent, which have access to the brake pedal, and, according to some, the karma propensities you bring into this life with you.

Let's take something you would like to manifest and look at the process.

You want a new car. As soon as that desire is expressed, the car is on its way to you. Now let's look at the Monkeys that could exist to slow down the coming of the car. Maybe you have a subconscious belief: (1) you do not deserve a new car, (2) new cars are too expensive; (3) your brother deserves a new car before you; or (4) your financial situation absolutely has no room for a new car. Each one of these thoughts are a Monkey with its foot on the brake of the energy for getting a new car. These Monkeys need to be tamed or discarded in order to get their feet off the brakes.

The act you are focused on (getting a new car) brings up the fact you do not have a new car. This vibration of lack actually says *send me more of what I lack*—no new car, because your focus is there. So, three things have to happen to change this.

Identify the subconscious Monkey beliefs that stop the car from coming and transmute them to supporting beliefs. This can be done with the Psych-K process.

Focus on having a new car and let go of how or when it will arrive. Give the details of the coming of the new car over to God/Universe or Quantum Physics and forget about it. Others teach to focus on what it will *feel* like when you have the new car. Smell the new car smell. Go car shopping and find a car you want and go for a test drive. Shop as if you are buying it now. Focus on what it feels like to have that new car.

Put it out to the Universe/God that you need a new car and the coming of the new car is now in His/Her/Its hands.

I have to tell you the story about my new used car. I did exactly what I said in number three. I put my need out there and put it in God's hands. At the same time, I had a wonderful car, which had been with me 14 years through all the hard times, but now kept breaking down. I didn't want to put any more money in it and saw no possibility of being able to pay a car payment for several more months (dark language). So, I kept fixing it.

A good friend said to me one day, "If you keep focused on fixing that old car, the new one will not come." Of course, I knew she was right, but what was I to do? I needed transportation. So, I fixed it again to the tune of $800.00. That was a lot of money for me then and would take over six months to pay off. I settled into that decision and one week later the timing belt went—another $1500 worth of repairs. Well, I no longer had room on my credit cards for that repair so had to let old Betsy go to the mechanic, who vowed to make the repairs and fix her up so his wife could drive a convertible for the summer.

There I was without a car and no ability to pay for a newer one for at least four months. I did not worry about it because I had put the solution into God's hands.

Almost the next day, my roommate told me he was buying his son's Audi. That meant he was going to get rid of his Honda and I could drive it until he sold it. Wow, Ok, not what I wanted, but transportation, nonetheless. I couldn't buy his car for two reasons: 1) it was a stick and, although I knew how to drive sticks, my knee could no longer handle the constant aggravation of a clutch, especially in Atlanta traffic; and 2) I had no money to pay outright for the car and banks would not make such a small loan for it.

In the month I drove his car, I started looking for that new car, still not knowing how I was to pay for it. At the same time, I started inquiring about getting a modification to my mortgage. I had not done that up to this point because I believed help from the Hardest Hit Fund in Georgia and a modification to my loan was an either/or situation. Don't know what made me call to investigate the possibility with that belief floating in my head, but I did. After calling around and getting my questions answered about the modification, I applied. What blew my mind—in only 12 days, including a weekend, I received notification I was accepted into the program. That fast, I had a reduction in my mortgage payment of $300 monthly, which covered my new used-car payment of $270 and the increased insurance. Wham, I had a new 2013 Hyundai Sonata within a month, one week before my roommate sold his car.

I couldn't believe how fast everything manifested once I let go of old Betsy. (By the way, the mechanic who bought Betsy fixed everything and a couple of weeks later she blew up. He explained that sometimes the new parts put too much stress on the older parts. Imagine where I would be if I had fixed her again.)

"Everything is energy and that's all there is to it. Match the frequency of the reality you want and you cannot help but get that reality. It can be no other way. This is not philosophy. This is physics." Albert Einstein

I am not sure this is a direct quote from Albert Einstein but it should be, if it isn't. The study of Quantum Physics certainly is bearing this quote out. How fast it comes depends on the Monkeys.

POSITIVE VS. NEGATIVE/LOVE VS. NONLOVE ENERGY

This chapter describes the second level of communication...energy. Where the linear/words level has many hierarchies and degrees in words, this level is very simple...positive or negative, love or hate. That's it!

There is no neutral and no degrees of positive or degrees of negative. Aligning with hate and only feeling a mild discomfort does not mean that your hate is less than a stronger word description of hate. It is the EXACT same energy. There is no emotion in energy...positive vs. negative...period. Most people I talk to recoil at the word hate, so, to be heard here, I changed the words to Love/Nonlove. Because virtually everyone functions at the linear/words level, using Love/ Nonlove vs. Love /Hate keeps the listener from tuning me out. This level is where emotion is added thus the need for degrees. With emotion, there are different levels of feeling the energy. It is, however, still love vs. hate energy.

Why is this important you ask? Well Dr. Hawkins put it very succinctly. He would often say that in each moment we choose either Heaven or Hell. So, if you are unaware of this, you are allowing the Monkeys to make your choice. If you can't tell by now, the Monkeys are not the best to be left in charge of choosing. Here is what you can do to become more aware of your choices...ask questions.

Many of my friends and family expressed dislike for the choice of Mr. Trump for President. They did not *feel* right about it. That feeling was coming from the energetic level of understanding. Something was off that made them *feel* uneasy. They would then drop down into the linear/words level, disregard the feeling of uneasiness and justify their choice of Trump because he represented change or they liked how he spoke his mind, or they disliked Hillary, etc.

All they had to do to see what energy they were aligning with was to ask yes or no questions to get at the energy behind the behaviors, such as:

1. Is making fun of disabled people coming from love?
2. Is condoning grabbing a woman's pussy without permission coming from love?
3. Is advocating taking 24M people off healthcare coming from love?

Because the answer is no to all of the questions, the feelings show an open alignment with nonlove (hate) energy.

People supporting these nonlove energies are often unwittingly and unknowingly aligning with that hate energy. There may be things that he does that you support...I would encourage you to explore if those actions you support come from love. If not, what is it about you that aligns with that energy (probably your fear of something)? Be careful about justification...remember energy does not acknowledge justification. That is an action of man. Even if you do not agree with any of Trump's actions and you support him anyway you've aligned with the negative energy and somewhere in you is that same energy thus the attraction. (This is an example of nonlove energy not a political position for or against anything.) It is clear to me that many made this alignment because the country needed to become clear as to what direction it wanted to seek...love or nonlove. Like I said before most must hit bottom before they can turn their life around. The country had to become clear on what the two energies were in order to make a choice.

Using this form of questioning to determine the energy you align with will help you understand, especially if you have an uneasy *feeling* about anything. If you are lower on the consciousness scale, the easier it will be for the Monkeys to pull the resistance cloak over you and the more you will argue your points from the linear level where confusion resides.

The world of energy needs no words as feelings start to replace words.

CHAPTER 15
COMMUNICATION—
THERE ARE TWO LEVELS: WORDS AND ENERGY

When you are praying, do not heap up empty phrases *as the Gentiles do; for they think that they will be heard because of their many words. Do not be like them,* for your Father knows what you need before you ask him.
—Matthew 6:7,8

Everything is connected at the subatomic level and, from that level, communication is instantaneous. *Communication at the subatomic level (energy) is not subject to time or space. (VTK)* This means we are all capable of communicating instantly at the subatomic level and need no words. Many of us have situations in our life where we get messages or feelings through cyberspace that we cannot explain. Most of the time, we do not pay attention to these messages or relegate these feelings to coincidences. This was the type of communication going on with me and the horses.

Even the Bible refers to the vibrational field, but it uses other words when discussing how prayer works, the way we communicate to God/Universe (whatever word you choose to describe the Source) and the natural Law of Attraction. The thoughts you have, already have sent the message of what your needs are, or more accurately stated, the feelings about your thoughts are already communicated and understood. The empty words talked about in Matthew seven (above) are not communicating to the same level as your feelings about your thoughts because there is little emotion (vibration) around them. The words spoken in a rote fashion do not have much, if any, emotion or vibration attached to them; therefore, they are not recognized as easily or as quickly.

Defining the word rote as: mechanically, automatically, unthinking, mindlessly; from memory, by heart, there is no emotion or elevated vibrational frequency. The more emotion (energy) around your thoughts, the faster the thoughts are recognized and the faster the manifestation. The important message here is **emotion** (our word for energy). One way to look at it is that emotion is the volume dial on the radio—the more emotion, the higher the volume.

Yea, I know what you are saying right about now, "If that is the case, why can't I get the money or car I want?" As discussed earlier, *this is where the Monkeys enter the picture. Remember, I told you the Monkeys live in your subconscious and they have an invisible cloak they use to keep you from seeing your behavior or what is really in your subconscious? This is where they send out the thoughts consisting of what I call your Subconscious Intent. (VTK) Here is where all of your subconscious programming supersedes your conscious intent and you are blind to it...just happily sitting under that invisible cloak. (VTK)*

Because the subconscious programming and beliefs usually have significant emotion tied to them, they are more powerful than the conscious thoughts. (VTK) This is why it becomes paramount for you to seek to uncover and transmute or recontectualize these untrue, unwanted beliefs in order to shift what manifests in your life.

I have a great example of how the Monkeys keep you from understanding what is in your subconscious and under their cloak. One day I posted an article about childhood obesity on Facebook with the comment FYI and tagged a friend with children. She attacked me with such vicious hateful energy coming through on a text, it about knocked me over--that post did not warrant a reaction like that and she clearly was making it mean something about her. Remember we are meaning-making machines. In this case she thought I was telling her how to raise her kids and was further mortified that I posted it on her wall so all her friends could see.

All of that anger was coming from her subconscious. She was showing her deep-seated beliefs about her own self-hatred. The Monkeys can misguide you and that is the reason for the suffering. I later told her she needed to do something about her anger or she would have a heart attack someday. (At 29 she already has heart problems) She at least asked a question because, clearly, she could not see the anger I was talking about. She was not conscious of her anger at all and completely unaware of the vicious hate she projected onto me. It has been my experience that most people, when I observe their anger and tell them that they are angry, can't see it.

The person having the anger storm is the only one that has that power to control his/her reaction and move that reaction to a logical more controlled response. You know the Monkeys are in charge when there are no questions being asked. Only when one asks questions to clarify to see if their perception is correct is one out from under the invisible cloak.

INTERPRETATION AND THE WORD IN COMMUNICATION

Language was brought to us by the Gods, or so they say (whoever they are). And with language comes interpretation; interpretation of a language, interpretation of a word, and interpretation-translation of one language to another. The study of language is called linguistics. The study of words is called etymology.

A friend of mine once asked, "Why do we study linguistics?" Of course, he had no interest in that particular endeavor and, therefore, was someone who would go to war over the misinterpretation of a word and not even know why there was a war.

Why am I taking time to discuss this? Because I believe all misunderstanding is simply miscommunication and the study of words and language can give one a great deal of insight into why there is misunderstanding. Except when malice enters the picture and people use opinion to attack.

"The difference between the right word and the almost right word is the difference between lightning and a lightning bug." Mark Twain[1]

He was right on the money with this quote. Words and all of

their nuances can, when misinterpreted or misunderstood, cause all kinds of consternation.

Each word has three sides to it:

Its **etymology**, its history of meaning and how that meaning may have changed over the years. In other words, the literal side;

The **consciousness level** of the one interpreting the word. People at different consciousness levels can and will understand the same word differently; and

The **energy** each word manifests and is magnified when in a set of thoughts—the power of the word. Adding energy to a word is like going from a two-dimensional drawing to a multidimensional hologram. All of a sudden one is giving life or power to that word. "I will do for you <u>exactly</u> what you have said." Numbers 14:28

But let's look at interpretation from the literal side and consciousness level first.

Take the term Word in this quote, "In the beginning was the Word, and the Word was with God, and the Word was God." John 1:1

Some think this Word is a moniker representing Jesus, which is why it is capitalized, and some think Word simply represents language. Or maybe Word represents vibration, which would flow with the idea of the Word actually being God.

Because interpretation is the creation of man, you may choose which facet or combination of facets you like. The interpretation is influenced by the facet of the diamond the interpreter associates with as well as the interpreter's consciousness level and the energy (emotion) applied to the word.

Consciousness levels affect one's ability to see different interpretations. The lower the consciousness level, the fewer the available interpretive possibilities, which is the reason many MUST interpret literally. They can see only one possible interpretation—theirs and, of course, theirs is the right one. Everything is black and white. Conversely, the higher the consciousness level, the greater the understanding of different possible meanings. The higher the consciousness level the more compassion in the interpretation.

Whether you interpret the term, Word, in the above quote as Jesus or whether you interpret the term as a representation of language and vibration, or whether you interpret the term God as representing the supreme Creator or some alien from another planet is all based on what facet of the diamond you have chosen to reside and *not whether you are the keeper of the ultimate truth.* Each facet of the diamond simply represents different possibilities of truth. However, the truth was different on each facet. Each person spoke his or her truth. When one takes the position that one's facet represents the real truth, the only truth, the Monkeys are proclaiming to be right. If those living on that facet had the education and view of the whole diamond, they would see their way was simply one possible way to the Source (truth), not the only way.

There is no way to prove any of the above possibilities. So, taking a position one way or the other is simply the Monkeys in control, wanting to fight and be right. There are different understandings of these possibilities at different levels of consciousness. Which is why, I believe, Jesus taught using parables.

Thus, the Mystery Schools are simply different levels of interpretation of the same truths. One's ability to understand is predicated on one's consciousness level. Make no mistake, we humans are all spirits having a human experience in this beautiful earthly school. Earth is a school for spiritual initiates and everyone is at a different grade level. We are all on a spiritual path. Some of us are moving slowly and some fast. Some of us are moving away from the Source in order to move closer to the Source and some of us are moving closer to the Source. *Regardless, the Path, for everyone, leads to the Source and there is only one Source. (VTK)*

Our ancestors have written their thoughts and many of those stories have ended up in various books. One of the most famous is the Bible. In order to learn the truth from a contextual point of view, one must study all of the possible interpretations. *The more literal one interprets the Bible and other books, the less likely one will*

truly learn and grow from a Spiritual Perspective. Literal interpretation
does not allow for historic understanding of the words used, perspective
or vibrational feelings and keeps one at the level of intellect and below
the level of love (500). One cannot truly cross over into the level of love
without letting go of reliance on the intellect or the need to prove. (VTK)
These are exciting times because every day we uncover more and
more old manuscripts and ancient places. Their interpretations
give us even more perspective of the way things were and how
the ancients thought.

ANCIENT MANUSCRIPTS AND PUNCTUATION

I had another important revelation while studying with
Jehovah's Witnesses and that had to do with punctuation.

I had two different Bibles in front of me so I could compare—
the one bought in the beginning of my quest and the one Jehovah
Witnesses use. We were discussing something concerning the crucifixion and I was reading the words of Jesus when he was on the
cross telling the thief who had asked for forgiveness he would join
him in paradise. Both Bibles used the same exact words but each
had a comma in different places, completely changing the meaning of the sentence.

"Truly I tell you today you will be with me in Paradise." No
punctuation.

"Truly I tell you, today you will be with me in Paradise." Luke
23:43[2]

"Truly I tell you today, you will be with me in Paradise." Luke
23:43[3]

As you can see, the position of a comma totally changes the
meaning of the sentence.

One says I am telling you this day that you will join Me at some
future date. The other says *this day* you will join Me in paradise.
Jehovah's Witnesses believe one does not go to Heaven after death
but remains unconscious in the grave until Jesus comes back to
Earth and resurrects everyone. The New Oxford Bible writers

believed that as soon as one dies, s/he goes to Heaven or Hell depending on God's judgment.

I thought this was very interesting and went to a friend, Don Tolman, who has studied ancient documents all his life and reads Hebrew, Aramaic, Greek and other ancient languages.

I asked, "Don, does ancient Hebrew have punctuation?"

He smiled, "No ancient languages have punctuation."

"Then where does all of the punctuation come from that is in the Bible?"

He smiled again, "There are approximately 1300 different versions of the Bible, one to fit any interpretation you would like to follow."

The point? Each was punctuated to emphasize the belief of the editor based on what facet of the diamond s/he resided upon.

Q. So where did the punctuation in the Bible come from?

A. Man.

Q. Why did we add punctuation?

A. So we could add our *individual interpretation.*

Q. And why did man do that?

A. To show that his particular way of thinking was the correct or right way of thinking.

The people adding this punctuation thought they were making the writings clearer and felt they knew what was best for the masses and what the *real* truth was. Of course, that is not true since the more powerful would elevate their translation and declare the less powerful as heretics for not following *their* way of thinking. This is an indication that the Monkeys are in control. The Monkeys want to *control* and *force* their way of believing when the reality is that there is plenty of room for all the different ways to God and different beliefs. *Those who force their way of thinking are simply representing the antithesis of God, or to be clearer—the dark side.* (VTK)

Back then, only a select few had literate education and the common course of action was to restrict people's accessibility to knowledge and education, especially for women and the oppressed. All of this was done to control the masses by the powerful and educated, usually government and the clergy. *So, in truth, the different interpretations come from a desire to control and be right, which is the domain of the Monkeys. (VTK)* If this weren't true, history would not be littered with book burnings and examples of restrictive education. The most recent infamous example is the youngest winner of the Nobel Peace Prize in 2014, Malala Yousafzai, who was shot by the Taliban in Pakistan because she was vocal on education for women.

Interestingly, those who push this backward position calibrate well below 200 at the lower levels of shame (20), guilt (30), grief (75), fear (100), and anger (150). Notice these are feeling words, not good or bad feelings, just feelings. They anthropomorphize their God and create a God who is vengeful, punitive, condemning and vindictive. Those are not the behaviors of God but their own behaviors that they project onto their God.

"At the time of the birth of Buddha, mankind collectively calibrated at 90. The collective consciousness level had reached 100 by the time of the birth of Jesus Christ and climbed slowly to level 190, where it remained for many centuries. Only in the late 1980's did the level jump from 190 to above the critical level of 200, to 204 and later to 207. It then went back down in the year 2007 to the level of 204 and currently is 200 for about 80% of mankind. In the United States, 55% of the population is below 200, which is significant because it had been only 49% in 2005."[4]

LANGUAGE AND ENERGY LEVELS

Talking about communication is difficult because of the need to separate the etymology of a word from the energy of the word and the different levels of understanding or consciousness levels of man, which affect the word or the word's interpretation.

There are basically two levels of communication: 1) Language and 2) Energy. *When Jesus talked about teaching in parables, he was talking about language. When he mentioned the Mysteries of Heaven, he was talking about communication through energy or a Knowing. (VTK)*

I read somewhere in *A Course in Miracles* that language is four times removed from the actual truth. So, communication through language is, at best, a flawed, misunderstood art form and often may not communicate the truth. When people go down the road of literal interpretation, they are sorely missing the boat, especially when the documents they are reading are thousands of years old, because of the flaws of language. At all levels, language is subject to interpretation, changing meanings of a word, the use or misuse of words, and interpretation from one language to another. Often when going from one language to another, there are words that defy interpretation, there is no word in the other language with the same meaning. The result: misguided interpretation that cause all kinds of misunderstanding and resulting fights and arguments. Pay attention to the energy here. Language is the mind's way of communication when at the levels of the linear. It is a flawed process at best, causing much misunderstanding.

As I began to discover the Monkeys, my Monkeys, I could see where the Monkeys disrupt communication when they experience threat. They shut down, deflect, and do anything but converse about the issue.

The mind and its mental process is the realm of the lower consciousness levels (1-499). The 400s are even called *reason*. This is where most of our scientists calibrate. As long as people are of a mindset that everything needs proof, they will remain below 500. One cannot cross over the line into the 500s (love) until they give up the notion of needing to prove everything scientifically.

Once you learn to allow the heart to lead the mind rather than the other way around, then, and only then, will you have conscious access to communication through energy and be able to cross over into the 500s. Once this leadership shifts, you will no longer need words or proof or the Bible or any other book to guide you. For when you come from the heart, you are coming from love. When you come from love, you will always be in alignment with the Creator's love energy and treat others lovingly, so you (personally) would no longer need laws, rules or words. There will be people, however, who have not made this transition who, because of where they are, will take a position against this energy, using words, simply because they do not understand the shift. It is too scary for them and comprehension is blocked by the Monkeys.

I am not talking about understanding at an intellectual level, which is more of the mind leading the way. I am talking about understanding at a heart level, where one *knows* what is the right loving path. *At the subatomic level, communication is not subject to time or space and is an instant knowing and alignment with what most of us call God. (VTK)*

Until you reach this level, you will always be studying, worshiping or believing in God. *Once you make the transition, you will have the privilege of becoming one <u>with</u> God with instant loving connectedness. This level of knowingness is where studying, worshiping or believing is no longer necessary. (VTK)*

Understanding the study of ancient languages and how meaning shifts over time and across cultures is key to understanding human communication. Add that different consciousness levels have different abilities to understand, and we see the importance of studying linguistics and etymology. *There is a correlation between communication styles and consciousness levels. (VTK)* This correlation does not happen 100% of the time, which adds an element of confusion that causes some with a more scientific mind to totally disregard the premise because it is not provable all of the time.

The Mystery Schools are nothing more than moving from the quantum physics (the physical) to the metaphysics (the unseen). (VTK) Quantum Physics has shown, your thoughts, beliefs and perceptions concerning any and every event, condition or circumstance determine how your life experience will unfold in the physical world. (VTK)

COMMUNICATION 101 LINEAR/WORDS

Diagram III is the basic way humans function and communicate. It represents linear thinking. Because we live in a linear world and because most of humanity believes in duality, this is how we often see life. This continuum line shows concepts going from one side to the other, such as, going from bad to good or from dark to light, wrong to right, hot to cold, etc. This is dualistic thinking. *Dualistic thinking is fraught with judgment. (VTK)* Man, on this level of thinking, uses a position model of communication. They draw a line in the sand and make people choose which side they are on and, of course, one side is judged as bad and one side is judged as good and the line drawer determines which side is good—the one they are on. See the Monkey folly?

Continuum: Bad To Good

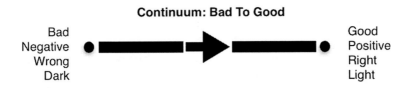

Bad		Good
Negative		Positive
Wrong		Right
Dark		Light

Diagram III—Dualistic/Linear Thinking

Dualistic thinking is simply the world of opposites, when, in fact, they are not opposite. Dark is not the opposite of light, but the absence of light. Cold is not the opposite of hot, but the absence of heat.

There is no good or bad except what lives in our minds. What is judged good for one man can be judged bad for another. Too much good can be bad and too much bad can be good. Yea, I can hear you now—you are saying, "How can too much good be bad?" Let's look at the striving musician who finally makes it big. S/he now has all the money, fame and notoriety. What happens? All that *good* often takes them to the depths of the alcohol and drug world, thus too much good can become bad. However, by hitting bottom too much, bad can be good. A modern-day maxim is *humans must hit bottom to turn their lives around* and go in a different direction. That was the case for me. I had to lose everything in order to deal with my insecurities. Once I lost all my money and assets at age 60, I had to face where my insecurities *really* came from and, therefore, where does security really come from? So too much bad ended up being good for me and my spiritual growth.

Diagram IV shows positionality where people draw a line in the sand and choose a position making the other side of that position wrong. People who see the world in a dualistic manner also live in a world of positionality which, by the way, is most of humanity because 80% calibrate below 200. *The 80% whose Monkeys are in control will often take a position on an issue and draw a line in the sand, as President Bush did after 9/11. "You are either with us (on our side of the line) or you are against us (on the other side of the line)." (VTK)* This is the win/lose mentality, the I-must-kill-you-in-order-for-me-to-live thinking. It is the communication tactic used by all those who take positions on issues. It is the I'm-right, you-are-wrong mentality. This mentality has no room for possibility. If you remain neutral with this person and do not join them in their way of thinking, they will make you the enemy anyway. They will automatically apply the view of what you do as the enemy. With this type of thinking, people die, often literally, as evidenced by the war casualties following 9/11.

This is precisely what Cox did when I became a threat. They drew a line in the sand and put me on the side of the enemy and then proceeded to try to kill me as best that they could rather than understand and deal with my issues.

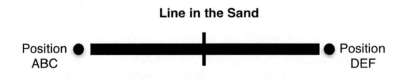

Diagram IV—Positionality

Let me be clear here. Because one calibrates above 200 does not mean that s/he does not use this form of communication style. *Communication styles do not have a 100% correlation with consciousness levels. (VTK)* The reason is that consciousness levels can be fluid, meaning they can vacillate. Additionally, we all have storms within our consciousness climate. One can calibrate in the 300s and have life create a temporary storm that takes them to the levels below 200. A good example of this is when people, usually of normal mindsets, totally loose it on the road creating road rage. When this happens, the Monkeys happily take you on a nosedive down your anger well to a level below 200 that resonates with your way of being and has never been healed.

The more narcissistic a person is the more capable s/he is of rewriting her/his own history and most people who calibrate below 200 are in varying degrees of narcissism. *People who calibrate below 200 are not capable of dialogue. (VTK) The intention of communication at that level is manipulation not understanding.* This is scary given that roughly 80% of the people in the world calibrate at those lower levels.

Because you may calibrate above 200 does not mean you never use this positional communication tactic. In my effort to understand the correlation between calibration levels and communication styles, I recently had four people in the media calibrated. My theory -- because of their behavior of taking a position on everything, they would calibrate below 200. The hypothesis turned out to be incorrect, much to my surprise. Of the four people, three calibrated between 250 and 350, which represents neutrality, willingness and acceptance in that order. Only one was calibrating below 200. However, here is the important part: Their bodies of work (TV shows or books written) ALL calibrated below 200. Why? My assumption is each, at some subconscious level, understood that taking a position and vilifying the other side of that position, thus angering and stirring up their base, *made them money.* This understanding I can assure you is at the level of the Monkeys. *The Monkeys tend to make decisions that benefit the individual (or Corporation) at the expense of the masses.* (VTK)

Interestingly, the one person on this list who calibrated below 200 is recently being called out as a liar by much of the press (and more recently was fired from his very powerful media position). The person calibrating at 250 writes books, regurgitating the same vilifying premise of the other side over and over. Neutrality (250) can be described as exercising in a hamster wheel. The one who calibrates at the acceptance level, (350), is showing signs of shifting and the last person calibrating at willingness (about 310) continues to thrive monetarily on the consternation he creates. He and many others view this as success in this world.

So, there is a correlation between consciousness levels and behavior or in this case communication styles but it is not a 100% correlation. *The reason is Monkeys need to be tamed at all levels below 600. If the Monkeys are allowed to run amuck without awareness, guidance and taming, what level you are at below 600 doesn't matter. You, too, will run amuck spiritually in your life. (VTK)*

People who usually rely solely on religion for spiritual guidance can get spiritually stuck in their religious dogma. "As long as I go to church every week and say my prayers every night or do as the priest or minister says, I will meet God's spiritual requirements." This is not a true assumption. That position is simply taking the lazy man's way out, which is also the reason people fall into the belief that *their* religion is the only way to God. This is a very dangerous position from a spiritual growth perspective and can add many lifetimes to the process of enlightenment. Dr. Hawkins warned us, "Religious zealots are the most dangerous people in the world."[5] Before you start pointing out certain examples in religions other than yours, let me caution you—all religions have religious zealots or extremists, as we call them today.

The Need for Balance

Diagram IV allows for a position of neutrality to exist. It is the beginning of understanding the need for balance and exists only in the linear world. There is no neutral at the energetic level.

My Native American teacher taught me that one needed to strive for balance, in the continuum of good to bad, light to dark, etc., in order to learn where there is a balance of energies and to be able to choose that balance. *It is in the balance that people become harmonious and thrive. (VTK)*

In my opinion, a good example of this of late is our Congress.

When Reagan was elected, the vast majority of Congress fell in the middle moderate range, whether they were Democrat or Republican. (In Diagram V Neutral represents moderate.) That is why they could get a lot done for the good of the country and work across the aisle. In 1994, 36% of Republicans were more liberal than typical Democrats and 30% of Democrats were more conservative than typical Republicans. In 2014, eight percent of Republicans were more liberal than typical Democrats. Six percent of Democrats were more conservative than typical Republicans. The ideological overlap in the House in 2002 was 137 members; in 2013, it was four members. The ideological overlap in the Senate in 2002 was seven, and in 2013 zero. [6]

The Tea Party did much to cement this divide when, in 2009, after Obama's first inauguration, born out of hatred for a black President, they ran on the stand of *no compromise.* That stand took us back to the line in the sand, to the *you are either with me or against me* position. It was no longer what was good for everyone, it was my way or the highway. They behaved like spoiled little kids. I want what I want and I want it now. So, what if I shut down the government and the country suffers...I am right. There was no longer room for neutrality or compromise.

Diagram V—Positionality

For me, I always thought I was moving from bad to good, all of my work was taking me to the light. But I was programmed with the you-are-born-with-sin software, so obviously life was all about moving toward the good. Of course, that is fallacious programming one must learn to undo.

The understanding of the intellect will allow you to get to only 499 on the consciousness scale. To move to love on the consciousness scale, one must cross from the intellect, mind, prove-it-to-me mentality, to coming from the heart and *feeling* harmony and love. This is the side where things cannot be *proven*. To get there, one must let go of having to prove things and start feeling, *feel the love. One can't prove love*. One can't get there by studying anything. *Study is an activity of the intellect. Feeling is an activity of the heart.*

DIALOGUE VS. POSITIONALITY

There are two elements to communication… *dialogue and positionality*. Dialogue fosters communication via understanding, compassion and mutual respect. This side of communication results in cooperation, win-win behavior and harmony. Positionality fosters indifference, noncaring and results in win-lose, fighting and war. The I-am-right-you-are-wrong thinking fosters positionality and feeds the war energy regardless of which side of the discussion you stand on. Positionality fosters the vilification of the other side. So, you can rest assured that if someone is vilifying the other side, s/he is at least functioning with that behavior below 200. As Dr. Hawkins often likes to say, "You don't have to hate chocolate in order to like vanilla." [7]

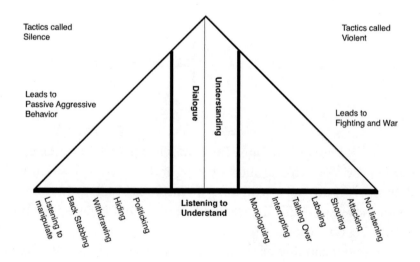

Diagram VI—Communication Styles [8]

The right side of Diagram VI[8] represents communication styles and tactics which are labeled *violent*, such as monologuing, talking over another, interrupting, name calling, raising the voice and shouting. All of which show no respect for the other person and, of course, there is no listening for understanding. These tactics can and often do lead to violence.

I am not talking about debate here. If one is in a debate, one has rules of communication to follow, which are supposed to keep emotion, for the most part, out of the interchange and introduce civility, respect and dialogue to the discourse.

The left side of the diagram are communication tactics which are labeled as *silent* styles and lead to passive aggressive behavior. These include but are not limited to hiding, silence, talking behind someone's back and politicking. All of them lead to the individual not speaking up for themselves, which eventually leads to passive/aggressive behavior. Both the left side of the diagram and the right side of the diagram represent different aspects of anger, disrespect and positionalities and will lead to fighting and war.

The only difference between the two sides is that the right side is *in-your-face with its intent* like a person who comes at you from the front with a knife to kill you. You are clear of his intentions. The left side is silent and its true *intent is hidden,* like a Southern lady who comes to you with a smile on her face as she drives the knife into your back. Both styles calibrate below 200 and are non-integrious. These communication tactics always distance the parties and result in fighting, misunderstanding and eventually war. The extremes of positionalities will bring societies to their knees and can result in the societies' destruction.

Dialogue is where compassion, mutual respect and understanding reside and calibrates above 200. Individuals who calibrate below 200 are incapable of dialogue. Their communication is always about manipulation and proving their side of a position right...winning. People who calibrate above 200 are also capable of positionalities but do not necessarily exercise the negative tactics on a regular basis.(VTK)

Dialogue with mutual respect includes the drive for understanding of the other's view. Understanding does not necessarily mean agreement but does lead to the development of possible solutions, taking everyone's concerns into consideration. Rarely to never do you see the communication skills to achieve dialogue modeled on our television today. Why? Because being nice to one another does not foster ratings. Why? Because most people calibrate below 200 and thrive on drama, bullying, hate mongering and now killing.

Some of the models we are subjected to on our media today are in no way a mature form of debate as they are mostly subject to un-proven opinion and fallacious material served up to intentionally arouse the emotional side of the audience rather than a maturely de-bated presentation of proven facts to inform. It is all about ratings. The purpose of these media shows is not only ratings but to manip-ulate the audience to a positional way of thinking—the one sup-ported by the network or particular show or show's host. Remember, our media outlets are owned by only six companies, which represent big business…beware of the wolf in sheep clothing. I am pointing all of this out to you so you can become aware of the tactics and become more discerning viewers. Stop watching the people who push posi-tionality, use vilification of the other side and treat opinion as fact.

If you want to study the energy the subconscious is picking up on news shows try this: Turn off the sound and just watch the video. You will very quickly see/feel what your subconscious is picking up. When in advertising, I did this all of the time. I often could see that the visual being put out was saying exactly the op-posite of the words being spoken. Your subconscious is not fooled…only you are.

The 2016 election year was a perfect example of this. I believe Donald Trump has a definitive violent communication style devel-oped as a reality show ratings host. The utterance of "You're Fired" delivered in his infamous way has nothing to do with win-win communication and everything to do with competition and the win-lose emotional drama of a reality show. This emotionality has a very low energetic pattern, which is why people who calibrate below 200 and those still breaking away from that energy absolutely love it.

These communication tactics applied to a network reality show where the main purpose is ratings is amazingly effective. Just look at The Jerry Springer Show, Donald Trump's Apprentice and the like. Audiences at these energy levels love win-lose emotional fighting and for them it is entertaining.

Apply these communication tactics to a presidential election and the country is in trouble. Politicians are supposed to be above this emotional communication behavior and those who aren't, pay a price. A good example of this was when Trump started calling every one of his opponent's names, like Little Marco and Lyin' Ted. When the politicians responded in kind, they were hurt by the interchange. Trump was right when he said, "I could shoot someone and not lose voters." He brought out that element of humanity that loves the gladiator confrontations and massacre on a huge scale. Trump got away with it because he is a reality show host and not a politician. Did that make it acceptable?

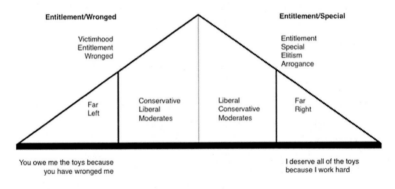

Diagram VII — The Political Divide

Diagram VII shows how the extremes of the triangle, both left and right, represent communication behaviors that create the environment for a fight and war. These are immature I-want-what-I-want, win-lose positions. The intent on both sides is to kill the other side whether that intent is covert or overt. The middle of the diagram represents the mature, balanced approach where people are in dialogue to reach a solution that is a win-win for all and creates balance and harmony in life. Both the violent communication and the silent tactics can be seen on either side, however, only at the extremes.

The far-right and the far-left tactics are both driven by fear or pride. The middle is driven by mutual respect. Mutual respect can exist even if there is not total trust.

If you would like to put some of this into Judeo-Christian terms...the devil rules on the extremes of the triangle or in my world...The Monkeys Rule. This does not mean the people who exhibit these behaviors are bad. It means they are being *used by external energetic forces*. In other words, they are feeding life-depleting energies...the bad wolf.

The Native Americans have a teaching in which everyone has two wolves inside of them—a bad wolf and a good wolf. The question is always which one do you feed?

Can we turn this around? Yes! If you are one of those people who are aware that watching the news leaves you feeling badly, then continue to pay attention to this and continuously move toward what makes you feel better and good. Find a channel that talks about facts objectively and not opinions to anger. By raising your vibrational frequency, you help to offset the lower frequencies, which is good for everyone.

Why am I talking about communication styles? Because when you ask the question put forth in the front of this book about the energy coming from human actions, paying attention to a person's communication style will help you see the energy being exhibited. Most people have no idea what I am talking about when I say, "Pay attention to the energy." Awareness takes practice.

Let's look at Diagram VIII, a somewhat complicated diagram of the school we must attend in order to become one with the Source or one with God. Let's also assume that in order to become one with the Source, we must learn everything possible to learn in our realm of existence. All the space in the triangle represents all the possible knowledge or truths from all the possible perspectives available. Your current lifetime is like taking a semester of learning in this school.

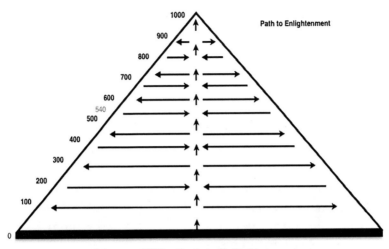

Diagram VIII—Path to Enlightenment

Your overall goal is to get the God degree, so to speak. The God degree, for sake of discussion, is simply learning to recontextualize things so you always come from the perspective of love or, better put, to become one with God.

Fortunately for you, there is no time limit to get this degree. You can take as many lifetimes as you choose. So, each time you prepare for your next semester of learning, you evaluate the learning of the past life and chart a course for what you want to learn in the next life. You pick out the courses you plan to study by planning what will happen to you in this lifetime that will help you learn those lessons.

For instance, I apparently was a very chauvinistic male in several past lives, so I came back to learn a different perspective, that of a woman in Corporate America, who is to experience how the behavior I dished out felt to my victims. This new perspective could allow me to become a more loving person, unless I have more to learn in that area.

For those of you who do not believe in a God, think of this as a school that allows you to study energy. From that perspective, you will be learning how to come from a place of love energy or life-enhancing energy in all of your life's activities. Some of us must disavow a belief in a God, so to speak, to remove all disingenuous dogma and hypocrisy in order to discover the true essence of the energy of love. At the lower grade levels, there is little discernment between the true love energy and behaviors that look like love but are really coming from control, hate and anger. At these levels, the Monkeys thrive and keep that invisible cloak at the ready.

So, the diagram shows arrows going from the outside to the inside and back or up the ladder. You can travel in any direction, away from the Source as easily as toward the Source. If you travel away from the Source, you usually need to hit bottom personally in order to reverse the direction.

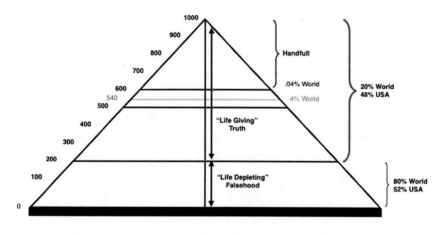

Diagram IX—Humanity Today on the Path to Enlightenment

Diagram IX simply shows where humanity is today on the path to enlightenment.

80% of us still are below 200 with only 20% above 200 and most of that 20% (16%) fall between 200 and 500. Only 4% are above 500 (love) and .04% above 540 (unconditional love). In the USA, 52% are below 200 and the rest are falling between 200 and 500 with maybe a few over the 500 mark. The good news is these numbers are logarithmic, and the power of love far exceeds the force of hate, for example one person at a level of 1000 will offset millions at a level below 200. Also remember that consciousness levels are fluid and constantly shifting, so the numbers are subject to change.[9]

We, as humans, not only evolve physically, but also spiritually or consciously. As said earlier, humanity calibrated at 90 during the time of Buddha, 100 during the time of Jesus, stayed at 190 for centuries, then about 1988, jumped to 207, thus reaching a level where we have a chance of not destroying ourselves, because we are in the life-enhancing/energy level, although barely. [10]

COMMUNICATION 102 ENERGY

This is the second level of communication...energy. And as I said before, where the linear/words level has many hierarchies and degrees in words, this level is very simple...positive or negative, love or hate. This level has no emotion associated with it. Hate energy is no more hateful than dislike and dislike is as hateful as hate when it comes to energy. There are no degrees. So, in every moment you choose between positive energy and negative energy.

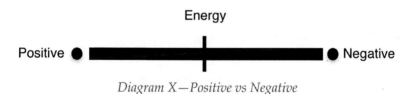

Diagram X—Positive vs Negative

Why is this important you ask? Well Dr. Hawkins put it very succinctly. He would often say, "In each moment we choose either Heaven or Hell."[11] So, if you are unaware of this, you are allowing the Monkeys to make your choice. If you can't tell by now, the Monkeys are not the best to be left in charge of choosing.

ENERGY/FEELINGS

Positive	Negative
Love	Nonlove (Hate)

LINEAR/LANGUAGE

Love Words	Nonlove Words
acceptance	separation
inclusion	anxiety
unity	fear
equal treatment	anger
non-judgment	judgment
joy	secrecy
peace	special consideration for some
fairness	exclusion
kindness	violence
like	dislike
gentleness	force
compassion	rage

Diagram XI — Energy/Feelings and Linear/Language

Diagram XI shows graphically what I have been trying to describe linearly or by words. As one goes higher on the consciousness scale, the energy level becomes much easier to comprehend. Below the line the words describing love vs. hate show degrees of love and hate. As one ascends the consciousness scale, those words start to merge and one begins to *feel* either good or not good. The choice between positive energy and negative energy becomes much clearer.

The Goal: Rise above the words…to feeling and choosing love.

CHAPTER 16
SO, WHAT'S IT ALL ABOUT, ALFIE?

It is all about (1) learning to be aware and (2) choosing to align with the right energy. This story is just one person's journey in doing that.

It is all about energy. Plain and simple. Learning to move from the linear world to the nonlinear world, the provable to the nonprovable, from nonlove to love energy. To learn this, I spent many hours with many teachers and reading every book that fell into my lap, studying with Jehovah Witnesses, Landmark, Dr. David Hawkins, the Native Americans, Psych-K, and *A Course in Miracles,* to name a few. It is a continuous path until one gets the lesson.

Some of you will find all of what I have learned a bunch of hogwash or woo-woo and the scientific among you will want proof. You may scoff at the use of applied kinesiology because you are uneducated in the process and can get different results. The black and white religious among you will claim Satan himself has possessed me (but then those people will not be reading this book). If you feel any resistance at all to what I have discovered, whether religious or scientific, then there is much for you to learn.

Resistance is simply a road sign telling you that. Resistance is also the Monkeys exerting their power over you. My advice: stop fighting for your position and start allowing the curiosity to lead you. I can assure you, you will not go to Hell or be judged badly by God because all mistakes (sin) will be forgiven. Remember, we do not know what we do not know. If you are not asking questions to understand, you are probably being right and in resistance.

Some of you will feel a glimmer of resonance, sense a smidgeon of truth in what I say, which will spark a bit of curiosity to propel

269

you toward exploration on your own path. Allow the learning and exploration to continue. The path will be challenging, difficult at times, and downright fun at others. Enable the boat to flow with the river and enjoy the trip.

In my lifetime, I've gone from a happy child to a collector of victimizations to the twilight zone to the peace of now (and it is not always peaceful). The last 20 years of *waking up* have been quite a journey for me. I have written this book to show anyone who cares to listen that a trip into victimhood does not necessarily mean a life sentence. On the other hand, for some, it means many lifetimes of blaming others. Peace comes when one is able to take responsibility for ALL of one's actions.

So, for all of you victims out there, the view from a higher spiritual place teaches that we are responsible for everything that happens to us. There *is an equal playing field* and we create everything that happens to us in order to learn the lessons we came here to learn. At the lower consciousness levels, this concept is impossible to grasp because victimization and victimhood are alive and well.

This concept was difficult for me to grasp until I did the Psych-K relationship balance with Jim Robbins. When we were both in balance it showed that our relationship on this earth was one of a karmic agreement. In other words, if he had done what I expected him to do—protect me from my slotters, in his words, I never would have written this book. In order for me to be pushed to write this book he needed to leave me hanging with my slotters. When this was realized there was instant forgiveness on my part.

CHOICE IS YOURS ... REMAIN IN VICTIMHOOD OR MOVE ON WITH LIFE.

My main message in writing this book was to rise above the words and learn to choose love energy. People <u>are</u> victimized and oppressed by the powerful, and, once victimized, people must wake up to their choice—stay in victimhood or move out of it and move on to a happier, more fulfilling life. Many people and groups of people choose to stay in victimhood to justify their anger, fear or martyrdom--the Jewish people, the Blacks in this country and the Indians to name a few groups. Many in those classifications have not learned there is a distinction between remembering what happened, so it doesn't happen again, and using the state of victimhood to choose to be offended or to blame others. There is a fine line--one side causes continued suffering and the other increases respect for humanity and all peoples.

"According to consciousness research, the likelihood of reaching Enlightenment is now approximately one thousand times more probable than it was in the past."[1] So, pay attention every day to what energies you choose. This takes discipline, courage and honesty.

You may or may not choose my path of experiential lessons. If not, I encourage you to simply focus on love at all times--rise above the words to energy. Those who are in fear about everything will find staying in love energy very difficult. In *A Course in Miracles* we read that Jesus tells us not to pray for him to remove the fear because you have created it. Rather he instructs, "You should ask, instead, for help in removing the conditions that have brought the fear about."[2]

As soon as I shifted my prayers from *remove the fear* to *remove the conditions that created the fear*, worry began to dissipate. This was **huge!**

RECAP

Let us review the some of the important concepts in the book:

1. Closely follow your heart with your mind, like an obedient dog.
2. Cognitive dissonance: If you are confronted by new information that conflicts with existing beliefs, ideas, or values, you must not refuse to incorporate the new learning or you will be guilty of cognitive dissonance.
3. The *repetition of a falsehood will eventually turn to truth in the mind.*

4. Everything is energy and everything has an energetic outcome, so pay attention to the energy coming from any interaction. Ask yourself the following question:

> Does the energy coming from any human interaction result in negative emotion nonloving energy, such as separation, anxiety, fear, anger, secrecy, exclusion, special consideration for some, judgment, fighting and violence; OR does the energy from this interaction result in positive emotion loving energy, such as acceptance, inclusion, unity, equal treatment, nonjudgment, joy and love?

When you answer that question you will have finally learned how to tell love energy from nonlove energy. Those who are working in the energy of God and those who are not.

5. Everything in the universe vibrates. We are all ONE!
6. Communication at the subatomic level is not subject to time and space.
7. The more emotion (behind thoughts) the higher the volume (of the request).
8. ***All things in your life manifest based on your thoughts and beliefs.***
9. The Monkeys Rule and live in your subconscious. All of your subconscious programming supersedes your conscious intent and you are blind to it—just happily sitting under that invisible cloak.

In the linear /words world there are two sides to communication, one of positionality and one of dialogue. Dialogue is where people seek to understand each other and their issues and then work together to find solutions that benefit everyone concerned. Taking a position on anything is simply preparing to fight, manipulate to prove a point or kill the other side. There is no goal for common good. It is kill or be killed.

Pay attention to what behaviors are being exhibited in any interchange and you will be able to see if there is interest in dialogue or a simple fight brewing. This process will not necessarily be instantaneous, although it can be. Patience is required. Don't force your will by trying to row upstream. Put out to the Universe/God what you want and forget about it. The allowing concept is contrary to the world's view of creating success.

POSITIONALITY in communication is:

1. Win/lose mentality
2. I am right and you are wrong thinking
3. Feeds life-depleting energies
4. Leads to fighting and war
5. Is noncompromising
6. Narcissistic immature behavior
7. Emotional manipulation

DIALOGUE in communication is:

1. Win/win mentality
2. I would like to understand your issues and for you to understand my issues
3. Feeds life-enhancing energies
4. Leads to the highest good for all
5. Compromising in nature
6. Mature concern and compassion for the good of all
7. Nonemotional, logical, balanced and harmonious

Rise above the linear/language to the energy/feeling. It is for the betterment of society that dialogue be chosen. Anyone who chooses positionality chooses death for everything and everyone. So how does one know they have chosen wisely? How do you know you have learned or are learning the lesson?

Materialism decreases
Fear decreases
Hate decreases
Feeling helpless decreases
Criticism for others decreases
Reactive behavior becomes responsive behavior
Love increases for everyone and everything
Peace increases
Happiness with little increases
Compassion for others increases
Tolerance increases
Joy comes from helping others or is just there

Remember one thing whether you understand it or not—in every moment you choose between love energy or hate energy. Those cumulative choices add up to make your consciousness level and your karma. If you choose negative energy, more of that energy will come to you. If you choose love energy, more of that energy will come to you. The more negative energy you choose the more power the Monkeys have in your life and the more apt they are to cover you with their invisible cloak so you cannot see what you choose.

Epilogue

At the start of this journey, I was angry and ready to kill everyone in the local vicinity. Instead I wrote this book, as I said when I quit The Brand Consultancy. In reality, I quit because I was no longer going to tolerate unethical behavior--writing was an excuse to leave and, for the first time, I did nothing to try to change what was happening. I just said *f- -k you* in my mind and left with a smile.

Alone and directionless, I started on the path to write. The section Anger Gathered, Anger Stored was written at that time. I then unknowingly fell into the Twilight Zone and for about the next 18 years, I was being exposed to the unprovable realm. And I can honestly tell you that this journey has dramatically changed me. Today I find myself sitting on the same couch where I contemplated suicide, often in a perfect state of happiness, even joy, laughing at the TV.

I am no more financially sound than I was. I am, however, no longer in fear about those finances. My fear around security no longer rules my life. In fact, I find it fun in seeing how things will come into my life based on what I put out that I want or need. I now know that when I need to pay the bills, the resources will come. My knowing how is no longer necessary.

Yes, I still do not have a partner but I am no longer alone. I know the power is with me always. Some of you call this power by different names: God, Jehovah, Universe, Allah, Krishna. To me God is simply Energy.

I divorced John less than ten years into our union. Sad to say, one of the reasons I married him, after two other proposals, was to show the world that, yes, someone loved me at one time. He is a good man and deserved better than what I could give him. He found that in Linda. We are friends on Facebook today.

Remember when I told you how angry I got when my coach and psychologist would ask what my passion was? My psychologist hinted at what it was way back in the beginning...that I was passionate about change. Well, one of the major positives out of all of this--I found clarity around my passion.

If you recall my trip to the cave with Gary, what the last Spirit said I must do to reclaim the loss of my resources was— *teach...teach many.* Well, now I understand that this book may be a vehicle to do that.

My focus is not making money but helping people when *they are ready* to increase their consciousness. This road leads to happiness and joy.

Many of my writer friends are all about making their books successful and doing what needs to be done to make money. My book is already successful because it has already helped several people. The rest will be gravy and fun for me.

I am so excited right now -- about developing all things around the Monkeys that can be comical. The t-shirts alone have me laughing, sometimes hysterically.

Remember, only your Monkeys think they are right all of the time. Pray for removal of the circumstances that create your fears and trust that the problems are solved. Then go watch a movie or play a round of golf.

The Universe has got this!

REFERENCES

CHAPTER 2 A LOSS OF INNOCENCE – THE CONTINENTAL STORY
1. The U.S. Bureau of Labor Statistics

CHAPTER 6 VICTIMIZATION VS. VICTIMHOOD
1. Edited by Bruce M. Metzger & Roland E. Murphy, New Oxford University Press.
2. Mitroff, Page 4.
3. Mitroff, Page 6.
4. Mitroff, Preface Page xix.
5. Redfield, *The Tenth Insight,* page 33
6. Louise Hay, page 182 Laryngitis
7. Louise Ha, page 192 Pneumonia

CHAPTER 7 ENTER NATIVE AMERICAN TEACHINGS
1. *The Karate Kid,* Columbia Pictures Corp., 1984.

CHAPTER 9 MOVING ON
1. Emoto, The True Power of Water
2. Emoto, The Hidden Messages in Water and Secrets of Water on You Tube
3. Miramax, (2008)
4. Lord of the Wind Film, LLC
5. See Bibliography, Lipton
6. See Bibliography, Williams
7. Hawkins, *Letting Go,* page 19,20.

CHAPTER 10 THE MONKEYS
1. Eckhart Tolle, A New Earth Awakening to Your Life's Purpose.

2. I don't know if this is an actual quote from Einstein as I could not find it attributed to him.
3. See bibliography, Gachot.
4. A Course in Miracles
5. See Bibliography, Strong

CHAPTER 11 SO MUCH TO LEARN

1. The New Oxford Annotated Bible with the Apocrypha.
2. *Truth vs Falsehood*, Page 295.

CHAPTER 12 CONSCIOUSNESS

1. *Transcending the Levels of Consciousness*, 2006, page 165
2. Power vs Force, Pages 100-101
3. See bibliography Maslow
4. Sam Littlefair, *Lion's Roar*, January 8, 2017
5. Sam Littlefair, *Lion's Roar*, January 8, 2017
6. *I: Reality and Subjectivity* (2003), page 526
7. Wikipedia

CHAPTER 13 TRUTH

1. Wikipedia, Direct to Consumer Advertising for full history.
2. See bibliography, Wilde
3. See Bibliography, Sorkin.
4. U.S. Bureau of Labor Statistics
5. See bibliography, Hill.

CHAPTER 14 ENERGY

1. Google Thomas Young Physicist biography.
2. See Bibliography, Puligandla
3. See Bibliography, Bryne

CHAPTER 15 COMMUNICATION

1. See Bibliography, Twain.
2. The New Oxford Annotated Bible with Apocrypha (1994)
3. The New World Translation of the Holy Scriptures
4. Reality, Spirituality, and Modern Man pg, 34-35
5. Hawkins Lecture entitled *God is The Infinite Field*
6. *Meet the Press 4-19-17.*
7. Hawkins, Disc One, *Verification of Spiritual Realities* 1:56.08 to 1:56.38.
8. Some of this diagram came from The Path of Dialogue and The Praxis Institute 1995.   I was unable to find the company to secure permission for reproduction because the company no longer appears to exist.
9. *Transcending the Levels of Consciousness*, 2006, page 239
10. *Transcending the Levels of Consciousness*, 2006, page 28
11. *I: Reality and Subjectivity* (2003), Chapter 22: Applications, p. 526

CHAPTER 16 SO, WHAT'S IT ALL ABOUT, ALFIE?

1. "Discovery of the Presence of God" (page 42)
2. *A Course in Miracles*, Second Edition, newly revised, Chapter Two, Section VI. Fear and Conflict, paragraph 4, sentence 3. Page 29.

Albom, Mitch. *Tuesdays with Morrie.* New York: Doubleday, 1997.

Arntz, William, Chasse, Betsy, and Hoffman, Matthew. What the Bleep Do We Know. Documentary Film. 2004.

Barker, Raymond Charles. *The Power of Decision.* Marina Del Rey, CA: DeVoss & Company, 1968,1988,1996.

Bohr, Niels. The Theory of Spectra and Atomic Constitution. London: Cambridge U. Press, 1922.

Braden, Gregg. *The Isaiah Effect.* New York: Three Rivers Press, —————, *The God Code: The Secret of Our Past, the Promise of Our Future.* Carlsbad, CA: Hay House, Inc., 2004

Bryne, Rhonda. *The Secret.* New York: Atria Books, 2006.

Carlson, Ph.D., Richard. *Don't Sweat the Small Stuff...and it's all small stuff.* New York: Hyperion, 1997.

Chopra, M.D., Deepak. *The Path to Love.* New York: Three Rivers Press, 1997.
—————, *The Seven Spiritual Laws of Success.* CA: Copublished by Amber-Allen Publishing and New World Library
—————, *Quantum Healing: Exploring the Frontiers of Mind/Body Medicine.* New York: Bantam Books, 1989.

Covey, Stephen R. *The 7 Habits of Highly Effective People.* New York: Simon & Schuster, 1989.

Dalai Lama, His Holiness the. and Howard C. Cutler, M.D. *The Art of Happiness, A Handbook for Living.* New York: Riverbed Books, 1998.

————, *The Joy of Living and Dying in Peace.* Edited by Donald S. Lopez, Jr., New Delhi: Library of Tibetan Works and Archives, 2008.

Diamond, M.D., John. *Your Body Doesn't Lie: Unlock the Power of Your Natural Energy.* New York: Grand Central Publishing, Machete Book Group, 1979.

Drosnin, Michael. *The Bible Code.* New York: Touchstone, 1997.

Dyer, Dr. Wayne W. *Change Your Thoughts-Change Your Life: Living the Wisdom of the Tao.* Carlsbad, CA: Hay House, Inc., 2007.

————, *Getting in the Gap.* Carlsbad, CA: Hay House, Inc., 2003.

————, *The Power of Intention.* Carlsbad, CA: Hay House, Inc., 2010.

————, *There is a Spiritual Solution to Every Problem.* New York: HarperCollins, 2003.

Eadie, Betty J. *Embraced by the Light.* Placerville, CA: Gold Leaf Press, 1992.

Emoto, Masaru. *The Secret Life of Water.* Hillsboro, Oregon: Beyond Words Publishing, Inc., 2005.

————, *The True Power of Water Healing and Discovering Ourselves.* Hillsboro, Oregon: Beyond Words Publishing, Inc., 2005.

————, *The Hidden Messages in Water.* Hillsboro, Oregon: Beyond Words Publishing, Inc., 2004.

Fox, Emmet. *The Ten Commandments: The Master Key to Life.* New York: Harper Collins Publishers, 1953.

Freke, Timothy and Peter Gandy. *Jesus and the Lost Goddess the Secret Teachings of the Original Christians*. New York: Three Rivers Press, 2001.

Gachot, Amanda. Upallhours.com

Goldsmith, Joel S. *Living the Infinite Way*. New York: Harper Collins Publishers, 1961.
————, *The Thunder of Silence*. New York: Harper Collins Publishers, 1961.
————, *Spiritual Interpretation of Scripture*. Longboat Key, FL: Acropolis Books, Inc., 1947.

Goleman, Daniel. *Emotional Intelligence*. New York: Bantam Books, 1995.

Grabhorn, Lynn. *Excuse Me, Your Life is Waiting*. Charlottesville, VA: Hampton Roads Publishing, Inc. 2000.

Grout, Pam. *E2 (E Squared)*. Carlsbad, CA: Hay House, Inc., 2013.

Hawkins, M.D., Ph.D. David. *Power vs Force*. Carlsbad, CA: Hay House, Inc., 1995.
————, *The Eye of the I From Which Nothing is Hidden*. W. Sedona, AZ: Veritas Publishing, 2001.
————, *I Reality and Subjectivity*. W. Sedona, AZ: Veritas Publishing, 2003.
————, *Truth vs. Falsehood: How to Tell the Difference*. W. Sedona, AZ: Veritas Publishing, 2005.
————, *Transcending the Levels of Consciousness: The Stairway to Enlightenment*. W. Sedona, AZ: Veritas Publishing, 2006.
————, *Discovery of the Presence of God: Devotional Nonduality*. W. Sedona, AZ: Veritas Publishing, 2007.
————, *Reality, Spirituality, and Modern Man*. W. Sedona, AZ: Veritas Publishing, 2008.

—————, *Healing and Recovery*, W. Sedona, AZ: Veritas Publishing, 2009.

—————, *Letting Go*. W. Sedona, AZ: Veritas Publishing, 2012.

—————, *God is the Infinite Field*.

—————, *Verification of Spiritual Realities*, Disc One. 1:56.08.

Hay, Louise L. *You Can Heal Your Life*. Carlsbad, CA: Hay House, Inc., 1984,1987.

Hicks, Jerry and Ester. *Ask and It Is Given: Learning to Manifest Your Desires*. Carlsbad, CA: Hay House, Inc., 2004.

—————, *A New Beginning I*. San Antonio, TX: Abraham-Hicks Publications, 2000.

—————, *Money and the Law of Attraction: Learning to Attract Wealth, Health, and Happiness*. United States: Hay House, 2008.

Hill, Napoleon. *Think and Grow Rich*. The Ralston Society, 1937.

Jehovah's Witnesses.

Jones, Laurie Beth. *The Path: Creating Your Mission Statement for Work and Life*. *New York: Hyperion, 1996.*

Kahn, Jill. *The Gift of Taking: Honor Yourself First, All Else Will Follow*. Impressions Pub., 2001.

Kahn, Matt. *Whatever Arises, Love That: A Love Revolution that Begins with You*. Boulder, CO: Sounds True, Inc., 2016.

Kaman, Robert Mark. *The Karate Kid*. Columbia Pictures Corp, 1984.

Kasl, Charlotte. *If the Buddha Dated:* A Handbook for Finding Love on a Spiritual Path. Penquin Books, 1999.

Kopp, Karen. *Remembering Our Spiritual Journey Home...The Twelve Keys*. Asheville, North Carolina: Magic Mountain Press, 2002.

Littlefair, Sam. *Lion's Roar Magazine. 2017.*

Lipton, Ph.D., Bruce. *The Biology of Belief.* Carlsbad, CA: Hay House, Inc., 2005.

Maslow, Abraham. <u>Psychological Review,</u> *A Theory of Human Motivation*. 1943.

McTaggart, Lynne. *The Field: The Quest for the Secret Force of the Universe.* New York: HarperCollins Publishers, 2002.

Metzger, Bruce M. and Roland E. Murphy, eds., *The New Oxford Annotated Bible with the Apocrypha/Deuterocanonical Books.* New York: Oxford University Press,1991, 1994.

Millan, Cesar. The Dog Whisperer (TV show).

Mitroff, Ian I., and Elizabeth A. Denton. *A Spiritual Audit of Corporate America: A Hard Look at Spirituality, Religion, and Values in the Workplace.* San Francisco, CA: Jossey-Bass Inc., 1999.

Monroe, Robert A. *Ultimate Journey.* New York: Bantam Doubleday Dell Publishing Group, Inc., 1994.

Mundy, Ph.D., Jon. *Living: A Course in Miracles.* New York: Sterling Publishing Co., Inc., 2011.

NBC News. Meet the Press. April 19, 2017.

New World Bible Translation Committee, trans. *New World Translation of the Holy Scriptures.* Brooklyn, New York: Watchtower Bible and Tract Society of New York, Inc., 1984.

Pagels, Elaine. *The Gnostic Gospels.* New York: Vintage Books Edition, 1979.

Pelzer, Dave. *A Child Called It.* Omaha NE: Omaha Press, 1993.

Puligandla, R. *Quantum Theory.* Sterling Publishers, 1977.

Redfield, James. *The Celestine Prophecy.* New York, NY: Warner Books, Inc., 1993.
————, *The Tenth Insight Holding the Vision: Future Adventures of the Celestine Prophecy.* New York: Warner Books, 1996.

Redfield, James., and Carol Adrienne. *The Tenth Insight: An Experiential Guide.* New York: Warner Books, 1995.

Rumi. The Essential Rumi. Coleman Barks, Ed., Harper One, 2004 (1st 1273).

S, Acharya. *The Christ Conspiracy: The Greatest Story Ever Sold.* Kempton, IL: Adventures Unlimited Press, 1999.

Schucman, Helen, Thetford William, Wapnick, Ken, Editors. *A Course in Miracles: Text Workbook for Students and Manual for Teachers.* NY: Penguin Group, 1996.

Singer, Michael A. *The Untethered Soul: The Journey Beyond Yourself.* Oakland, CA: New Harbinger Publications, Inc., 2007.

Sorkin, Aaron. *A Few Good Men.* Movie. NY: 1992.

Strong, James. Exhaustive Concordance of the Bible. Drew Theological Seminary, 1890.

Thomas of Celano. *The First Life of St. Francis of Assisi.* Italy, 1228.

Tolle, Eckhart. *The Power of Now: A Guide to Spiritual Enlightenment.* Novato, CA: New World Library and Vancouver, B.C., Canada: Namaste Publishing, 1999.
————, *A New Earth: Awakening to Your Life's Purpose.* New York: Penguin Random House, LLC, 2005.

Tolman, Don. *The Quest: Pulse & Water.* Rogersville, TN: Brain Forest Pub, 2000.

Twain, Mark. *The Wit and Wisdom of Mark Twain.* Dover Publications, 1998.

The U.S. Bureau of Labor Statistics, August 2017, report 1069 and similar.

Vanzant, Iyanla, *Fix My Life,* Host, OWN: Oprah Winfrey Network (2012–present)

Vincent, John. *Secrets of Water, Rice Consciousness Experiment,* 2013.

Walsch, Neale Donald. *Conversations with God: An Uncommon Dialogue, Book 1.* New York: G.P. Putnam's Sons, 1996.
————, *Conversations with God: An Uncommon Dialogue, Book 1, Guidebook.* Charlottesville, VA: Hampton Roads Publishing Company, Inc., 1997.
————, *Conversations with God: An Uncommon Dialogue, Book 2.* Charlottesville, VA: Hampton Roads Publishing Company, Inc., 1997.
————, *Conversations with God an Uncommon Dialogue Book 3.* Charlottesville, VA: Hampton Roads Publishing Company, Inc., 1998.

Wilde, Oscar. The Importance of Being Earnes. Leonard Smithers & Co., London, 1899.

Williams, Robert M. *Psyck-K: The Missing Piece, Peace in Your Life.* Crestone, Colorado: Myrddin Publications, 2004-2009.

Williamson, Marianne. *The Law of Devine Compensation.* New York: HarperCollins Publishers, 2012.

Young, Thomas. *The Bakerian Lecture. On the Theory of Light and Colours.* Royal Society of London, 1802.

Indiegogo Campaign Contributors

Without your help, the progress of the book would have been even slower than it was. With deepest gratitude, I honor you here.

Lisa 'Montana' Popienko
Bryan Mercer
Karen Paul Holmes
Jackie and Kent Dickie
Jim and Peggy Hall
Cathy Marolt Conn
Nancy Sellers
Cheryl Burney
Blair Enfield
Lin Lemmer
Melodie Ransom
Linda and Michael Baron
Keith and Jennifer Rocke
Bill and Karen Koegle
David Lemcoe, Jr.
Angelina Li
Kelly Schleier
Heather Schon
Cinthia Wade McEntire
Lori Sissel
Mark and Helen Maselli
Ed Vaught
Cindy Beckman

Victoria Koegle Barkan has always had a quest to understand why people do what they do and think the way they think. She entered the study of the mind through her art. Receiving a degree in art education with a focus on advertising design from Bowling Green State University she started her study on what motivates consumers. It is here that she was introduced to subliminal advertising and the subconscious mind. She applied that knowledge with consumers in the cable TV world for over 20 years.

Later she pursued additional information in the curriculum offered by Landmark Education, studies with Native Americans, the Psych-K process and the work of Dr. David Hawkins' Map of Consciousness.

Self-education became a drive as her voracious reading and

travels to all seven continents fueled her study of the human mind and later energy.

Visits to third-world countries presented different cultures, teaching particularly the role of traditions and how cognitive dissonance inhibits a person or culture's growth. She became her best test subject, learning how her unconscious beliefs and the energy she projected were directing her life and how she could reprogram her mind to change her world. She is pictured here with her horse Baron who became one of her best teachers about the unconscious energy emitted by the subconscious.

The subconscious mind is what she calls the Monkeys. *The Monkeys Rule* became her gift to you.